QUANTUM AND WOODY

THE
WORLD'S
WORST
SUPERHERO TEAM

JAMES ASMUS | TOM FOWLER | JORDIE BELLAIRE

CONTENTS

Quantum & Woody created by MD Bright & Priest

Collection Cover Art: Ryan Sook

Editors: Jody LeHeup (#1-4, Weekly) and
Alejandro Arbona (#3-4)
Editor-in-Chief: Warren Simons

VALIANT

Peter Cuneo
Chairman

Dinesh Shamdasani
CEO & Chief Creative Officer

Gavin Cuneo
Chief Operating Officer & CFO

Fred Pierce
Publisher

Warren Simons
VP Editor-in-Chief

Walter Black
VP Operations

Hunter Gorinson
Director of Marketing,
Communications & Digital Media

Atom! Freeman
Director of Sales

Matthew Klein
Andy Liegl
John Petrie
Sales Managers

Josh Johns
Associate Director of Digital Media and Development

Travis Escarfullery
Jeff Walker
Production & Design Managers

Tom Brennan
Editor

Kyle Andrukiewicz
Editor and Creative Executive

Peter Stern
Publishing & Operations Manager

Andrew Steinbeiser
Marketing & Communications Manager

Danny Khazem
Editorial Operations Manager

Ivan Cohen
Collection Editor

Steve Blackwell
Collection Designer

Lauren Hitzhusen
Editorial Assistant

Rian Hughes/Device
Trade Dress & Book Design

Russell Brown
President, Consumer Products,
Promotions and Ad Sales

Geeta Singh
Licensing Manager

Quantum and Woody®: The World's Worst Superhero Team. Published by Valiant Entertainment, LLC. Office of Publication: 350 Seventh Avenue, New York, NY 10001. Printed in the U.S.A. Third Printing.
ISBN: 9781939346186.

VALIANT

JAMES ASMUS | TOM FOWLER | JORDIE BELLAIRE

QUANTUM AND WOODY!

#1

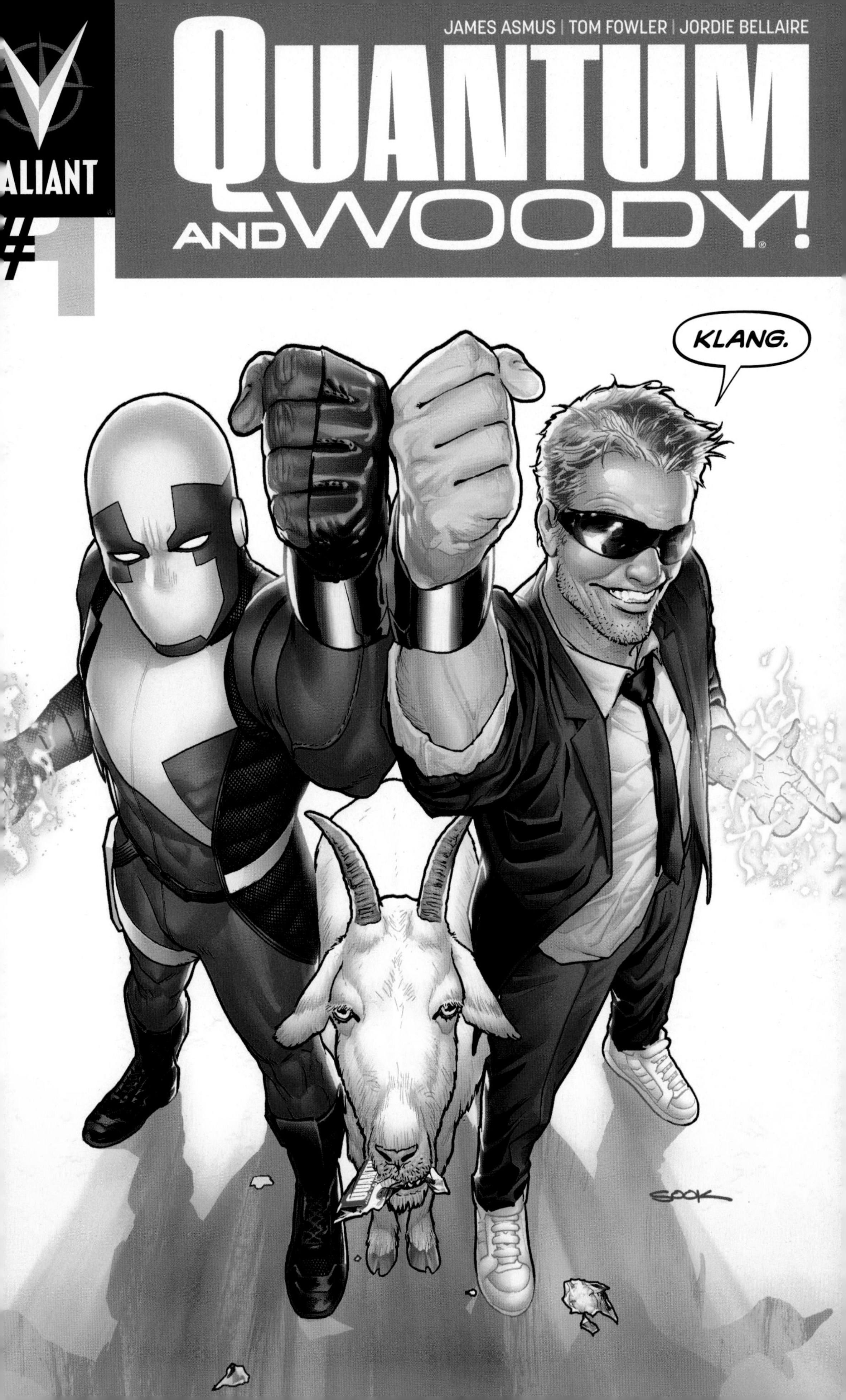

KLANG.

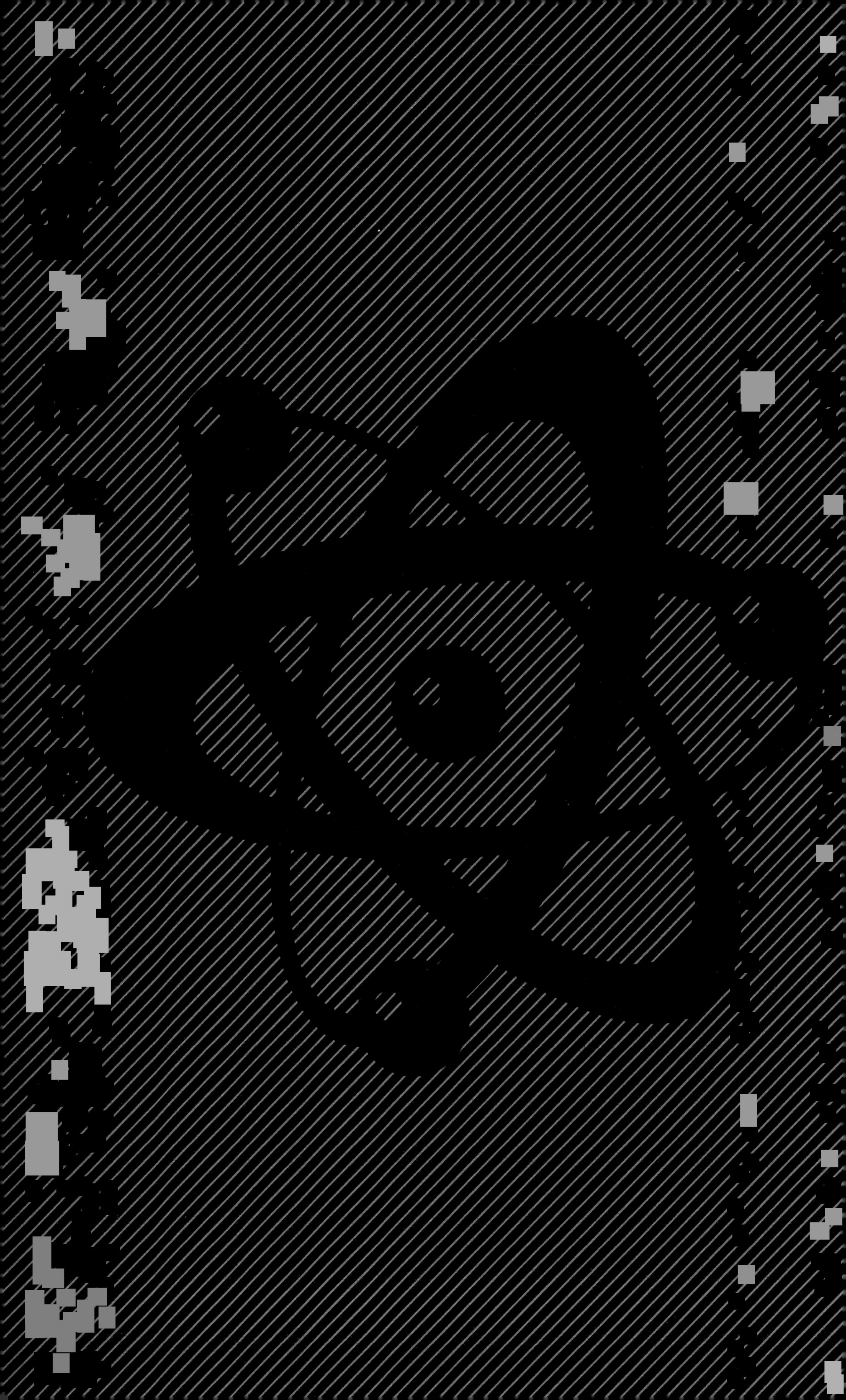

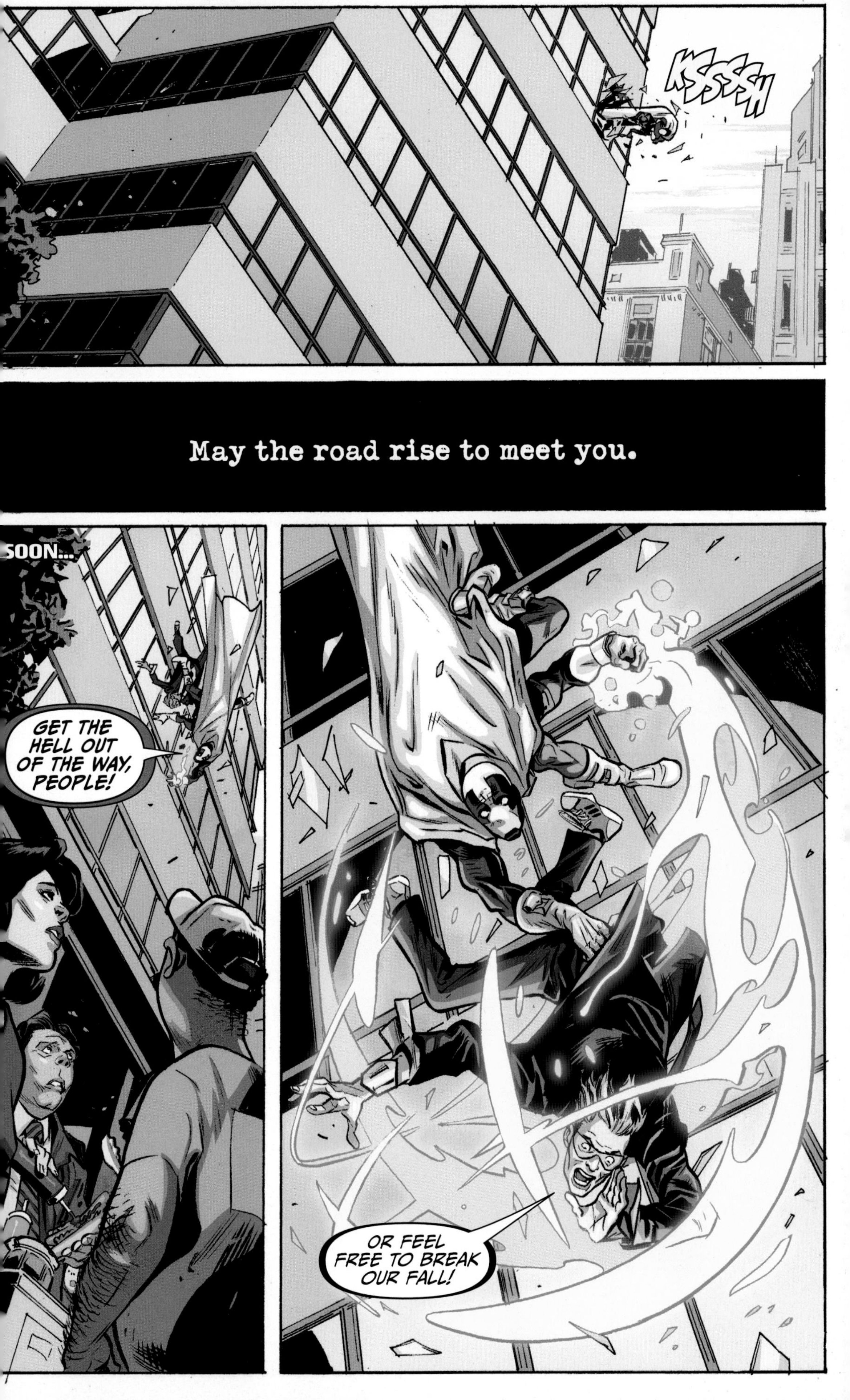
KSSSSH
May the road rise to meet you.
SOON...
GET THE HELL OUT OF THE WAY, PEOPLE!
OR FEEL FREE TO BREAK OUR FALL!

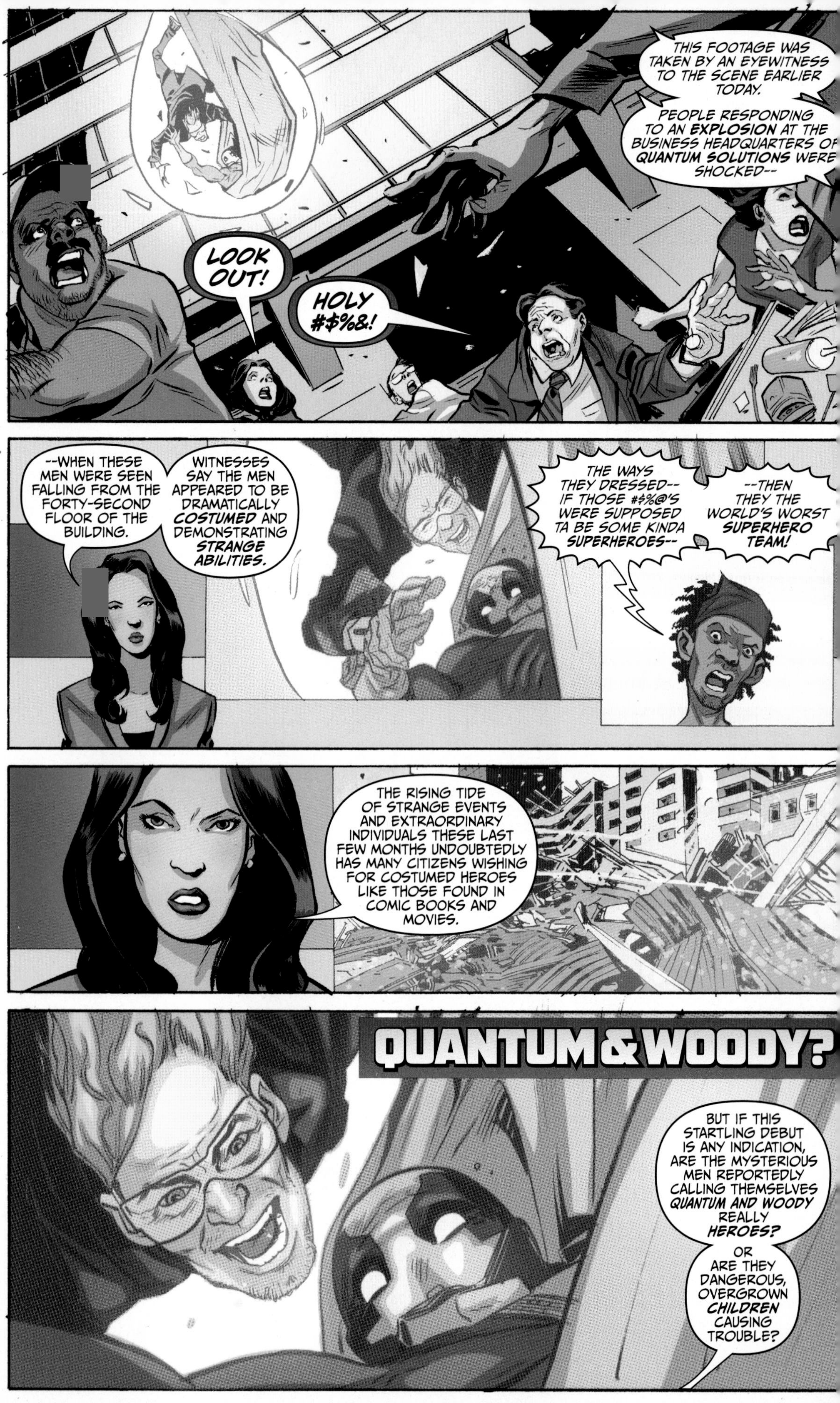
THIS FOOTAGE WAS TAKEN BY AN EYEWITNESS TO THE SCENE EARLIER TODAY.
PEOPLE RESPONDING TO AN **EXPLOSION** AT THE BUSINESS HEADQUARTERS OF **QUANTUM SOLUTIONS** WERE SHOCKED--
LOOK OUT!
HOLY #$%&!
--WHEN THESE MEN WERE SEEN FALLING FROM THE FORTY-SECOND FLOOR OF THE BUILDING.
WITNESSES SAY THE MEN APPEARED TO BE DRAMATICALLY **COSTUMED** AND DEMONSTRATING **STRANGE ABILITIES.**
THE WAYS THEY DRESSED-- IF THOSE #$%@'S WERE SUPPOSED TA BE SOME KINDA **SUPERHEROES**--
--THEN THEY THE WORLD'S WORST **SUPERHERO TEAM!**
THE RISING TIDE OF STRANGE EVENTS AND EXTRAORDINARY INDIVIDUALS THESE LAST FEW MONTHS UNDOUBTEDLY HAS MANY CITIZENS WISHING FOR COSTUMED HEROES LIKE THOSE FOUND IN COMIC BOOKS AND MOVIES.
QUANTUM & WOODY?
BUT IF THIS STARTLING DEBUT IS ANY INDICATION, ARE THE MYSTERIOUS MEN REPORTEDLY CALLING THEMSELVES **QUANTUM AND WOODY** REALLY **HEROES?**
OR ARE THEY DANGEROUS, OVERGROWN **CHILDREN** CAUSING TROUBLE?

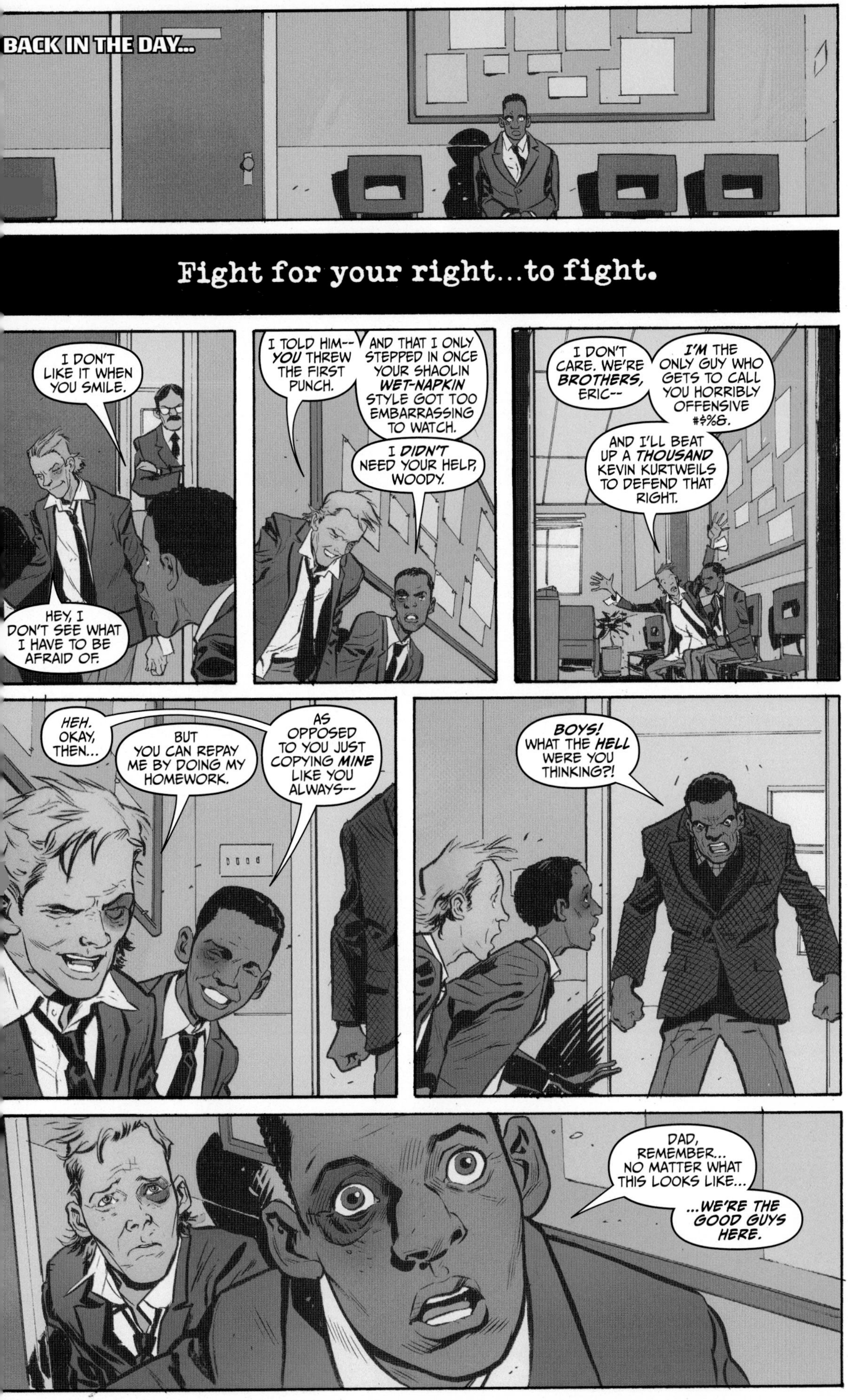
BACK IN THE DAY...
Fight for your right...to fight.
I DON'T LIKE IT WHEN YOU SMILE.
HEY, I DON'T SEE WHAT I HAVE TO BE AFRAID OF.
I TOLD HIM-- YOU THREW THE FIRST PUNCH.
AND THAT I ONLY STEPPED IN ONCE YOUR SHAOLIN WET-NAPKIN STYLE GOT TOO EMBARRASSING TO WATCH.
I DIDN'T NEED YOUR HELP, WOODY.
I DON'T CARE. WE'RE BROTHERS, ERIC--
I'M THE ONLY GUY WHO GETS TO CALL YOU HORRIBLY OFFENSIVE #$%&.
AND I'LL BEAT UP A THOUSAND KEVIN KURTWEILS TO DEFEND THAT RIGHT.
HEH. OKAY, THEN...
BUT YOU CAN REPAY ME BY DOING MY HOMEWORK.
AS OPPOSED TO YOU JUST COPYING MINE LIKE YOU ALWAYS--
BOYS! WHAT THE HELL WERE YOU THINKING?!
DAD, REMEMBER... NO MATTER WHAT THIS LOOKS LIKE...
...WE'RE THE GOOD GUYS HERE.

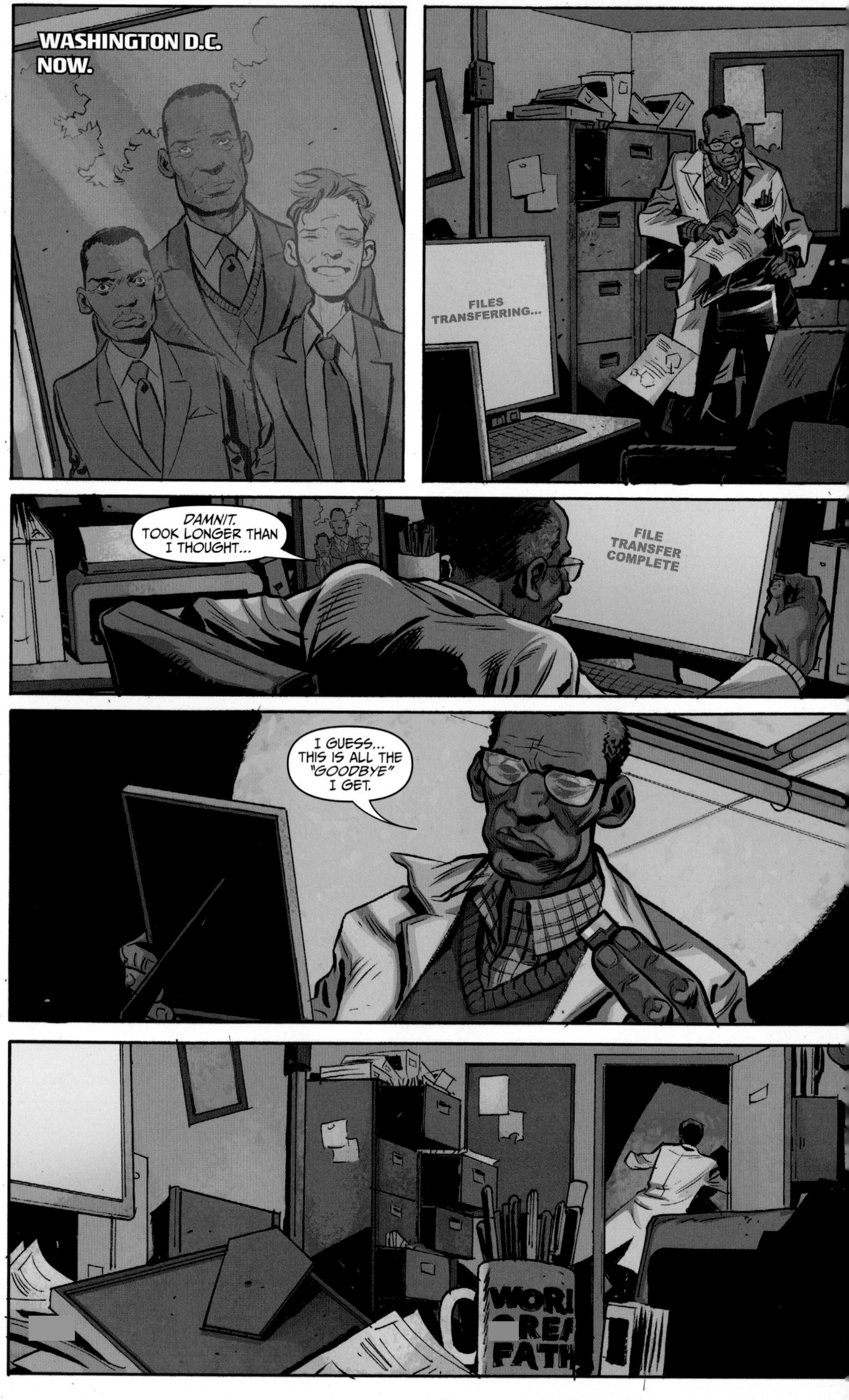

WASHINGTON D.C. NOW.
FILES TRANSFERRING...
DAMNIT. TOOK LONGER THAN I THOUGHT...
FILE TRANSFER COMPLETE
I GUESS... THIS IS ALL THE "GOODBYE" I GET.

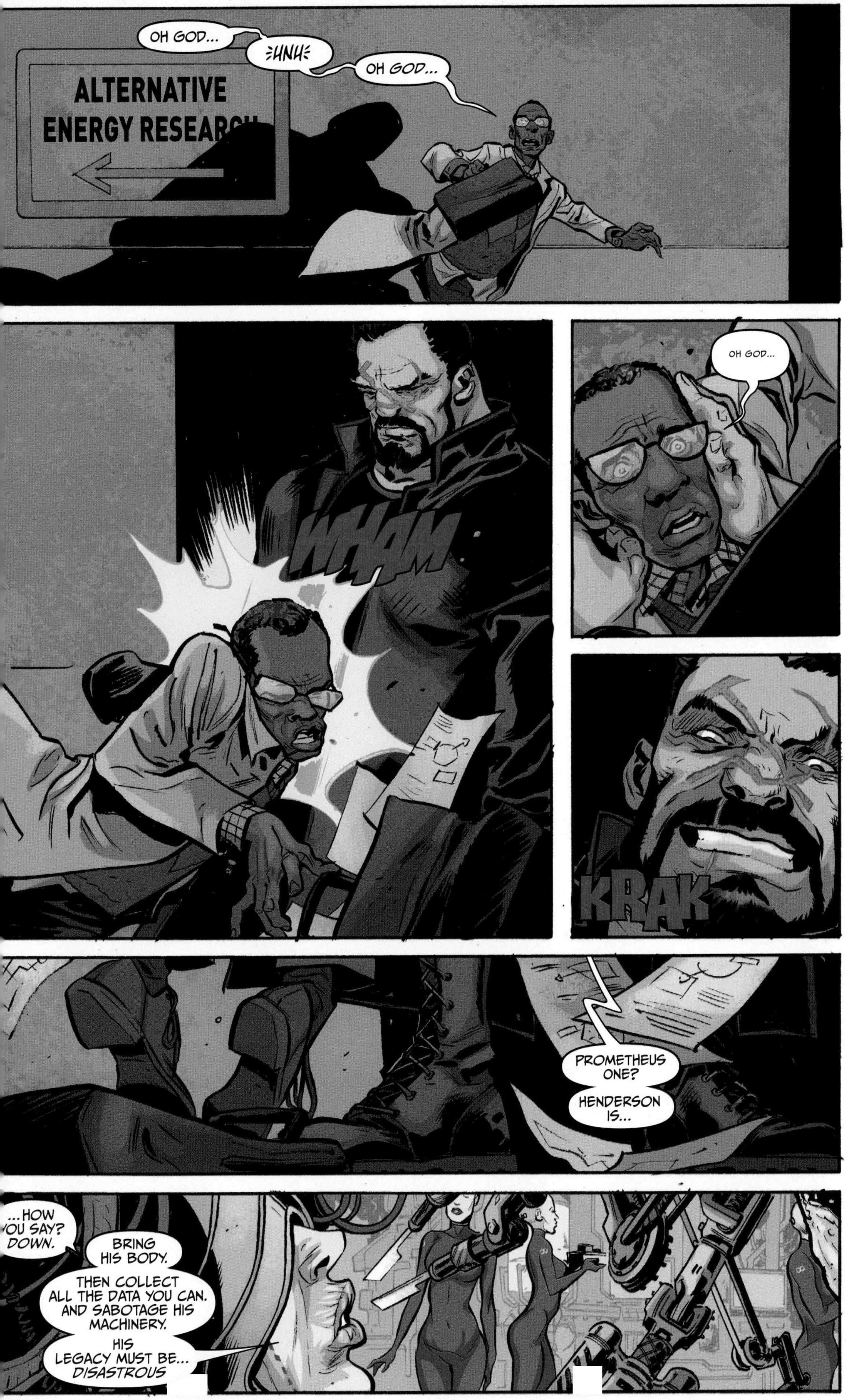
OH GOD...
UNH
OH GOD...
ALTERNATIVE
ENERGY RESEAR
WHAM
OH GOD...
KRAK
PROMETHEUS ONE?
HENDERSON IS...
...HOW OU SAY? DOWN.
BRING HIS BODY.
THEN COLLECT ALL THE DATA YOU CAN. AND SABOTAGE HIS MACHINERY.
HIS LEGACY MUST BE... DISASTROUS

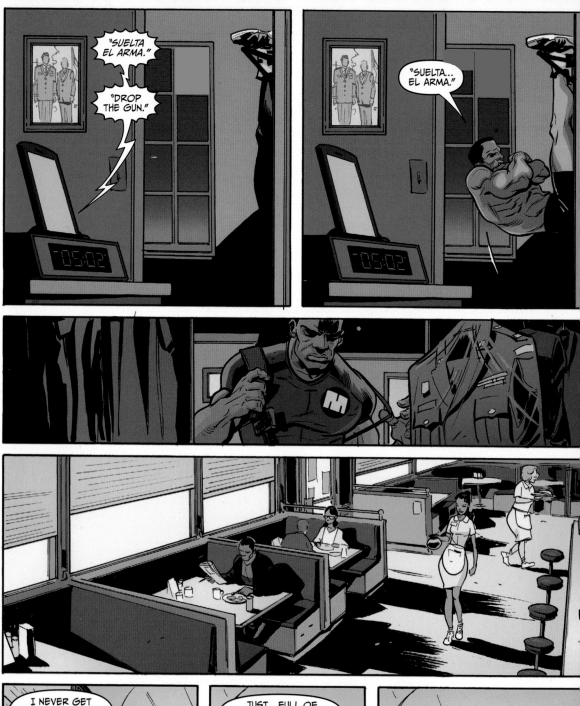

"SUELTA EL ARMA."

"DROP THE GUN."

"SUELTA... EL ARMA."

I NEVER GET OVER HOW YOU CAN DO THAT THING IN PEN.

AND BEFORE YOU CLEAR YOUR PLATE!

JUST... FULL OF USELESS INFORMATION, I GUESS.

DON'T WANT NO TROUBLE, LADY-- JUS' EMPTY OUT THAT REGISTER AN' NOBODY GETS SHOT TA DEATH.

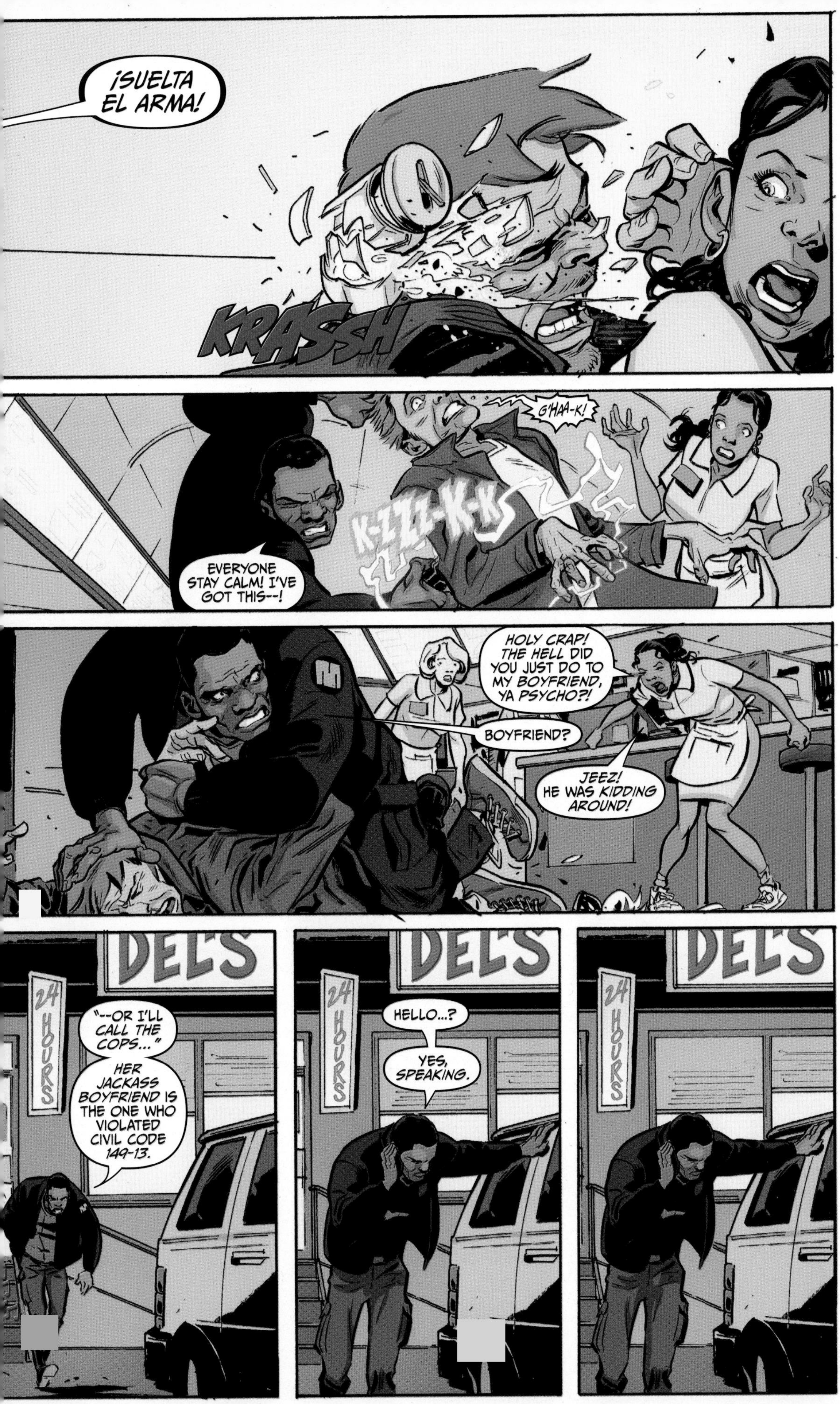

¡SUELTA EL ARMA!
KRASSH
G'HAA-K!
K-ZZZZ-K-K
EVERYONE STAY CALM! I'VE GOT THIS--!
HOLY CRAP! THE HELL DID YOU JUST DO TO MY BOYFRIEND, YA PSYCHO?!
BOYFRIEND?
JEEZ! HE WAS KIDDING AROUND!
DEL'S
24 HOURS
"--OR I'LL CALL THE COPS..."
HER JACKASS BOYFRIEND IS THE ONE WHO VIOLATED CIVIL CODE 149-13.
DEL'S
24 HOURS
HELLO...?
YES, SPEAKING.
DEL'S
24 HOURS

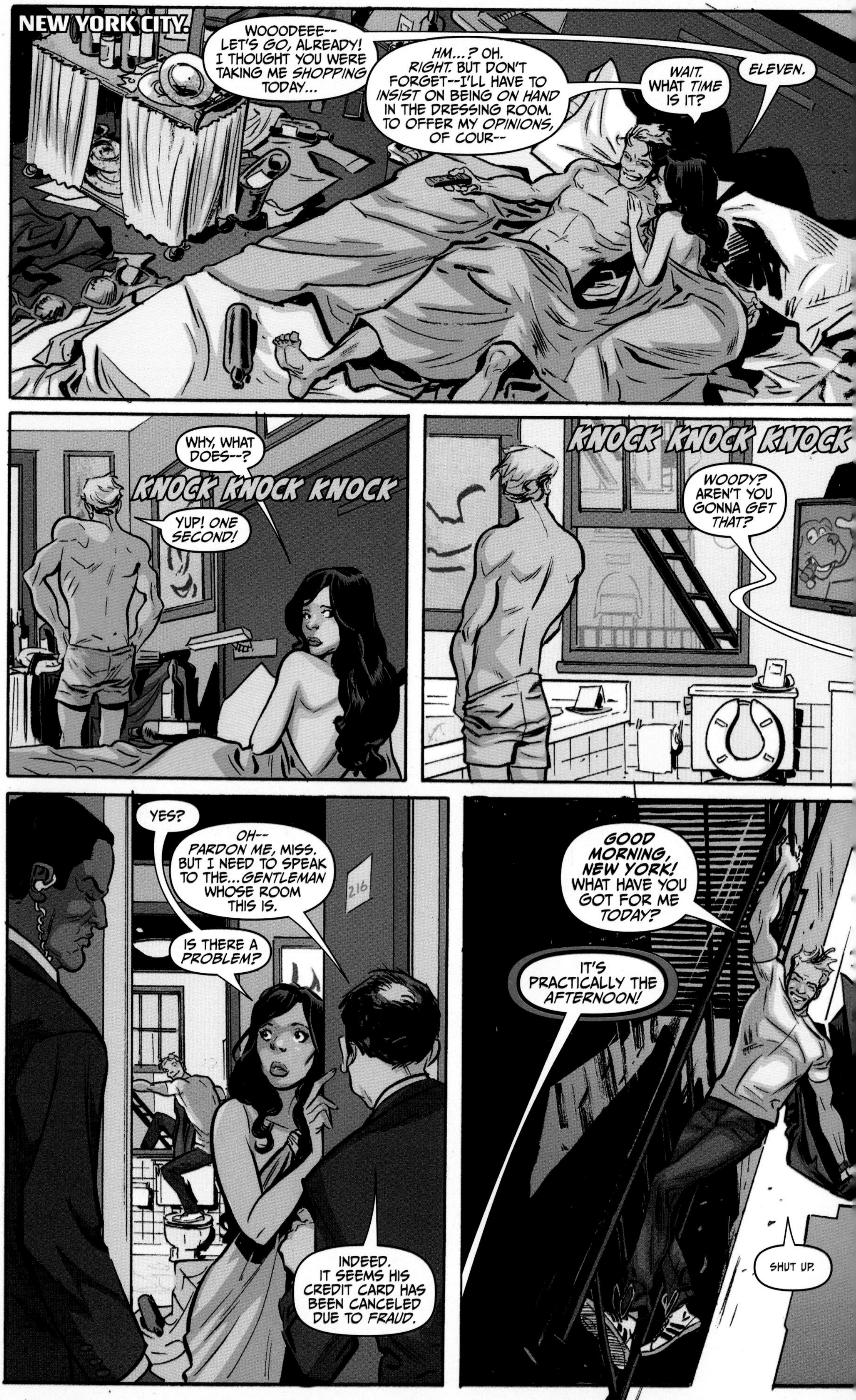
NEW YORK CITY.
WOOODEEE-- LET'S GO, ALREADY! I THOUGHT YOU WERE TAKING ME SHOPPING TODAY...
HM...? OH. RIGHT. BUT DON'T FORGET--I'LL HAVE TO INSIST ON BEING ON HAND IN THE DRESSING ROOM. TO OFFER MY OPINIONS, OF COUR--
WAIT. WHAT TIME IS IT?
ELEVEN.
WHY, WHAT DOES--?
KNOCK KNOCK KNOCK
YUP! ONE SECOND!
KNOCK KNOCK KNOCK
WOODY? AREN'T YOU GONNA GET THAT?
YES?
OH-- PARDON ME, MISS. BUT I NEED TO SPEAK TO THE...GENTLEMAN WHOSE ROOM THIS IS.
216
IS THERE A PROBLEM?
INDEED. IT SEEMS HIS CREDIT CARD HAS BEEN CANCELED DUE TO FRAUD.
GOOD MORNING, NEW YORK! WHAT HAVE YOU GOT FOR ME TODAY?
IT'S PRACTICALLY THE AFTERNOON!
SHUT UP.

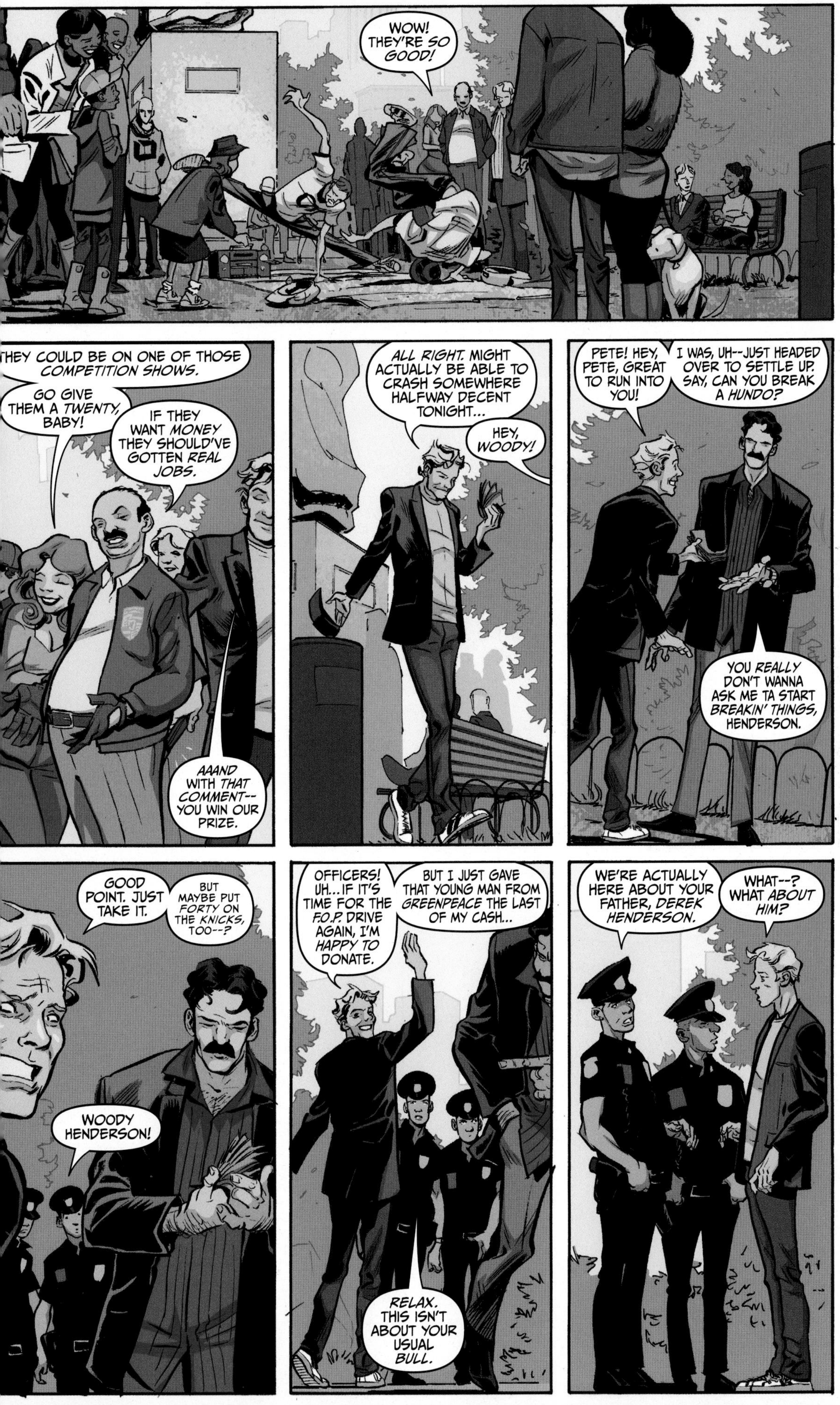
WOW! THEY'RE SO GOOD!
THEY COULD BE ON ONE OF THOSE COMPETITION SHOWS.
GO GIVE THEM A TWENTY, BABY!
IF THEY WANT MONEY THEY SHOULD'VE GOTTEN REAL JOBS.
AAAND WITH THAT COMMENT-- YOU WIN OUR PRIZE.
ALL RIGHT. MIGHT ACTUALLY BE ABLE TO CRASH SOMEWHERE HALFWAY DECENT TONIGHT...
HEY, WOODY!
PETE! HEY, PETE, GREAT TO RUN INTO YOU!
I WAS, UH--JUST HEADED OVER TO SETTLE UP. SAY, CAN YOU BREAK A HUNDO?
YOU REALLY DON'T WANNA ASK ME TA START BREAKIN' THINGS, HENDERSON.
GOOD POINT. JUST TAKE IT.
BUT MAYBE PUT FORTY ON THE KNICKS, TOO--?
WOODY HENDERSON!
OFFICERS! UH...IF IT'S TIME FOR THE F.O.P. DRIVE AGAIN, I'M HAPPY TO DONATE.
BUT I JUST GAVE THAT YOUNG MAN FROM GREENPEACE THE LAST OF MY CASH...
RELAX. THIS ISN'T ABOUT YOUR USUAL BULL.
WE'RE ACTUALLY HERE ABOUT YOUR FATHER, DEREK HENDERSON.
WHAT--? WHAT ABOUT HIM?

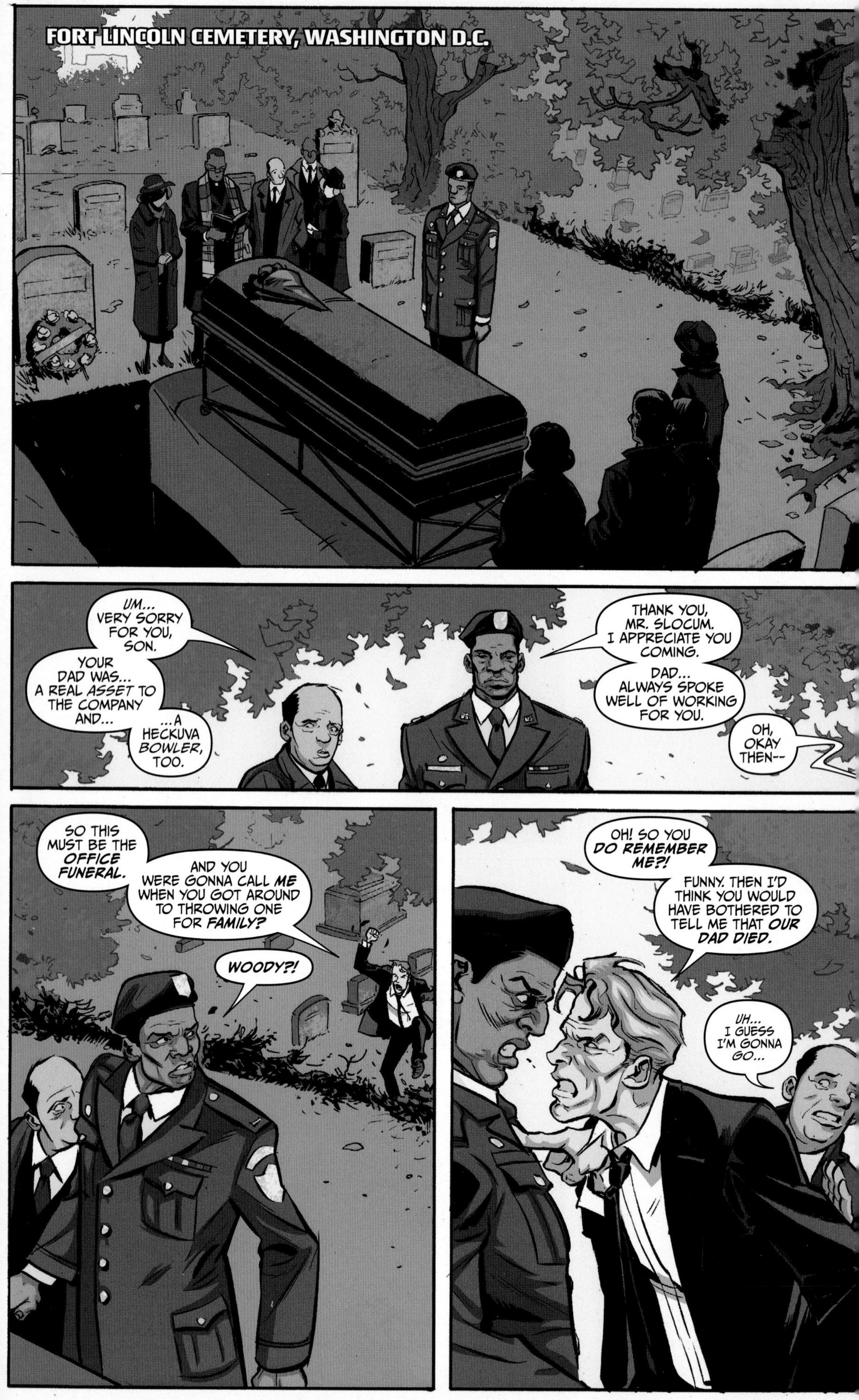
FORT LINCOLN CEMETERY, WASHINGTON D.C.
UM... VERY SORRY FOR YOU, SON.
YOUR DAD WAS... A REAL ASSET TO THE COMPANY AND...
...A HECKUVA BOWLER, TOO.
THANK YOU, MR. SLOCUM. I APPRECIATE YOU COMING.
DAD... ALWAYS SPOKE WELL OF WORKING FOR YOU.
OH, OKAY THEN--
SO THIS MUST BE THE OFFICE FUNERAL.
AND YOU WERE GONNA CALL ME WHEN YOU GOT AROUND TO THROWING ONE FOR FAMILY?
WOODY?!
OH! SO YOU DO REMEMBER ME?!
FUNNY. THEN I'D THINK YOU WOULD HAVE BOTHERED TO TELL ME THAT OUR DAD DIED.
UH... I GUESS I'M GONNA GO...

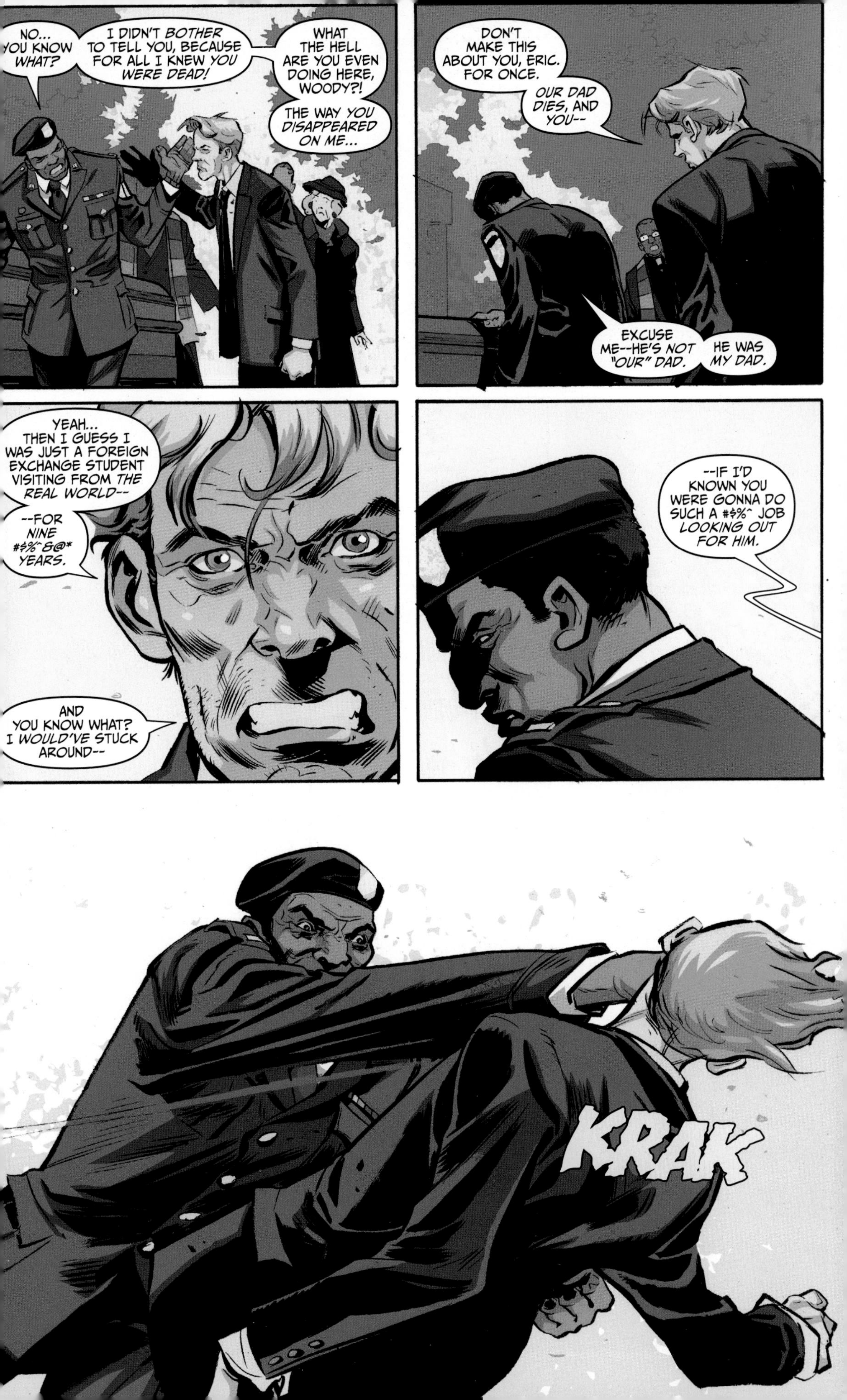
NO... YOU KNOW WHAT?
I DIDN'T BOTHER TO TELL YOU, BECAUSE FOR ALL I KNEW YOU WERE DEAD!
WHAT THE HELL ARE YOU EVEN DOING HERE, WOODY?!
THE WAY YOU DISAPPEARED ON ME...
DON'T MAKE THIS ABOUT YOU, ERIC. FOR ONCE.
OUR DAD DIES, AND YOU--
EXCUSE ME--HE'S NOT "OUR" DAD.
HE WAS MY DAD.
YEAH... THEN I GUESS I WAS JUST A FOREIGN EXCHANGE STUDENT VISITING FROM THE REAL WORLD--
--FOR NINE #$%^&@* YEARS.
AND YOU KNOW WHAT? I WOULD'VE STUCK AROUND--
--IF I'D KNOWN YOU WERE GONNA DO SUCH A #$%^ JOB LOOKING OUT FOR HIM.
KRAK

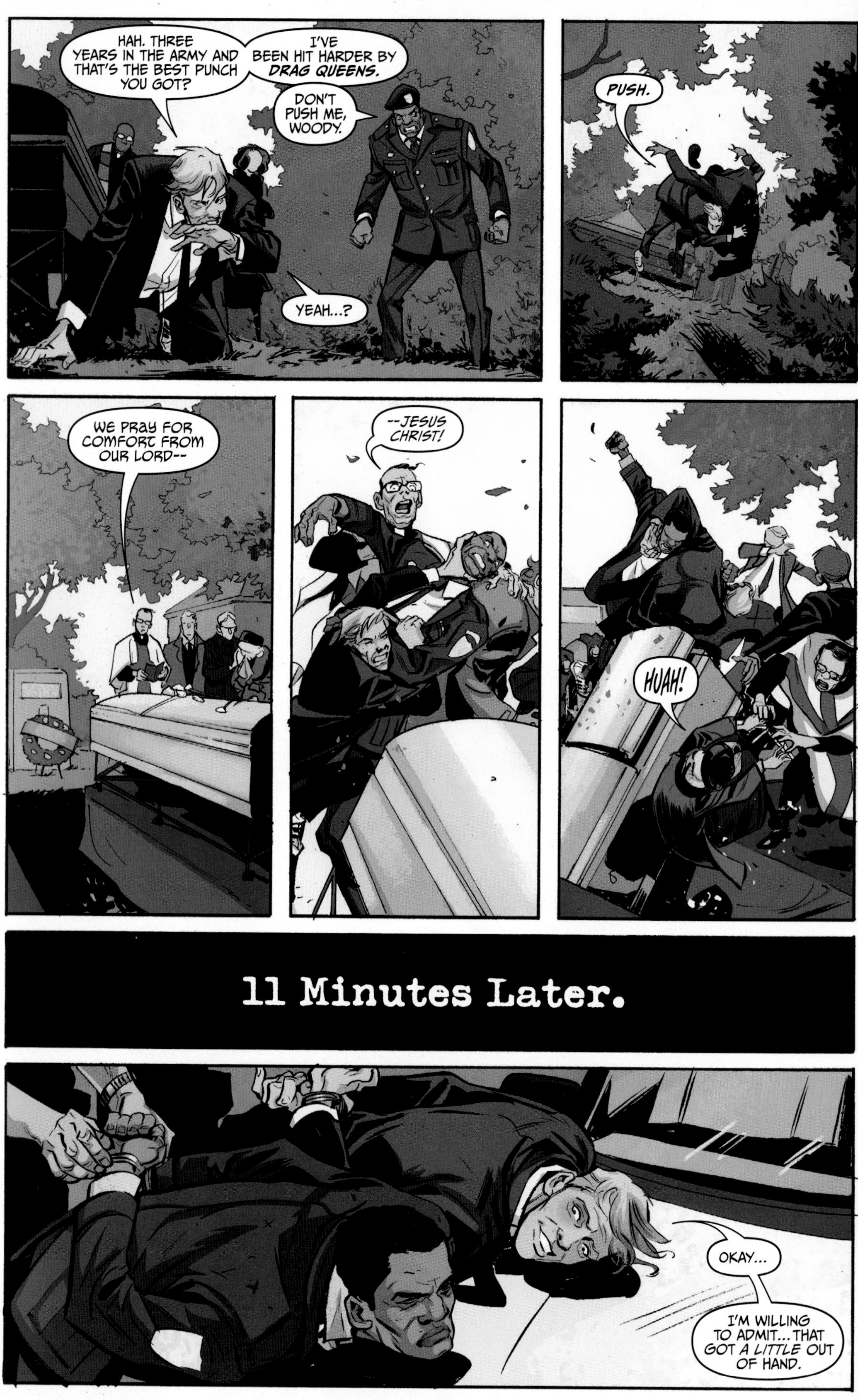
HAH. THREE YEARS IN THE ARMY AND THAT'S THE BEST PUNCH YOU GOT?
I'VE BEEN HIT HARDER BY DRAG QUEENS.
DON'T PUSH ME, WOODY.
YEAH...?
PUSH.
WE PRAY FOR COMFORT FROM OUR LORD--
--JESUS CHRIST!
HUAH!
11 Minutes Later.
OKAY...
I'M WILLING TO ADMIT... THAT GOT A LITTLE OUT OF HAND.

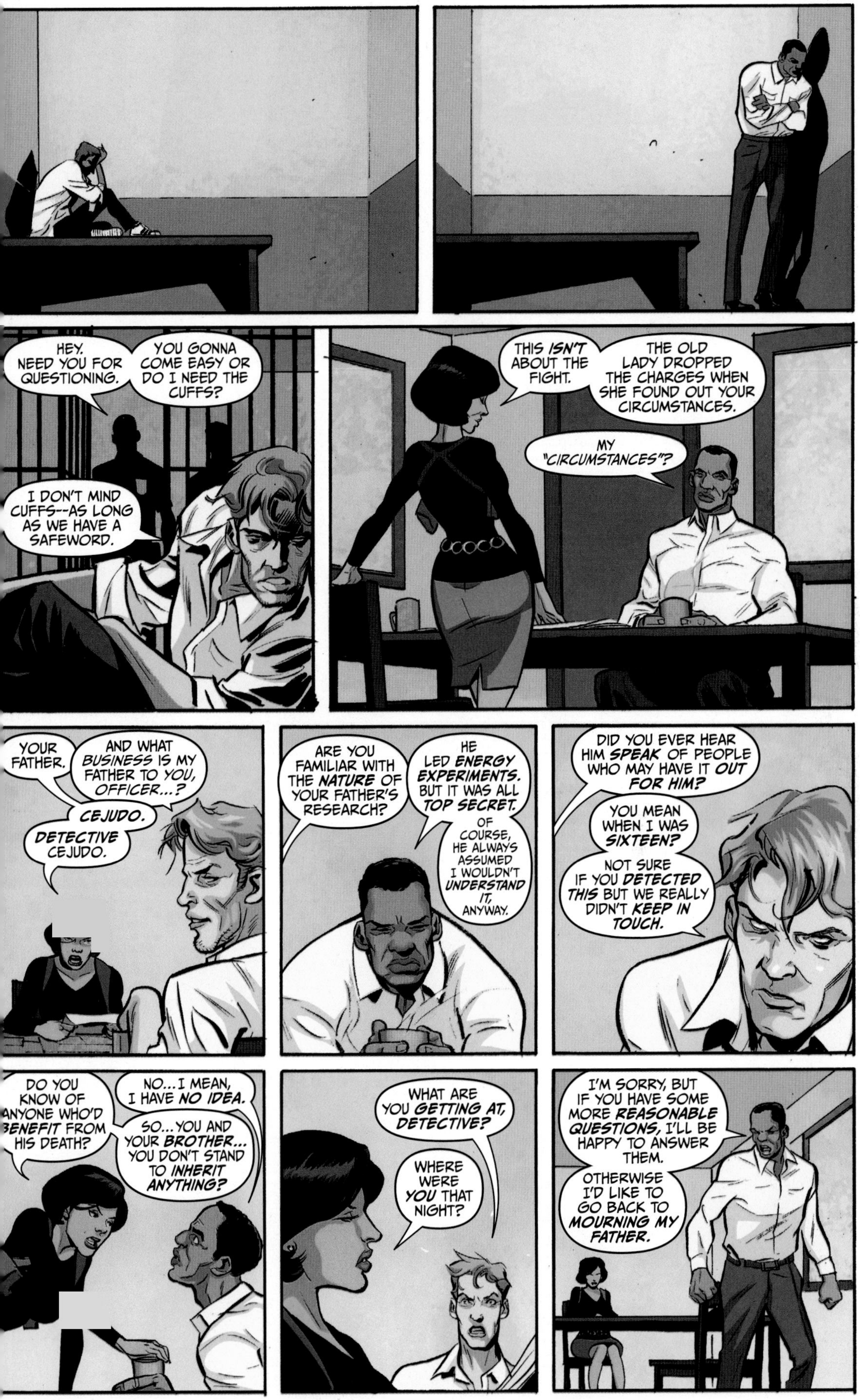
HEY. NEED YOU FOR QUESTIONING.
YOU GONNA COME EASY OR DO I NEED THE CUFFS?
I DON'T MIND CUFFS--AS LONG AS WE HAVE A SAFEWORD.
THIS ISN'T ABOUT THE FIGHT.
THE OLD LADY DROPPED THE CHARGES WHEN SHE FOUND OUT YOUR CIRCUMSTANCES.
MY "CIRCUMSTANCES"?
YOUR FATHER.
AND WHAT BUSINESS IS MY FATHER TO YOU, OFFICER...?
CEJUDO.
DETECTIVE CEJUDO.
ARE YOU FAMILIAR WITH THE NATURE OF YOUR FATHER'S RESEARCH?
HE LED ENERGY EXPERIMENTS. BUT IT WAS ALL TOP SECRET.
OF COURSE, HE ALWAYS ASSUMED I WOULDN'T UNDERSTAND IT, ANYWAY.
DID YOU EVER HEAR HIM SPEAK OF PEOPLE WHO MAY HAVE IT OUT FOR HIM?
YOU MEAN WHEN I WAS SIXTEEN?
NOT SURE IF YOU DETECTED THIS BUT WE REALLY DIDN'T KEEP IN TOUCH.
DO YOU KNOW OF ANYONE WHO'D BENEFIT FROM HIS DEATH?
NO...I MEAN, I HAVE NO IDEA.
SO...YOU AND YOUR BROTHER... YOU DON'T STAND TO INHERIT ANYTHING?
WHAT ARE YOU GETTING AT, DETECTIVE?
WHERE WERE YOU THAT NIGHT?
I'M SORRY, BUT IF YOU HAVE SOME MORE REASONABLE QUESTIONS, I'LL BE HAPPY TO ANSWER THEM.
OTHERWISE I'D LIKE TO GO BACK TO MOURNING MY FATHER.

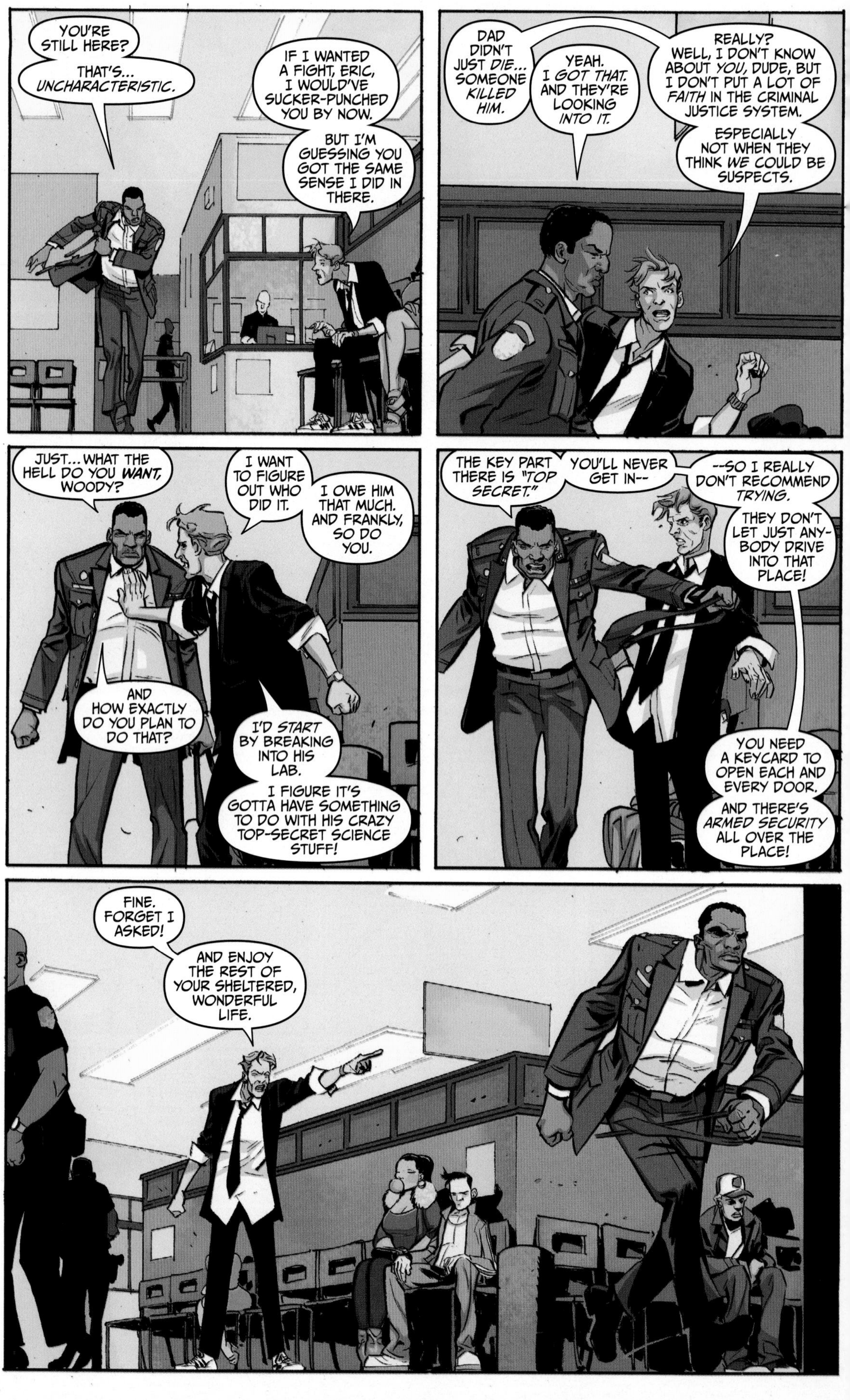
YOU'RE STILL HERE?
THAT'S... UNCHARACTERISTIC.
IF I WANTED A FIGHT, ERIC, I WOULD'VE SUCKER-PUNCHED YOU BY NOW.
BUT I'M GUESSING YOU GOT THE SAME SENSE I DID IN THERE.
DAD DIDN'T JUST DIE... SOMEONE KILLED HIM.
YEAH. I GOT THAT. AND THEY'RE LOOKING INTO IT.
REALLY? WELL, I DON'T KNOW ABOUT YOU, DUDE, BUT I DON'T PUT A LOT OF FAITH IN THE CRIMINAL JUSTICE SYSTEM.
ESPECIALLY NOT WHEN THEY THINK WE COULD BE SUSPECTS.
JUST... WHAT THE HELL DO YOU WANT, WOODY?
I WANT TO FIGURE OUT WHO DID IT.
I OWE HIM THAT MUCH. AND FRANKLY, SO DO YOU.
AND HOW EXACTLY DO YOU PLAN TO DO THAT?
I'D START BY BREAKING INTO HIS LAB.
I FIGURE IT'S GOTTA HAVE SOMETHING TO DO WITH HIS CRAZY TOP-SECRET SCIENCE STUFF!
THE KEY PART THERE IS "TOP SECRET."
YOU'LL NEVER GET IN--
--SO I REALLY DON'T RECOMMEND TRYING.
THEY DON'T LET JUST ANYBODY DRIVE INTO THAT PLACE!
YOU NEED A KEYCARD TO OPEN EACH AND EVERY DOOR.
AND THERE'S ARMED SECURITY ALL OVER THE PLACE!
FINE. FORGET I ASKED!
AND ENJOY THE REST OF YOUR SHELTERED, WONDERFUL LIFE.

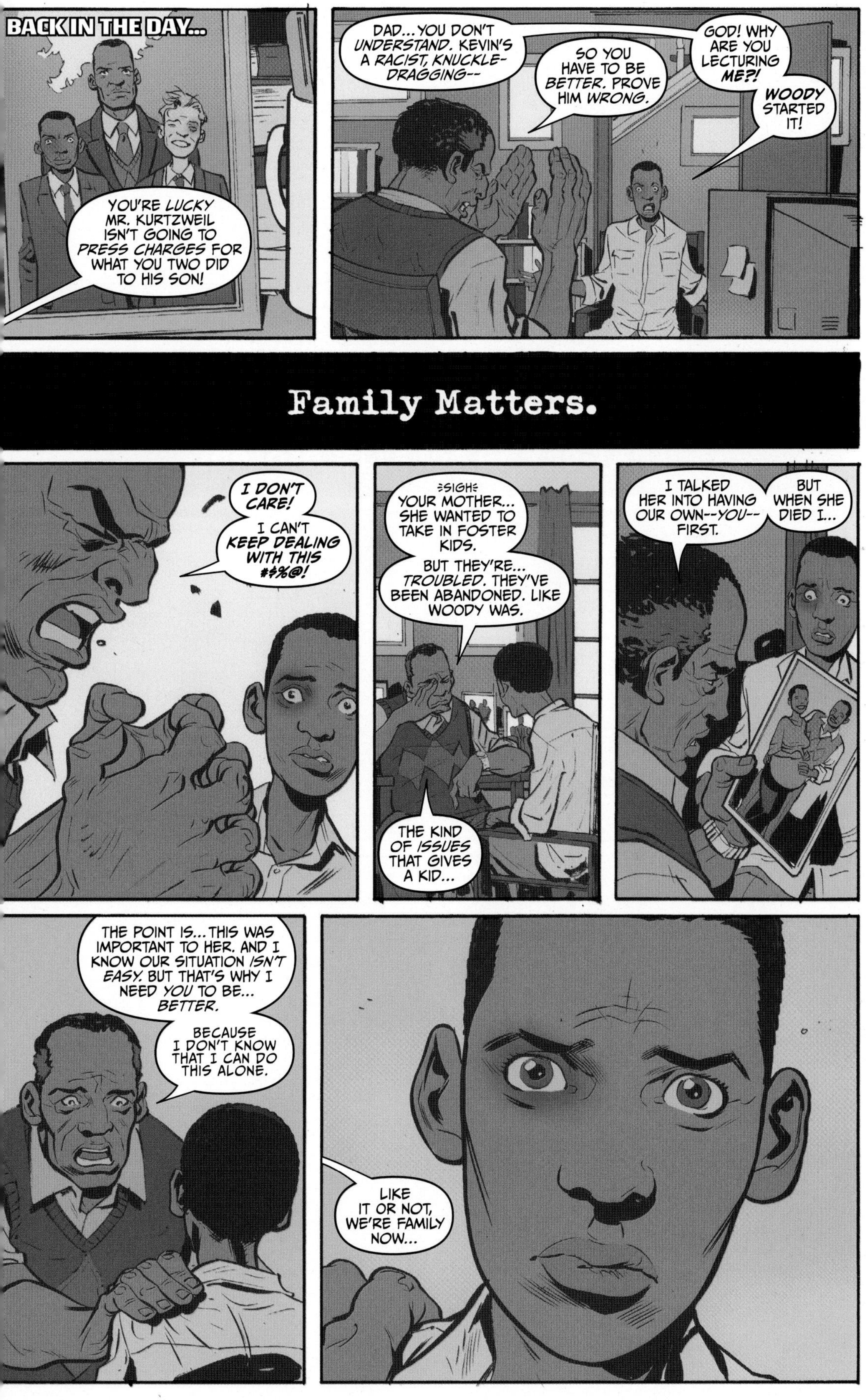
BACK IN THE DAY...
YOU'RE LUCKY MR. KURTZWEIL ISN'T GOING TO PRESS CHARGES FOR WHAT YOU TWO DID TO HIS SON!
DAD... YOU DON'T UNDERSTAND. KEVIN'S A RACIST, KNUCKLE-DRAGGING--
SO YOU HAVE TO BE BETTER. PROVE HIM WRONG.
GOD! WHY ARE YOU LECTURING ME?!
WOODY STARTED IT!
Family Matters.
I DON'T CARE!
I CAN'T KEEP DEALING WITH THIS #$%@!
=SIGH=
YOUR MOTHER... SHE WANTED TO TAKE IN FOSTER KIDS.
BUT THEY'RE... TROUBLED. THEY'VE BEEN ABANDONED. LIKE WOODY WAS.
THE KIND OF ISSUES THAT GIVES A KID...
I TALKED HER INTO HAVING OUR OWN--YOU--FIRST.
BUT WHEN SHE DIED I...
THE POINT IS... THIS WAS IMPORTANT TO HER. AND I KNOW OUR SITUATION ISN'T EASY. BUT THAT'S WHY I NEED YOU TO BE... BETTER.
BECAUSE I DON'T KNOW THAT I CAN DO THIS ALONE.
LIKE IT OR NOT, WE'RE FAMILY NOW...

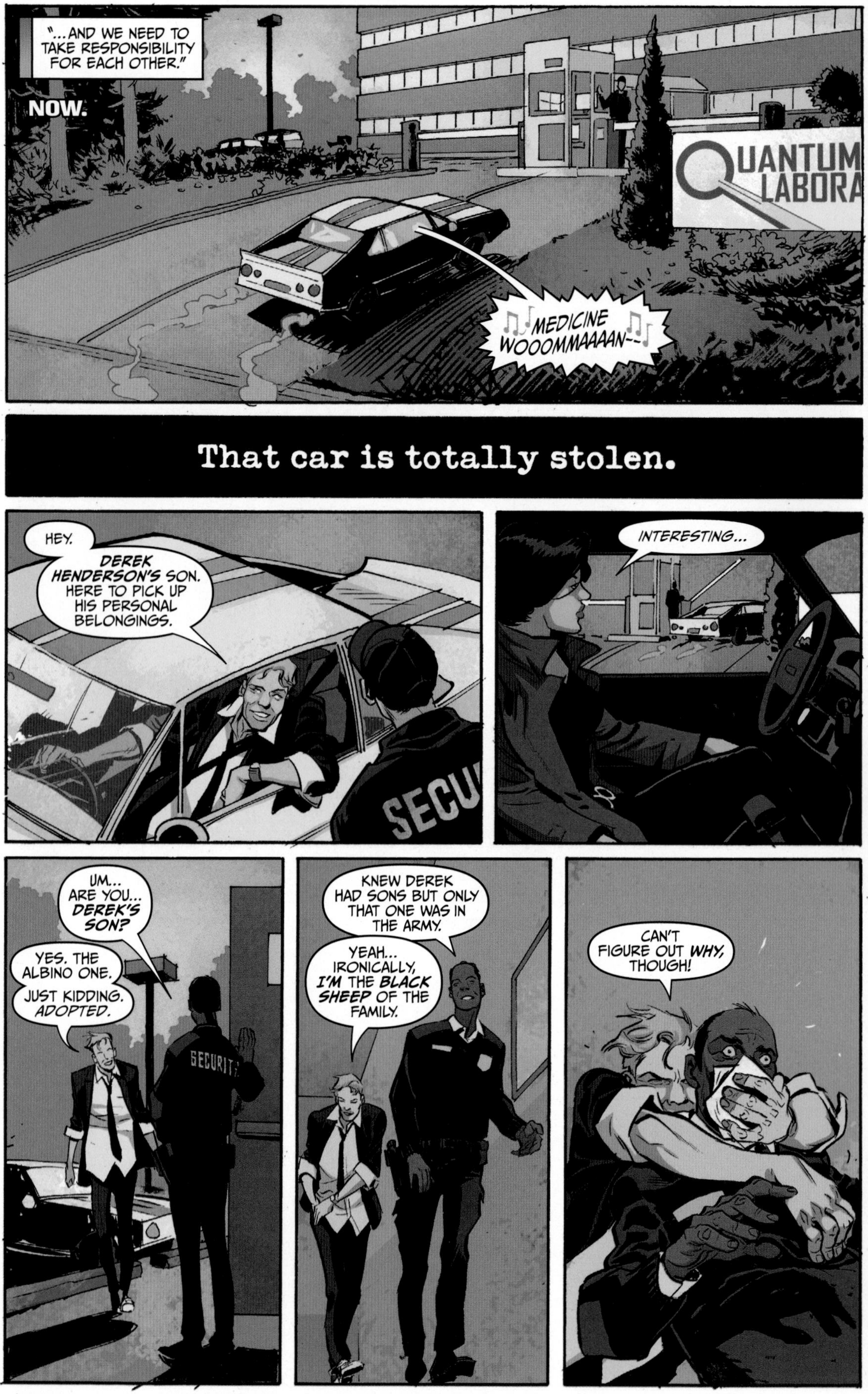
"...AND WE NEED TO TAKE RESPONSIBILITY FOR EACH OTHER."
NOW.
QUANTUM
LABORA
MEDICINE WOOOMMAAAAN--
That car is totally stolen.
HEY.
DEREK HENDERSON'S SON. HERE TO PICK UP HIS PERSONAL BELONGINGS.
SECU
INTERESTING...
UM... ARE YOU... DEREK'S SON?
YES. THE ALBINO ONE.
JUST KIDDING. ADOPTED.
SECURITY
KNEW DEREK HAD SONS BUT ONLY THAT ONE WAS IN THE ARMY.
YEAH... IRONICALLY, I'M THE BLACK SHEEP OF THE FAMILY.
CAN'T FIGURE OUT WHY, THOUGH!

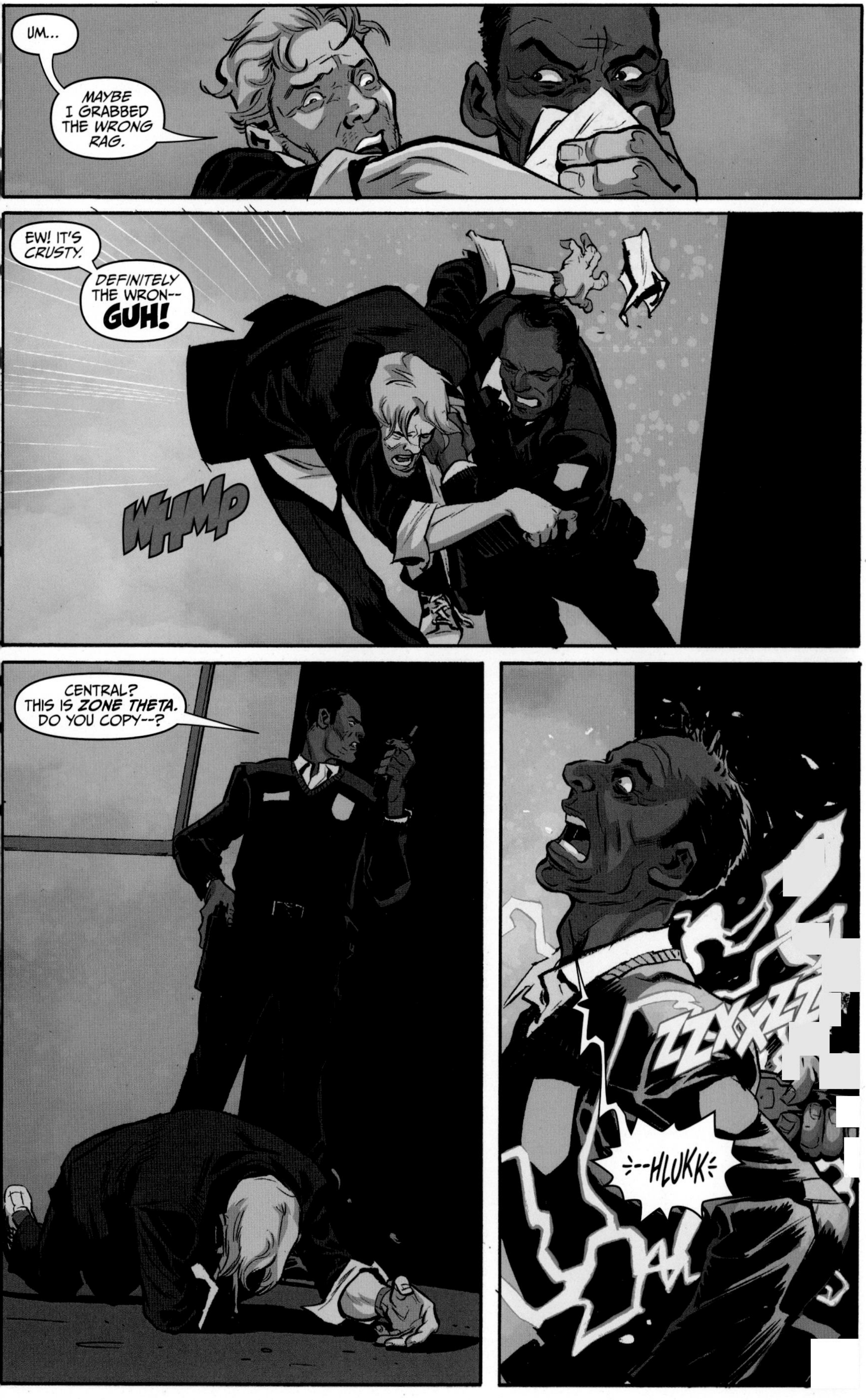
UM...
MAYBE I GRABBED THE WRONG RAG.
EW! IT'S CRUSTY.
DEFINITELY THE WRON-- GUH!
WHMP
CENTRAL? THIS IS ZONE THETA. DO YOU COPY--?
ZZ-XXZZ
--HLUKK

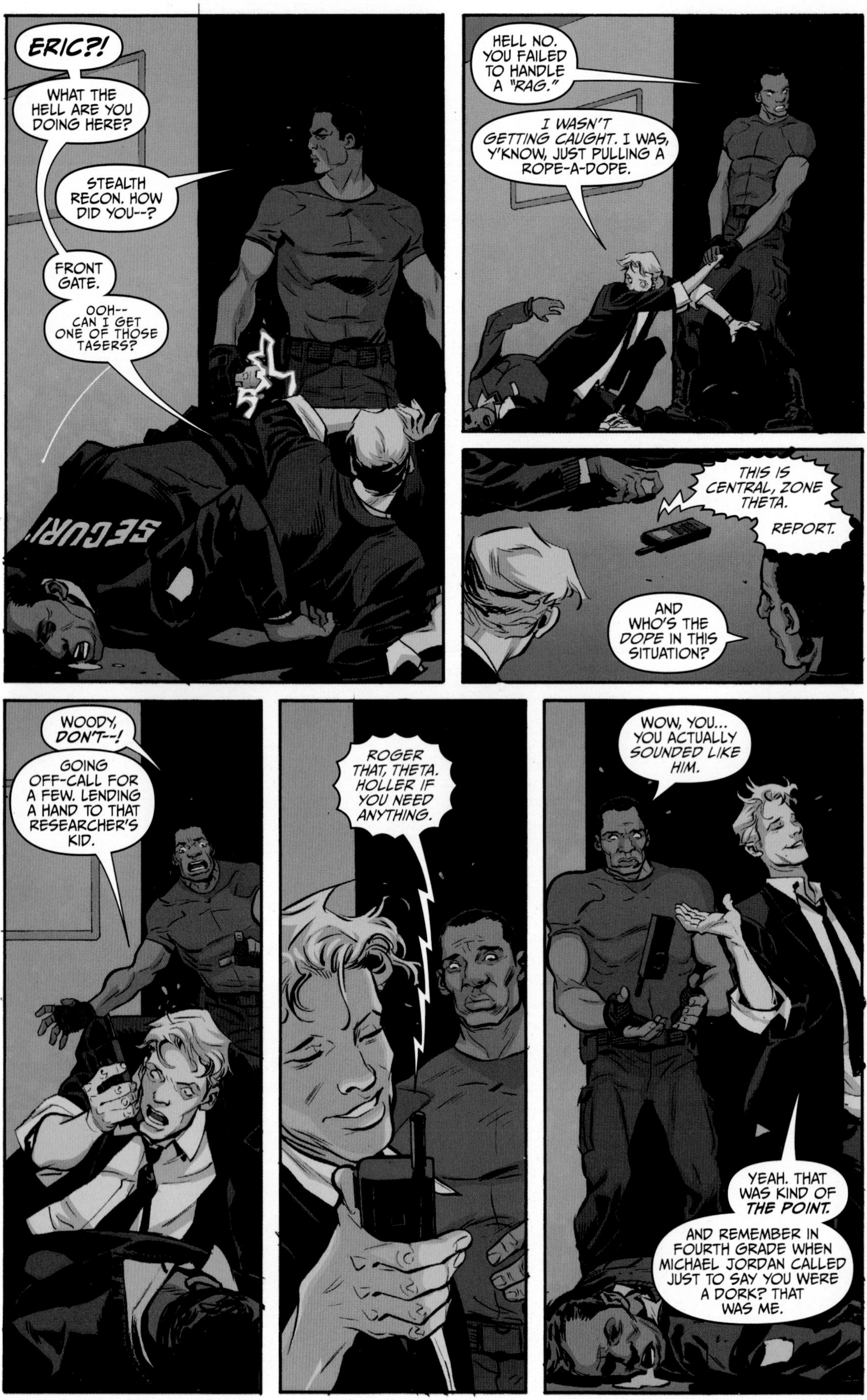
ERIC?!
WHAT THE HELL ARE YOU DOING HERE?
STEALTH RECON. HOW DID YOU--?
FRONT GATE.
OOH-- CAN I GET ONE OF THOSE TASERS?
SECURI
HELL NO. YOU FAILED TO HANDLE A "RAG."
I WASN'T GETTING CAUGHT. I WAS, Y'KNOW, JUST PULLING A ROPE-A-DOPE.
THIS IS CENTRAL, ZONE THETA.
REPORT.
AND WHO'S THE DOPE IN THIS SITUATION?
WOODY, DON'T--!
GOING OFF-CALL FOR A FEW. LENDING A HAND TO THAT RESEARCHER'S KID.
ROGER THAT, THETA. HOLLER IF YOU NEED ANYTHING.
WOW, YOU... YOU ACTUALLY SOUNDED LIKE HIM.
YEAH. THAT WAS KIND OF THE POINT.
AND REMEMBER IN FOURTH GRADE WHEN MICHAEL JORDAN CALLED JUST TO SAY YOU WERE A DORK? THAT WAS ME.

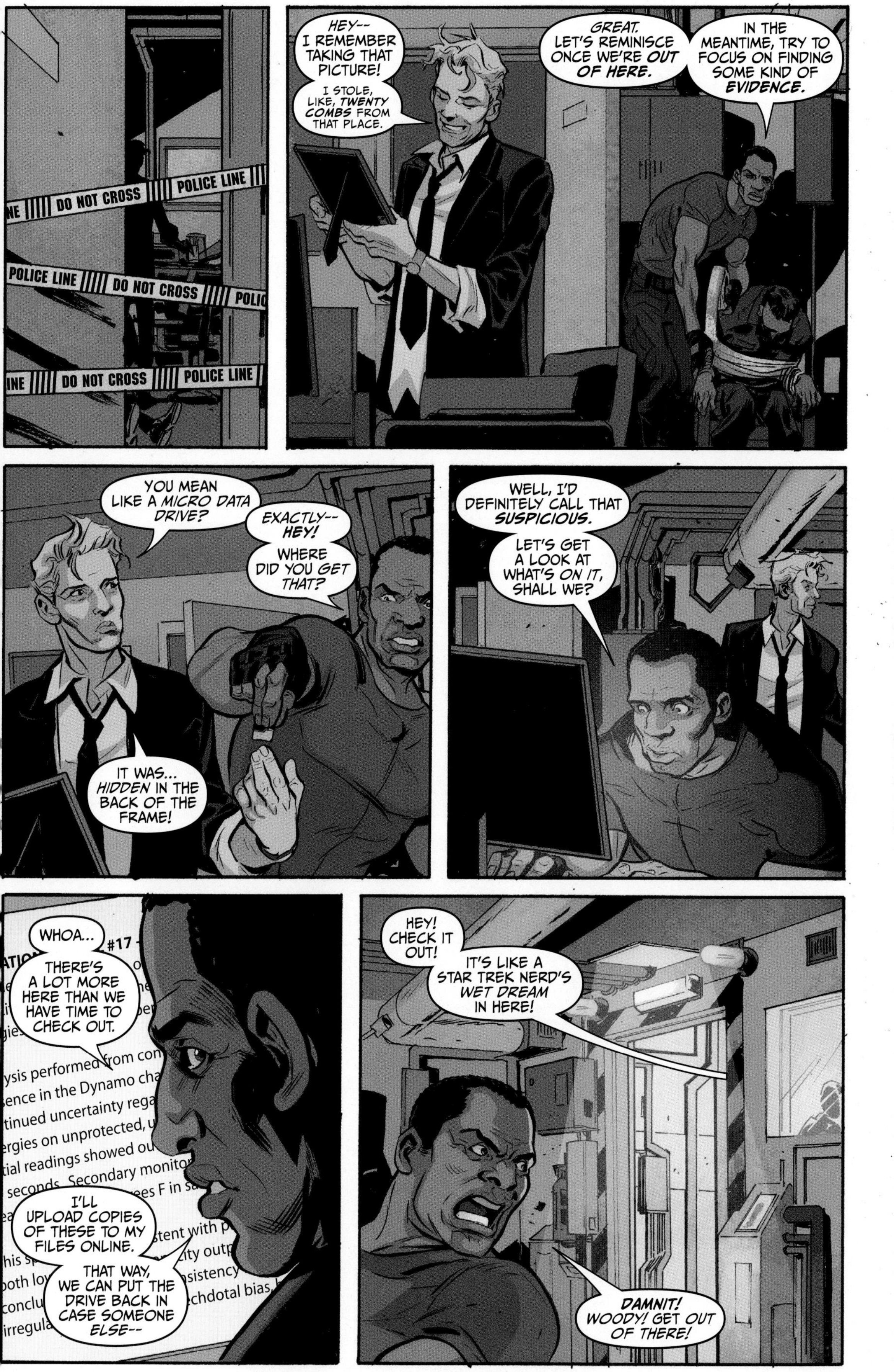

POLICE LINE
DO NOT CROSS
HEY-- I REMEMBER TAKING THAT PICTURE!
I STOLE, LIKE, TWENTY COMBS FROM THAT PLACE.
GREAT. LET'S REMINISCE ONCE WE'RE OUT OF HERE.
IN THE MEANTIME, TRY TO FOCUS ON FINDING SOME KIND OF EVIDENCE.
YOU MEAN LIKE A MICRO DATA DRIVE?
EXACTLY-- HEY!
WHERE DID YOU GET THAT?
IT WAS... HIDDEN IN THE BACK OF THE FRAME!
WELL, I'D DEFINITELY CALL THAT SUSPICIOUS.
LET'S GET A LOOK AT WHAT'S ON IT, SHALL WE?
WHOA...
THERE'S A LOT MORE HERE THAN WE HAVE TIME TO CHECK OUT.
I'LL UPLOAD COPIES OF THESE TO MY FILES ONLINE.
THAT WAY, WE CAN PUT THE DRIVE BACK IN CASE SOMEONE ELSE--
HEY! CHECK IT OUT!
IT'S LIKE A STAR TREK NERD'S WET DREAM IN HERE!
DAMNIT! WOODY! GET OUT OF THERE!

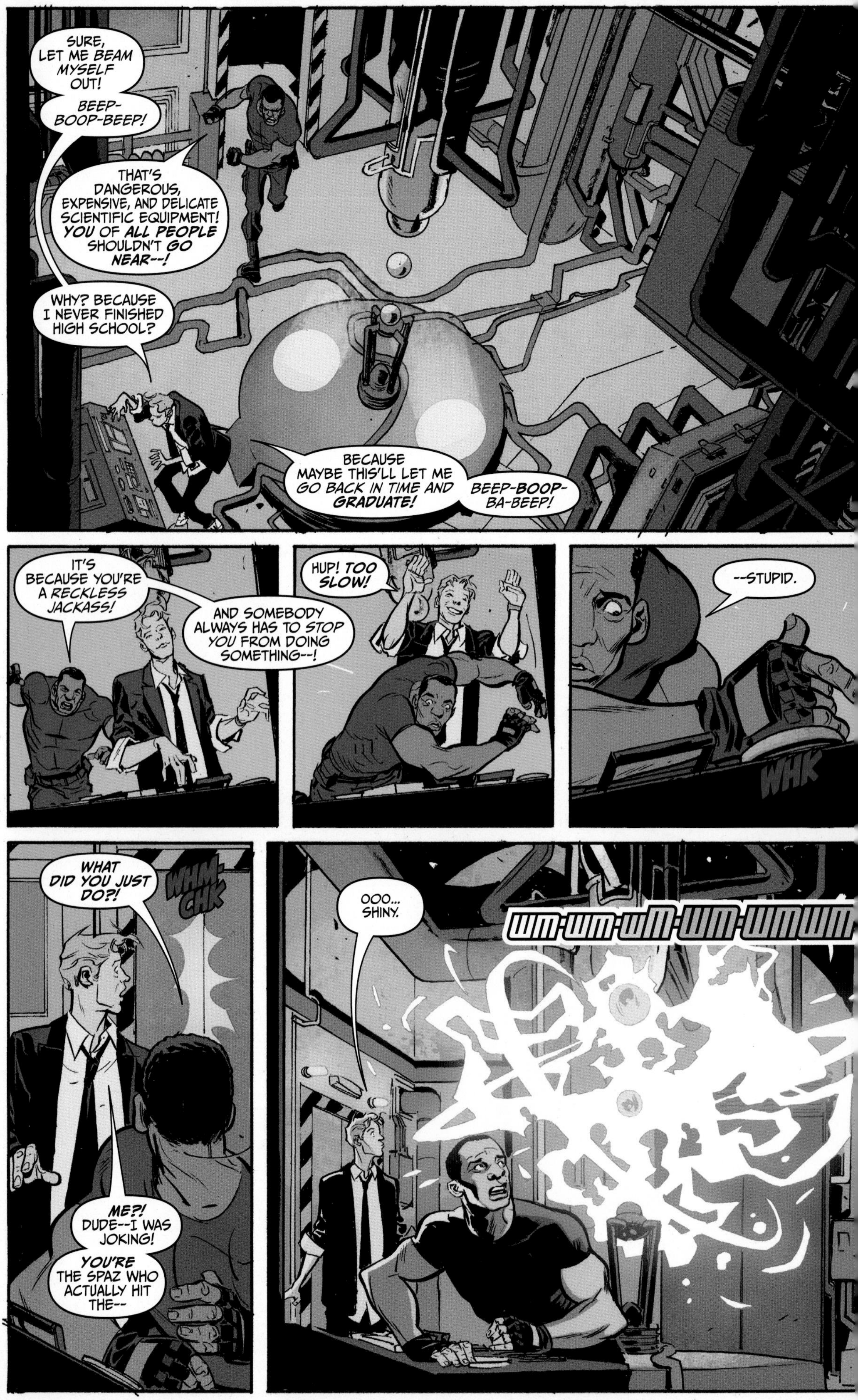
SURE, LET ME *BEAM* MYSELF OUT!
BEEP-BOOP-BEEP!
THAT'S DANGEROUS, EXPENSIVE, AND DELICATE SCIENTIFIC EQUIPMENT! ***YOU*** OF ***ALL PEOPLE*** SHOULDN'T ***GO NEAR--!***
WHY? BECAUSE I NEVER FINISHED HIGH SCHOOL?
BECAUSE MAYBE THIS'LL LET ME *GO BACK IN TIME AND* ***GRADUATE!***
*BEEP-**BOOP**-BA-BEEP!*
IT'S BECAUSE YOU'RE A *RECKLESS JACKASS!*
AND SOMEBODY ALWAYS HAS TO *STOP YOU* FROM DOING SOMETHING--!
HUP! ***TOO SLOW!***
--STUPID.
WHK
WHAT DID YOU JUST DO?!
WHM-CHK
ME?! DUDE--I WAS JOKING!
YOU'RE THE SPAZ WHO ACTUALLY HIT THE--
OOO... SHINY.
WM-WM-WM-WM-WMWM

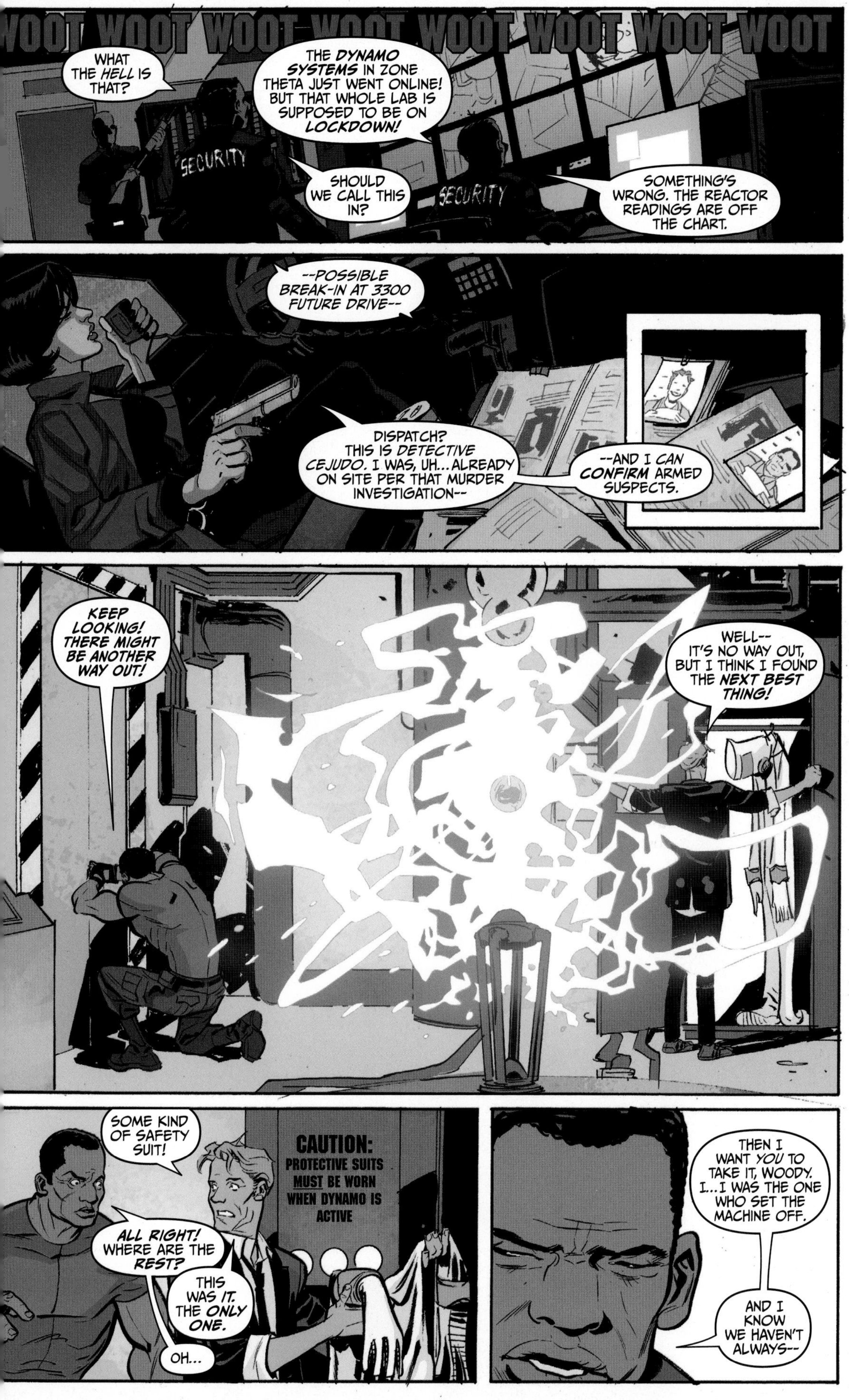
WOOT WOOT WOOT WOOT WOOT WOOT WOOT WOOT
WHAT THE HELL IS THAT?
THE DYNAMO SYSTEMS IN ZONE THETA JUST WENT ONLINE! BUT THAT WHOLE LAB IS SUPPOSED TO BE ON LOCKDOWN!
SECURITY
SHOULD WE CALL THIS IN?
SECURITY
SOMETHING'S WRONG. THE REACTOR READINGS ARE OFF THE CHART.
--POSSIBLE BREAK-IN AT 3300 FUTURE DRIVE--
DISPATCH? THIS IS DETECTIVE CEJUDO. I WAS, UH...ALREADY ON SITE PER THAT MURDER INVESTIGATION--
--AND I CAN CONFIRM ARMED SUSPECTS.
KEEP LOOKING! THERE MIGHT BE ANOTHER WAY OUT!
WELL-- IT'S NO WAY OUT, BUT I THINK I FOUND THE NEXT BEST THING!
SOME KIND OF SAFETY SUIT!
CAUTION: PROTECTIVE SUITS MUST BE WORN WHEN DYNAMO IS ACTIVE
ALL RIGHT! WHERE ARE THE REST?
THIS WAS IT. THE ONLY ONE.
OH...
THEN I WANT YOU TO TAKE IT, WOODY. I...I WAS THE ONE WHO SET THE MACHINE OFF.
AND I KNOW WE HAVEN'T ALWAYS--

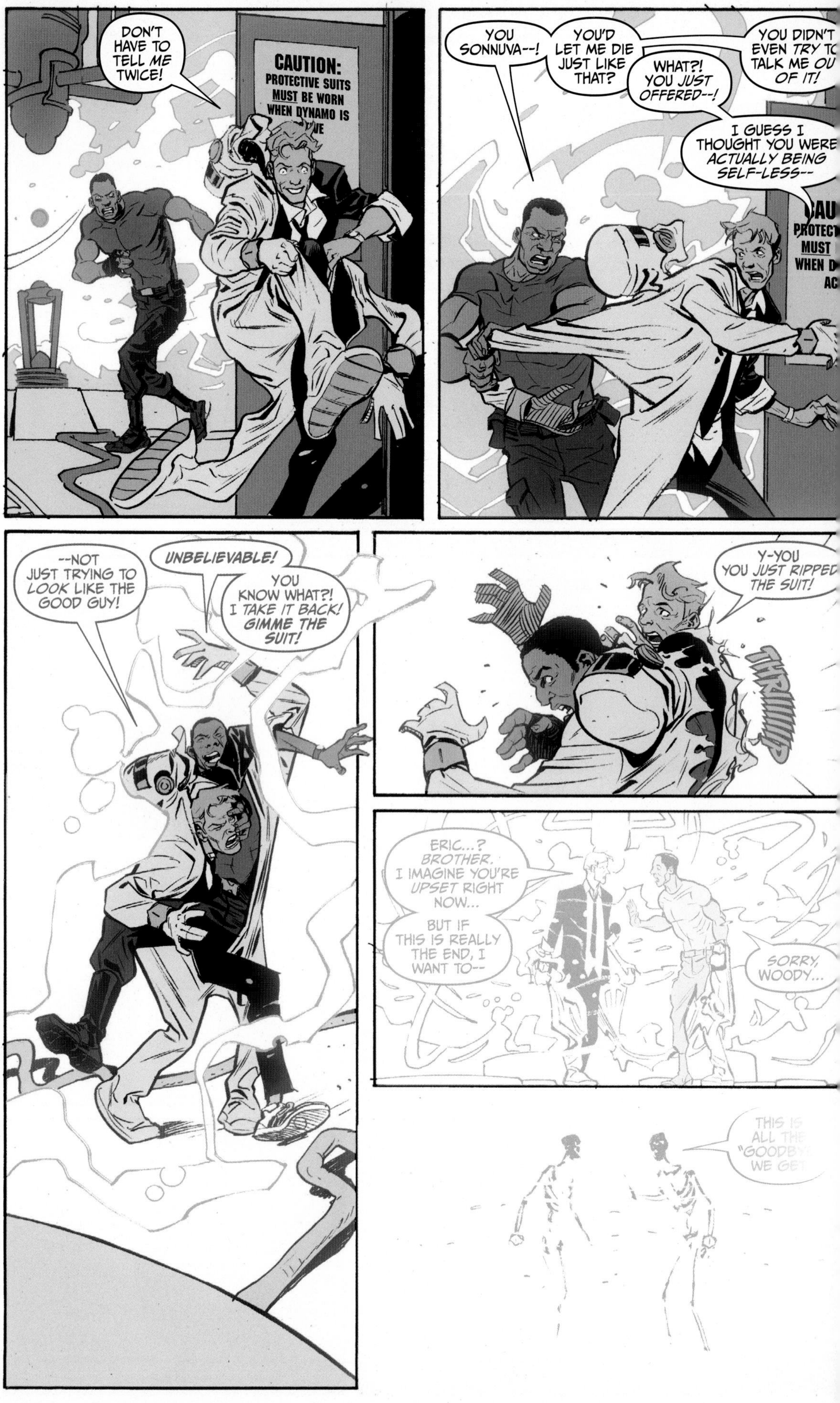
DON'T HAVE TO TELL ME TWICE!
CAUTION: PROTECTIVE SUITS MUST BE WORN WHEN DYNAMO IS
YOU SONNUVA--!
YOU'D LET ME DIE JUST LIKE THAT?
WHAT?! YOU JUST OFFERED--!
YOU DIDN'T EVEN TRY TO TALK ME OU OF IT!
I GUESS I THOUGHT YOU WERE ACTUALLY BEING SELF-LESS--
--NOT JUST TRYING TO LOOK LIKE THE GOOD GUY!
UNBELIEVABLE!
YOU KNOW WHAT?! I TAKE IT BACK! GIMME THE SUIT!
Y-YOU YOU JUST RIPPED THE SUIT!
ERIC...? BROTHER. I IMAGINE YOU'RE UPSET RIGHT NOW...
BUT IF THIS IS REALLY THE END, I WANT TO--
SORRY, WOODY...
THIS IS ALL THE

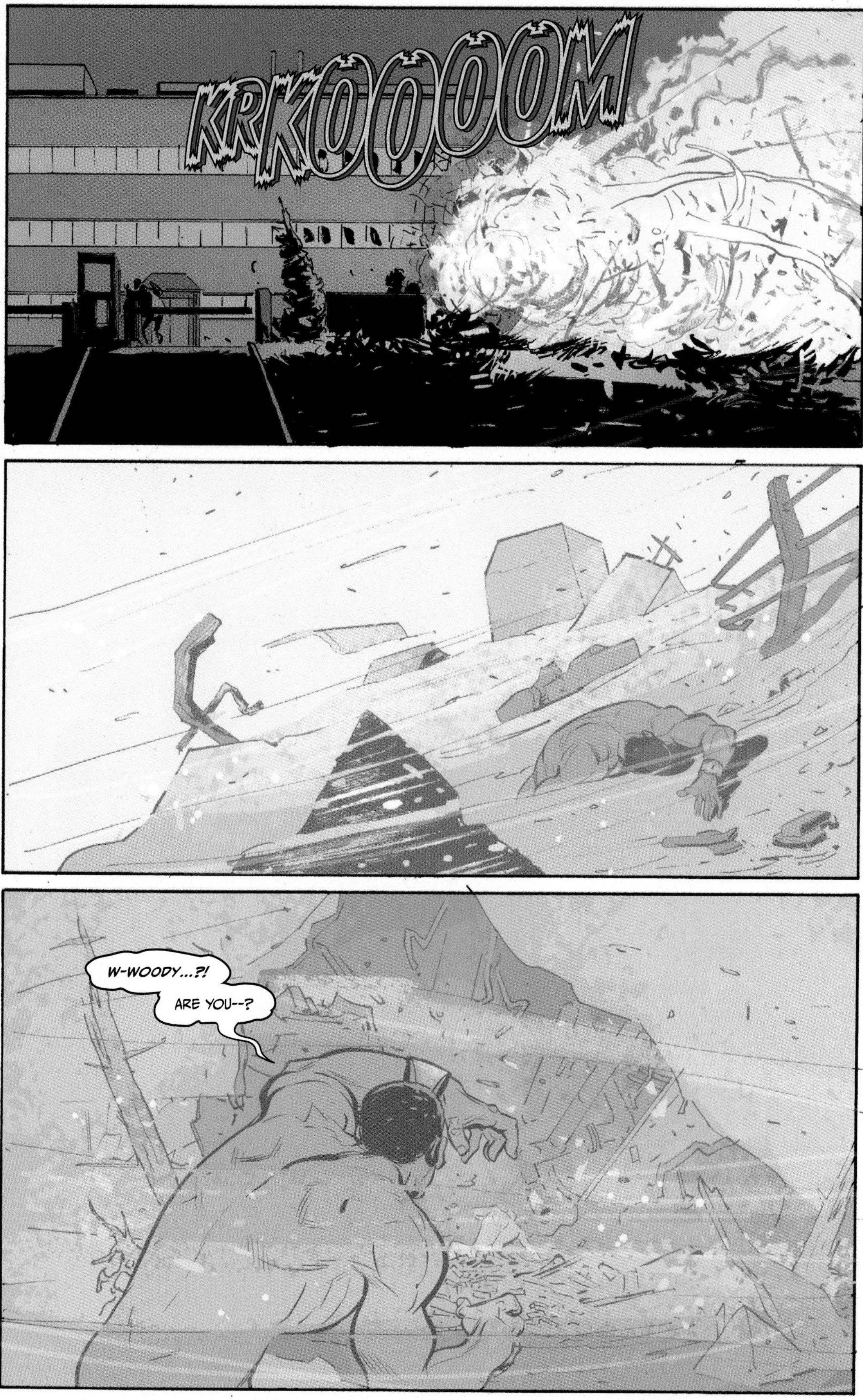
KRKOOOOOM
W-WOODY...?!
ARE YOU--?

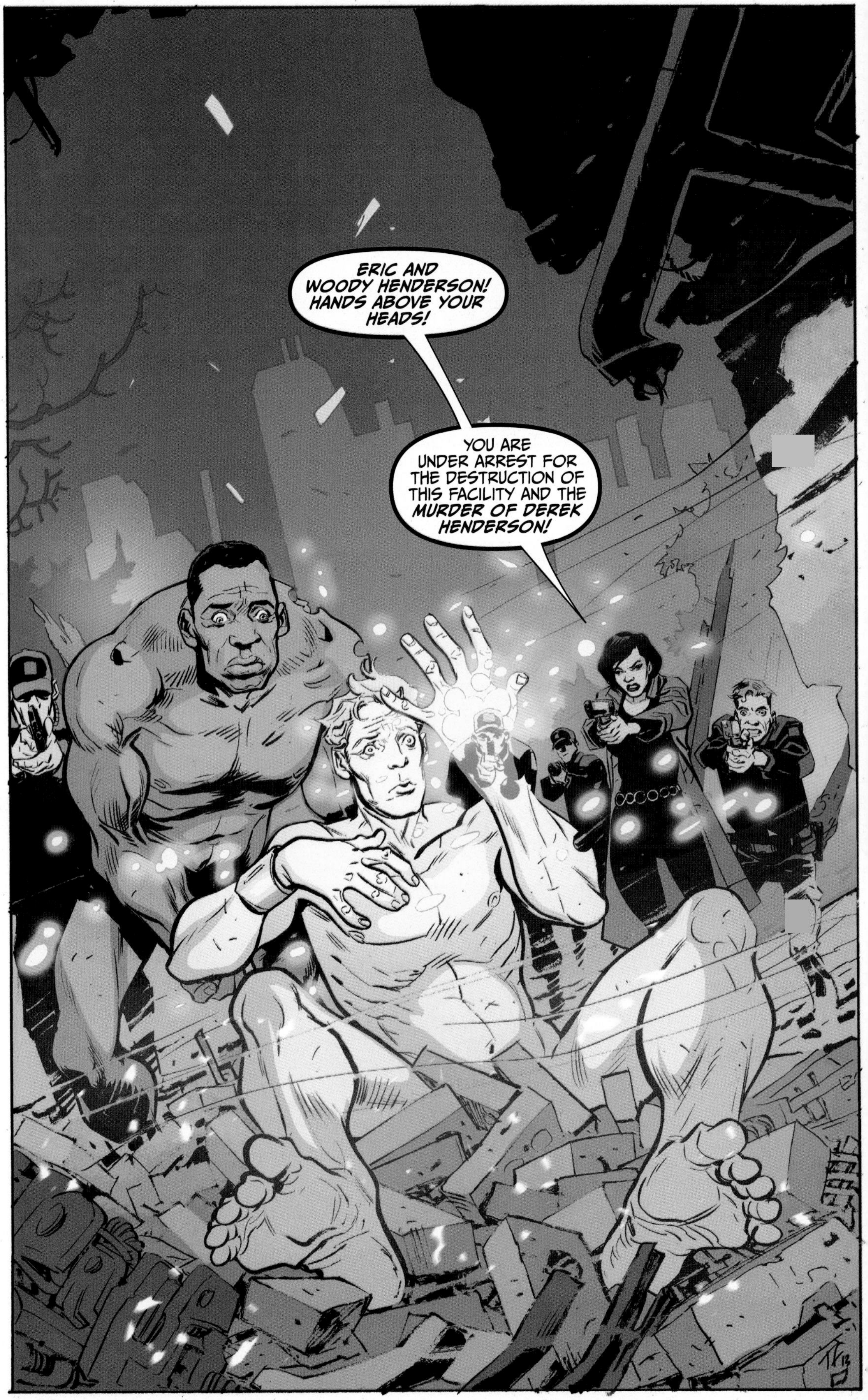
ERIC AND WOODY HENDERSON! HANDS ABOVE YOUR HEADS!
YOU ARE UNDER ARREST FOR THE DESTRUCTION OF THIS FACILITY AND THE MURDER OF DEREK HENDERSON!

VALIANT

JAMES ASMUS | TOM FOWLER | JORDIE BELLAIRE

QUANTUM AND WOODY!

#2

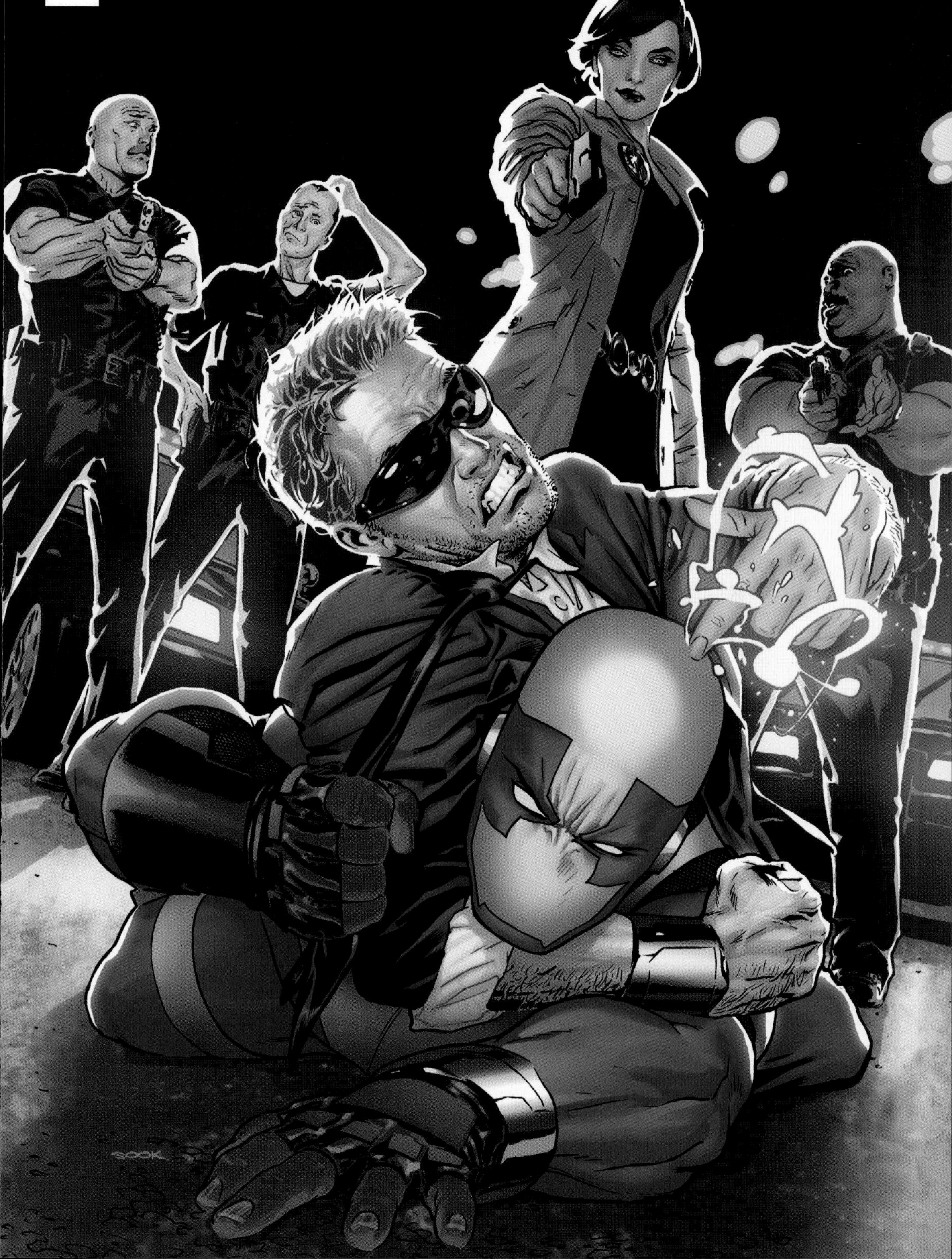

SOOK

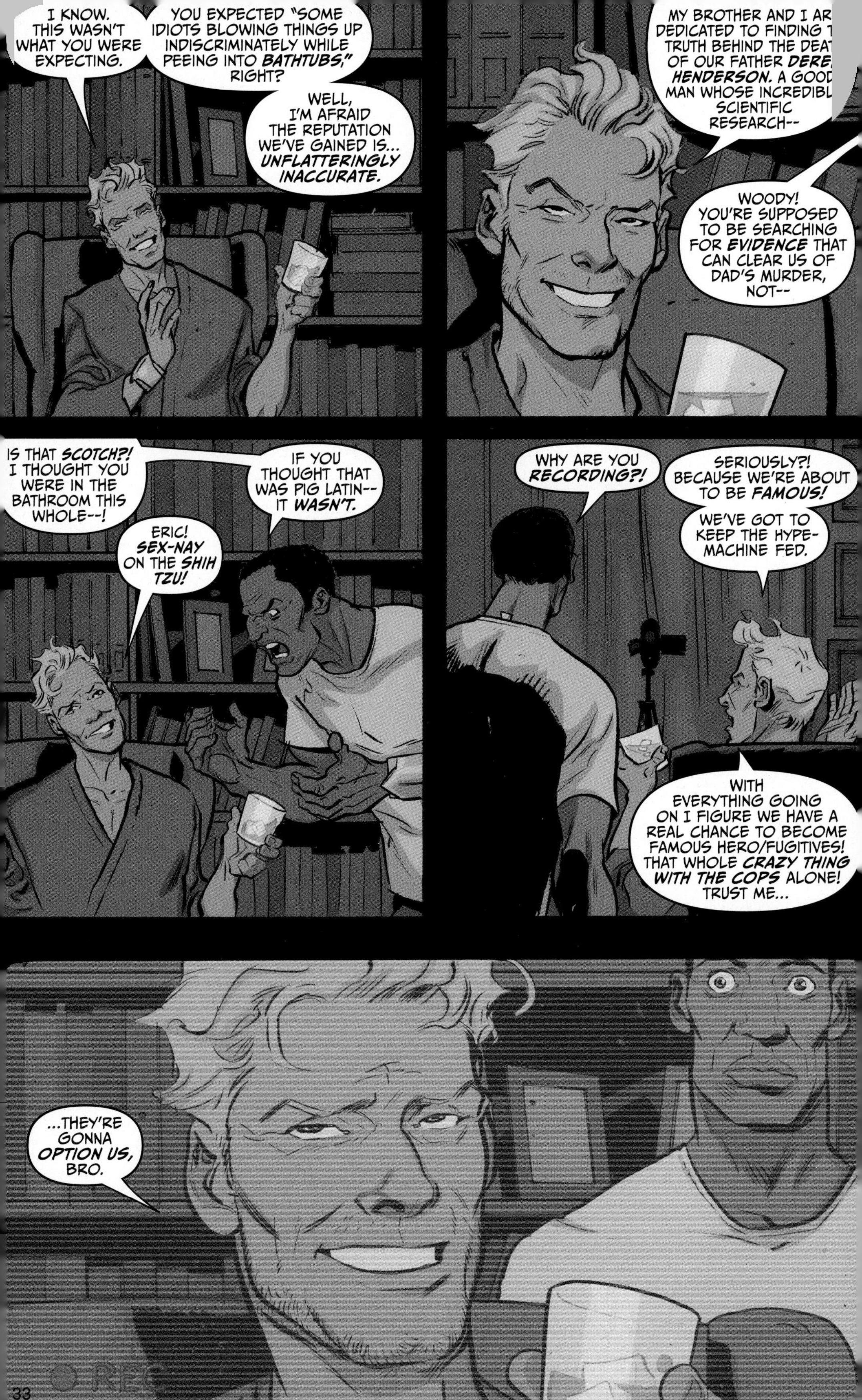
I KNOW. THIS WASN'T WHAT YOU WERE EXPECTING.
YOU EXPECTED "SOME IDIOTS BLOWING THINGS UP INDISCRIMINATELY WHILE PEEING INTO BATHTUBS," RIGHT?
WELL, I'M AFRAID THE REPUTATION WE'VE GAINED IS... UNFLATTERINGLY INACCURATE.
MY BROTHER AND I AR DEDICATED TO FINDING T TRUTH BEHIND THE DEAT OF OUR FATHER DERE HENDERSON. A GOOD MAN WHOSE INCREDIBL SCIENTIFIC RESEARCH--
WOODY! YOU'RE SUPPOSED TO BE SEARCHING FOR EVIDENCE THAT CAN CLEAR US OF DAD'S MURDER, NOT--
IS THAT SCOTCH?! I THOUGHT YOU WERE IN THE BATHROOM THIS WHOLE--!
ERIC! SEX-NAY ON THE SHIH TZU!
IF YOU THOUGHT THAT WAS PIG LATIN-- IT WASN'T.
WHY ARE YOU RECORDING?!
SERIOUSLY?! BECAUSE WE'RE ABOUT TO BE FAMOUS!
WE'VE GOT TO KEEP THE HYPE-MACHINE FED.
WITH EVERYTHING GOING ON I FIGURE WE HAVE A REAL CHANCE TO BECOME FAMOUS HERO/FUGITIVES! THAT WHOLE CRAZY THING WITH THE COPS ALONE! TRUST ME...
...THEY'RE GONNA OPTION US, BRO.
REC

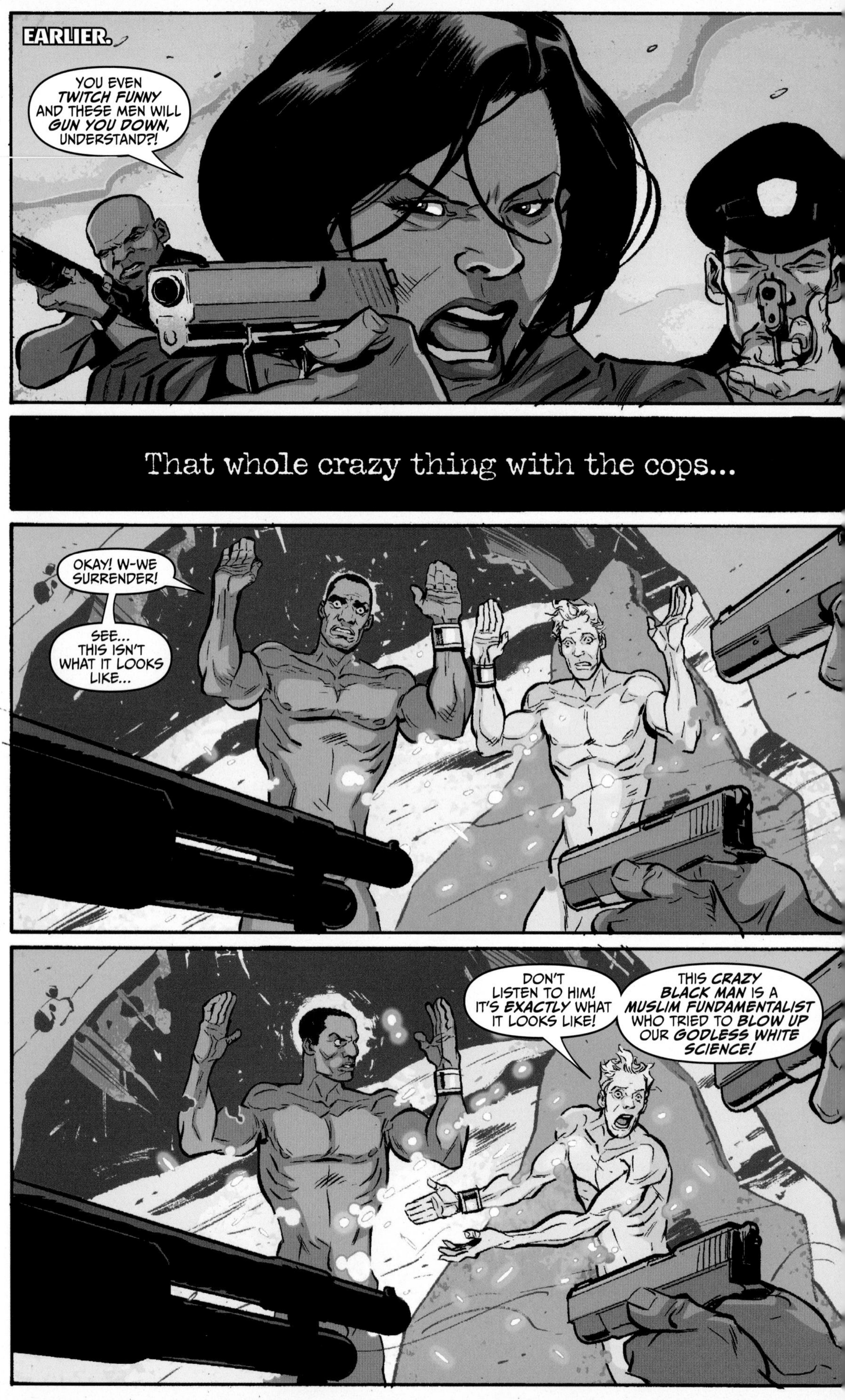
EARLIER.
YOU EVEN TWITCH FUNNY AND THESE MEN WILL GUN YOU DOWN, UNDERSTAND?!
That whole crazy thing with the cops...
OKAY! W-WE SURRENDER!
SEE... THIS ISN'T WHAT IT LOOKS LIKE...
DON'T LISTEN TO HIM! IT'S EXACTLY WHAT IT LOOKS LIKE!
THIS CRAZY BLACK MAN IS A MUSLIM FUNDAMENTALIST WHO TRIED TO BLOW UP OUR GODLESS WHITE SCIENCE!

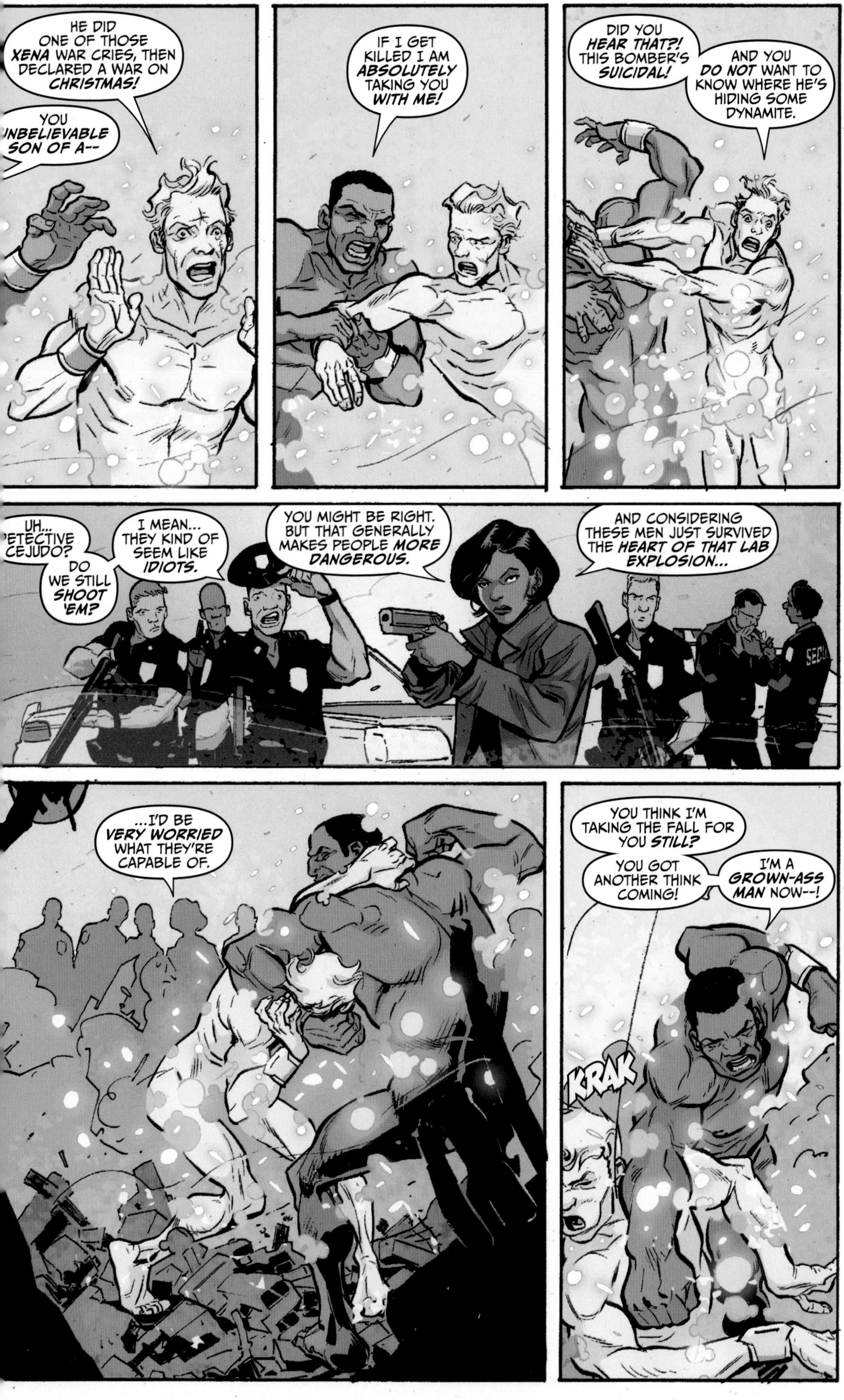
HE DID ONE OF THOSE XENA WAR CRIES, THEN DECLARED A WAR ON CHRISTMAS!
YOU UNBELIEVABLE SON OF A--
IF I GET KILLED I AM ABSOLUTELY TAKING YOU WITH ME!
DID YOU HEAR THAT?! THIS BOMBER'S SUICIDAL!
AND YOU DO NOT WANT TO KNOW WHERE HE'S HIDING SOME DYNAMITE.
UH... DETECTIVE CEJUDO?
DO WE STILL SHOOT 'EM?
I MEAN... THEY KIND OF SEEM LIKE IDIOTS.
YOU MIGHT BE RIGHT. BUT THAT GENERALLY MAKES PEOPLE MORE DANGEROUS.
AND CONSIDERING THESE MEN JUST SURVIVED THE HEART OF THAT LAB EXPLOSION...
...I'D BE VERY WORRIED WHAT THEY'RE CAPABLE OF.
YOU THINK I'M TAKING THE FALL FOR YOU STILL?
YOU GOT ANOTHER THINK COMING!
I'M A GROWN-ASS MAN NOW--!
KRAK

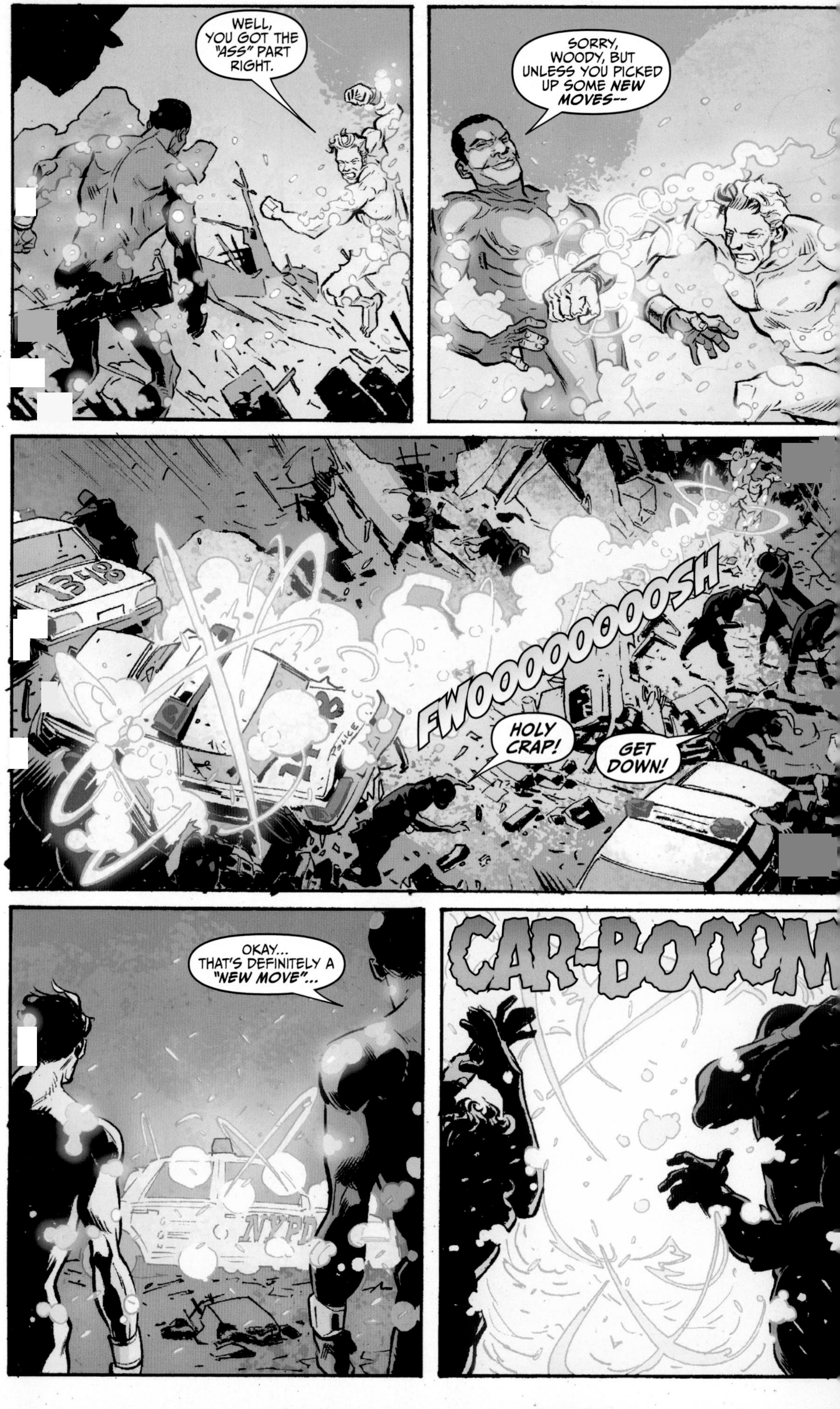
WELL, YOU GOT THE "ASS" PART RIGHT.
SORRY, WOODY, BUT UNLESS YOU PICKED UP SOME NEW MOVES--
FWOOOOOOOOOSH
HOLY CRAP!
GET DOWN!
POLICE
NYPD
OKAY... THAT'S DEFINITELY A "NEW MOVE"...
CAR-BOOOM

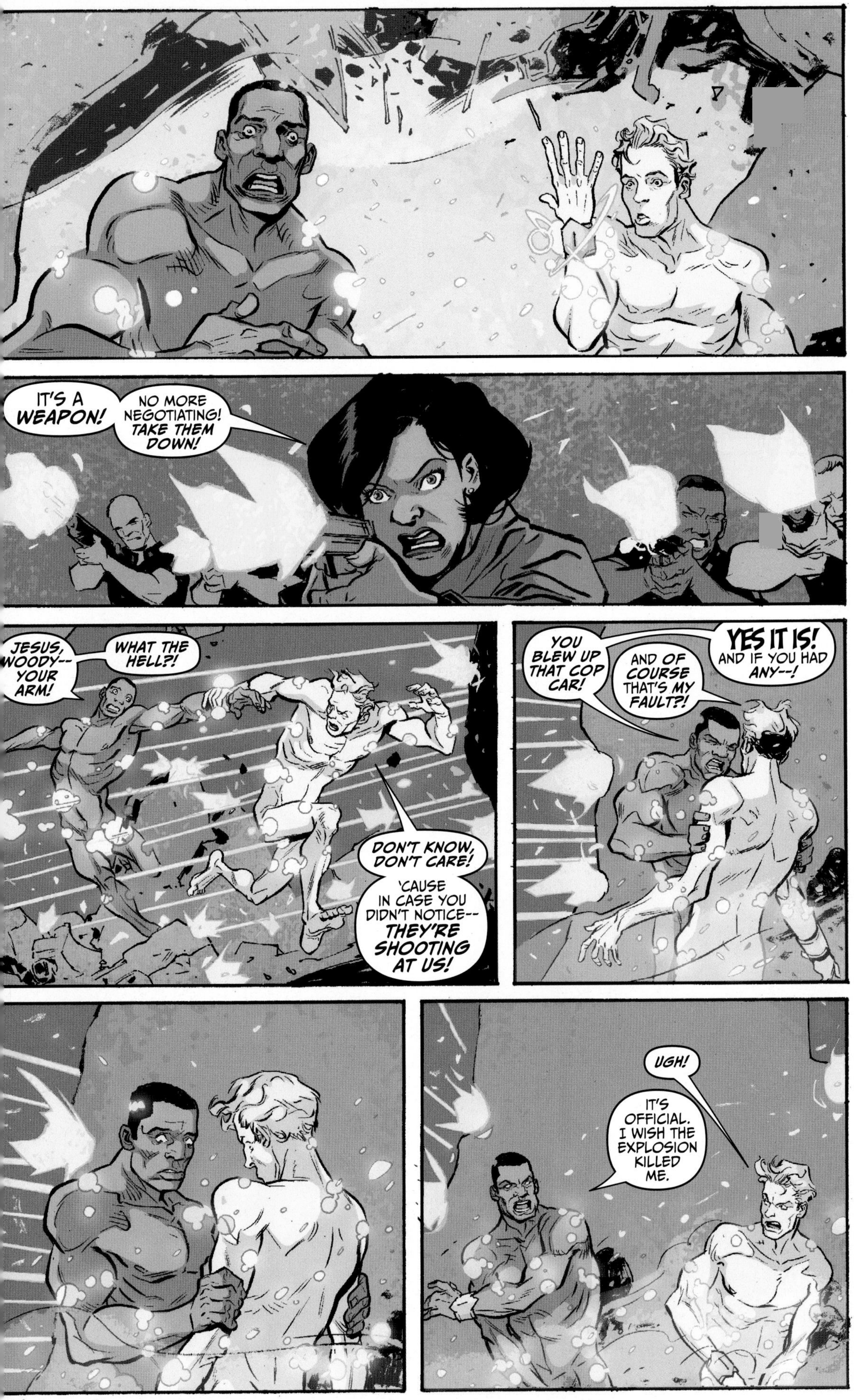
IT'S A WEAPON!
NO MORE NEGOTIATING! TAKE THEM DOWN!
JESUS, WOODY-- YOUR ARM!
WHAT THE HELL?!
DON'T KNOW, DON'T CARE!
'CAUSE IN CASE YOU DIDN'T NOTICE-- THEY'RE SHOOTING AT US!
YOU BLEW UP THAT COP CAR!
AND OF COURSE THAT'S MY FAULT?!
YES IT IS! AND IF YOU HAD ANY--!
UGH!
IT'S OFFICIAL. I WISH THE EXPLOSION KILLED ME.

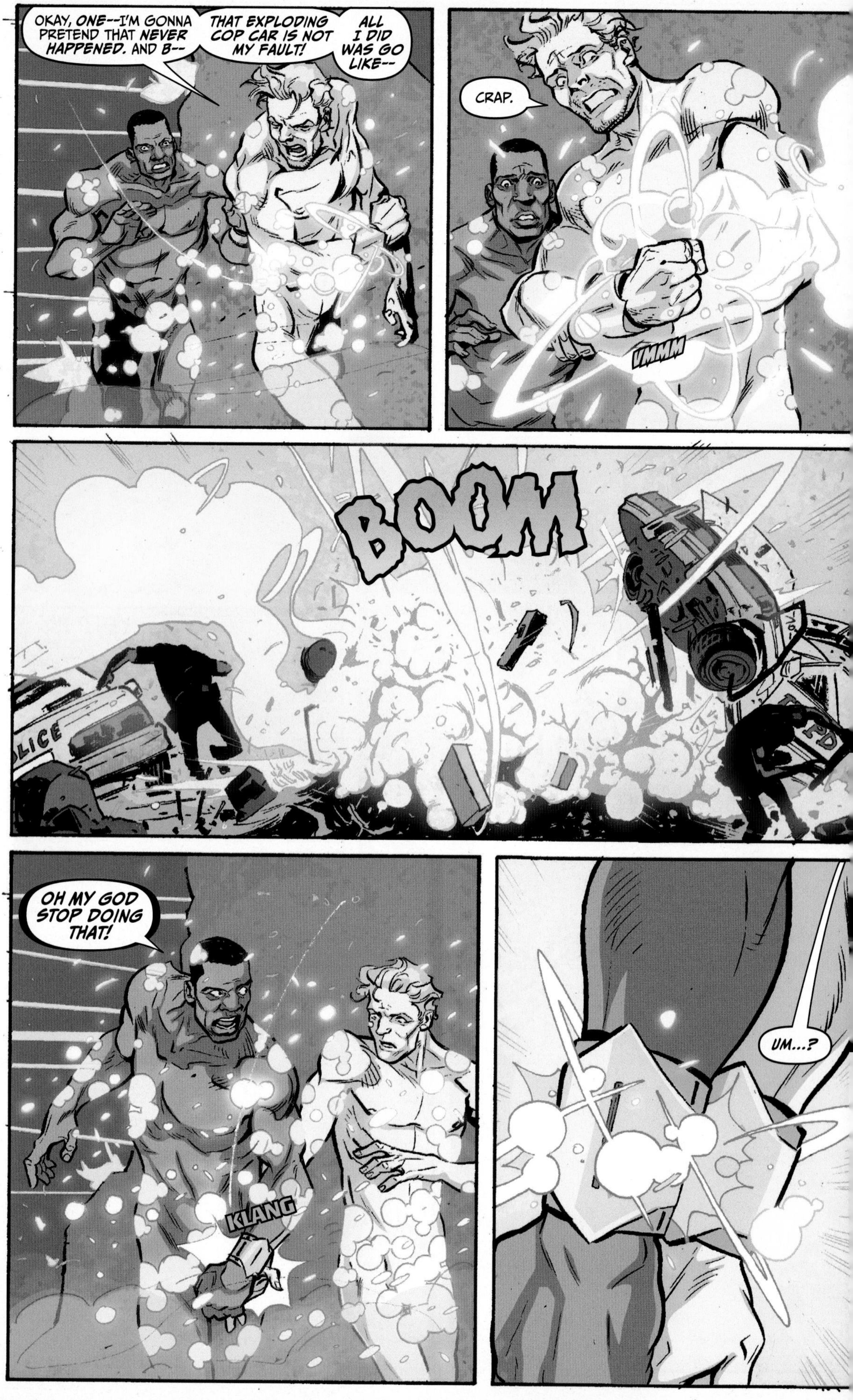
OKAY, ONE--I'M GONNA PRETEND THAT NEVER HAPPENED. AND B--
THAT EXPLODING COP CAR IS NOT MY FAULT!
ALL I DID WAS GO LIKE--
CRAP.
VMMM
BOOM
OLICE
PD
OH MY GOD STOP DOING THAT!
KLANG
UM...?

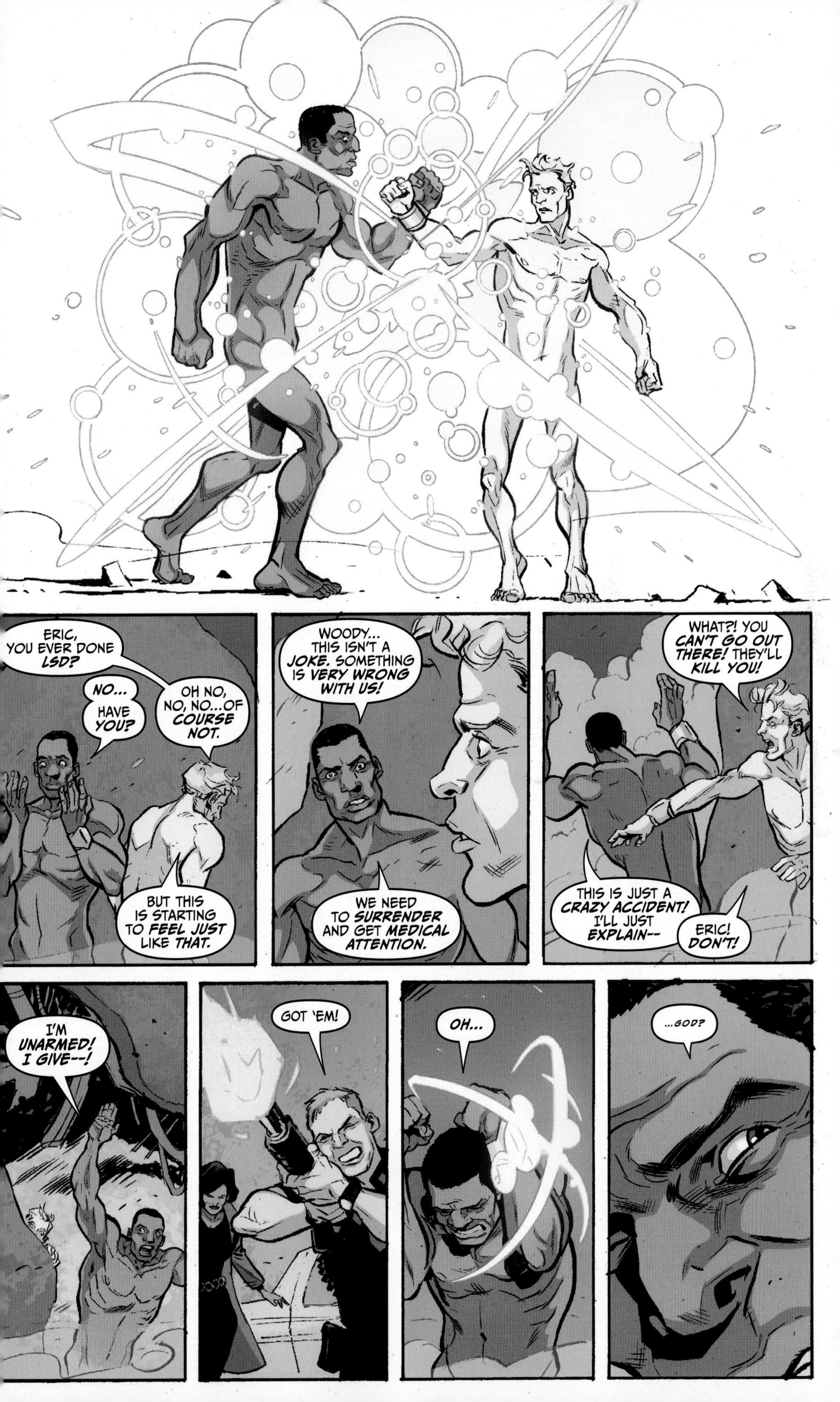

ERIC, YOU EVER DONE LSD?
NO... HAVE YOU?
OH NO, NO, NO...OF COURSE NOT.
BUT THIS IS STARTING TO FEEL JUST LIKE THAT.
WOODY... THIS ISN'T A JOKE. SOMETHING IS VERY WRONG WITH US!
WE NEED TO SURRENDER AND GET MEDICAL ATTENTION.
WHAT?! YOU CAN'T GO OUT THERE! THEY'LL KILL YOU!
THIS IS JUST A CRAZY ACCIDENT! I'LL JUST EXPLAIN--
ERIC! DON'T!
I'M UNARMED! I GIVE--!
GOT 'EM!
OH...
...GOD?

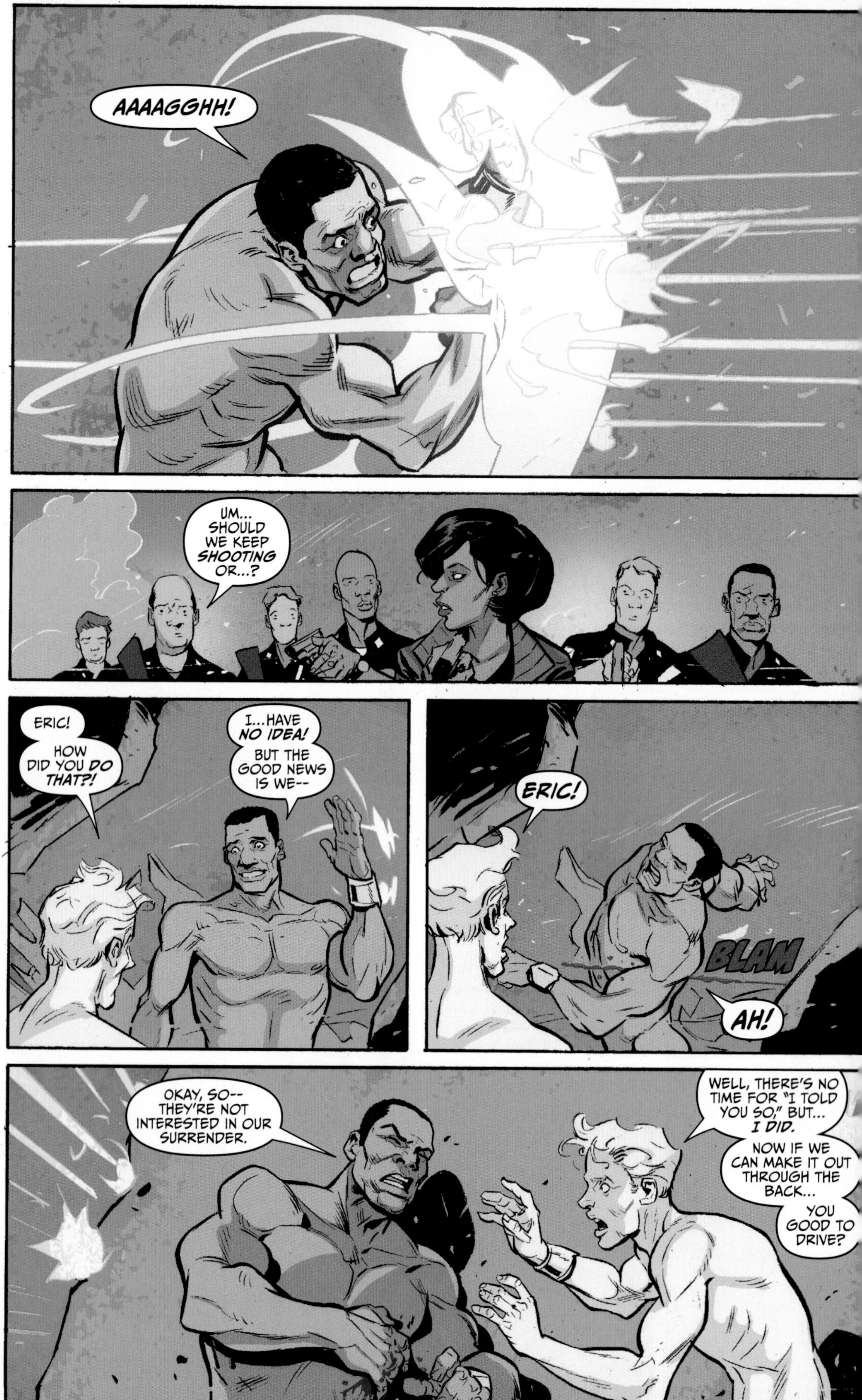

AAAAGGHH!
UM... SHOULD WE KEEP SHOOTING OR...?
ERIC!
HOW DID YOU DO THAT?!
I...HAVE NO IDEA!
BUT THE GOOD NEWS IS WE--
ERIC!
BLAM
AH!
OKAY, SO-- THEY'RE NOT INTERESTED IN OUR SURRENDER.
WELL, THERE'S NO TIME FOR "I TOLD YOU SO," BUT... I DID.
NOW IF WE CAN MAKE IT OUT THROUGH THE BACK...
YOU GOOD TO DRIVE?

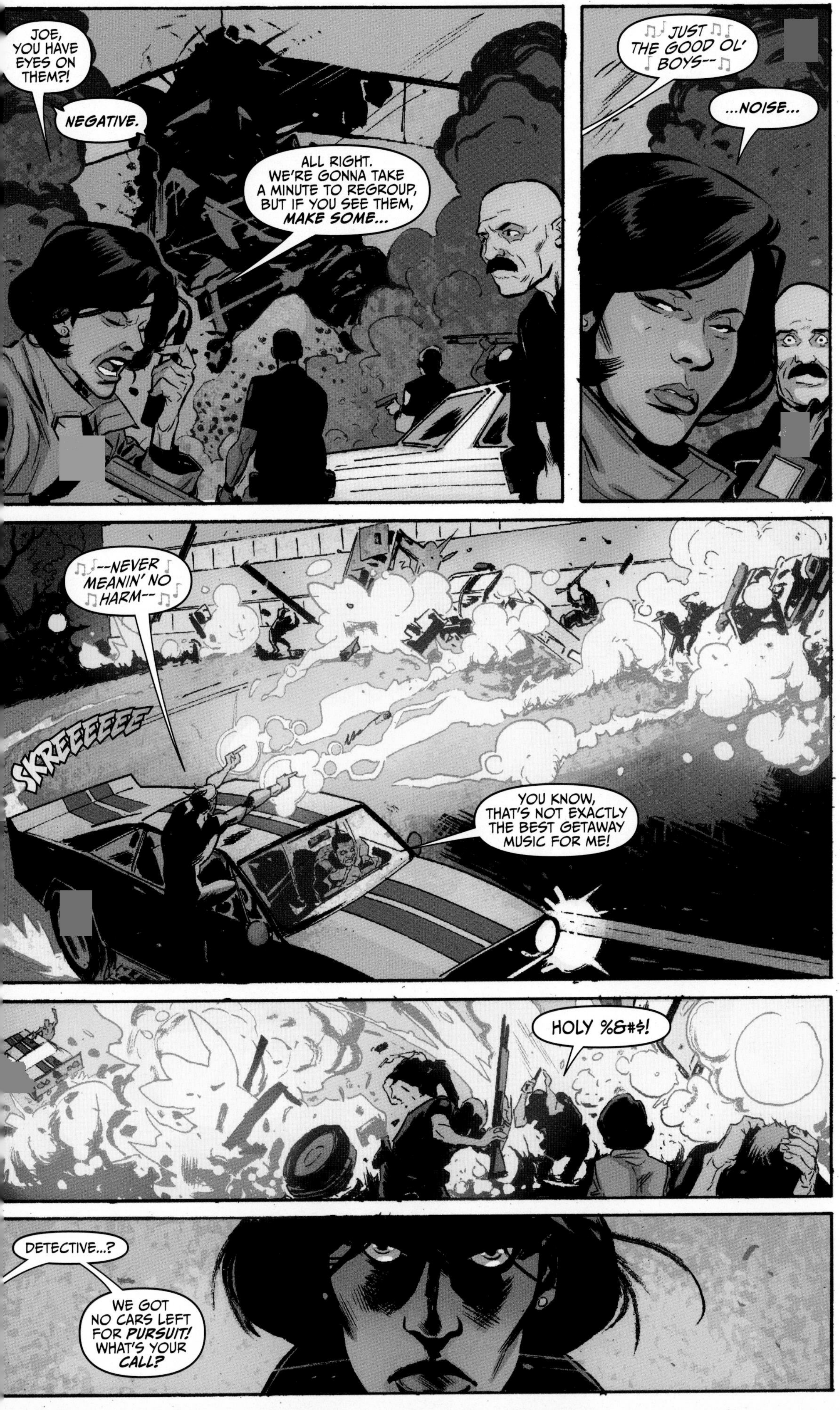
JOE, YOU HAVE EYES ON THEM?!
NEGATIVE.
ALL RIGHT. WE'RE GONNA TAKE A MINUTE TO REGROUP, BUT IF YOU SEE THEM, MAKE SOME...
♫ JUST ♫ THE GOOD OL' BOYS-- ♫
...NOISE...
♫ --NEVER MEANIN' NO HARM-- ♫
SKREEEEEEE
YOU KNOW, THAT'S NOT EXACTLY THE BEST GETAWAY MUSIC FOR ME!
HOLY %&#$!
DETECTIVE...?
WE GOT NO CARS LEFT FOR PURSUIT! WHAT'S YOUR CALL?

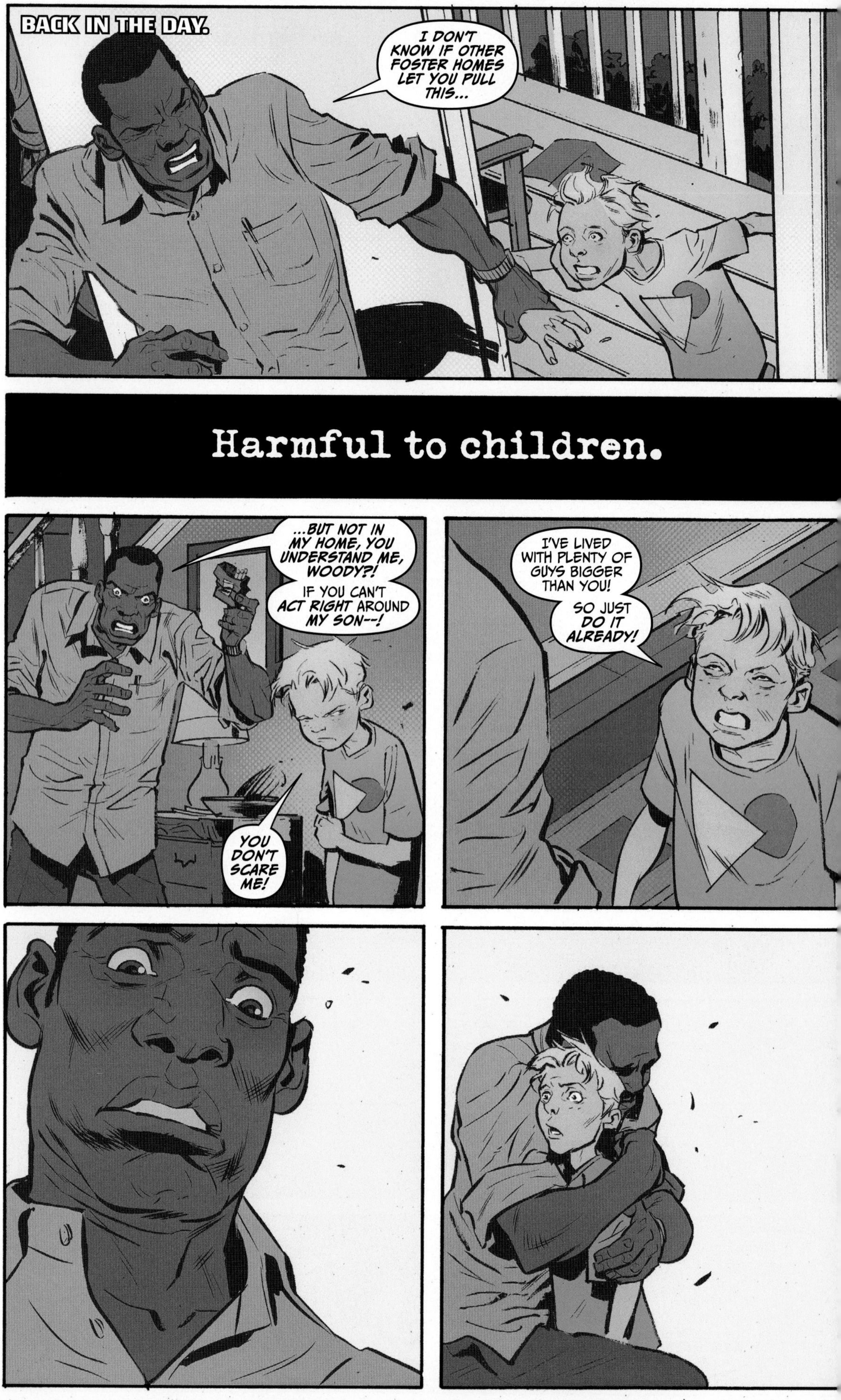
BACK IN THE DAY.
I DON'T KNOW IF OTHER FOSTER HOMES LET YOU PULL THIS...
Harmful to children.
...BUT NOT IN MY HOME, YOU UNDERSTAND ME, WOODY?!
IF YOU CAN'T ACT RIGHT AROUND MY SON--!
YOU DON'T SCARE ME!
I'VE LIVED WITH PLENTY OF GUYS BIGGER THAN YOU!
SO JUST DO IT ALREADY!

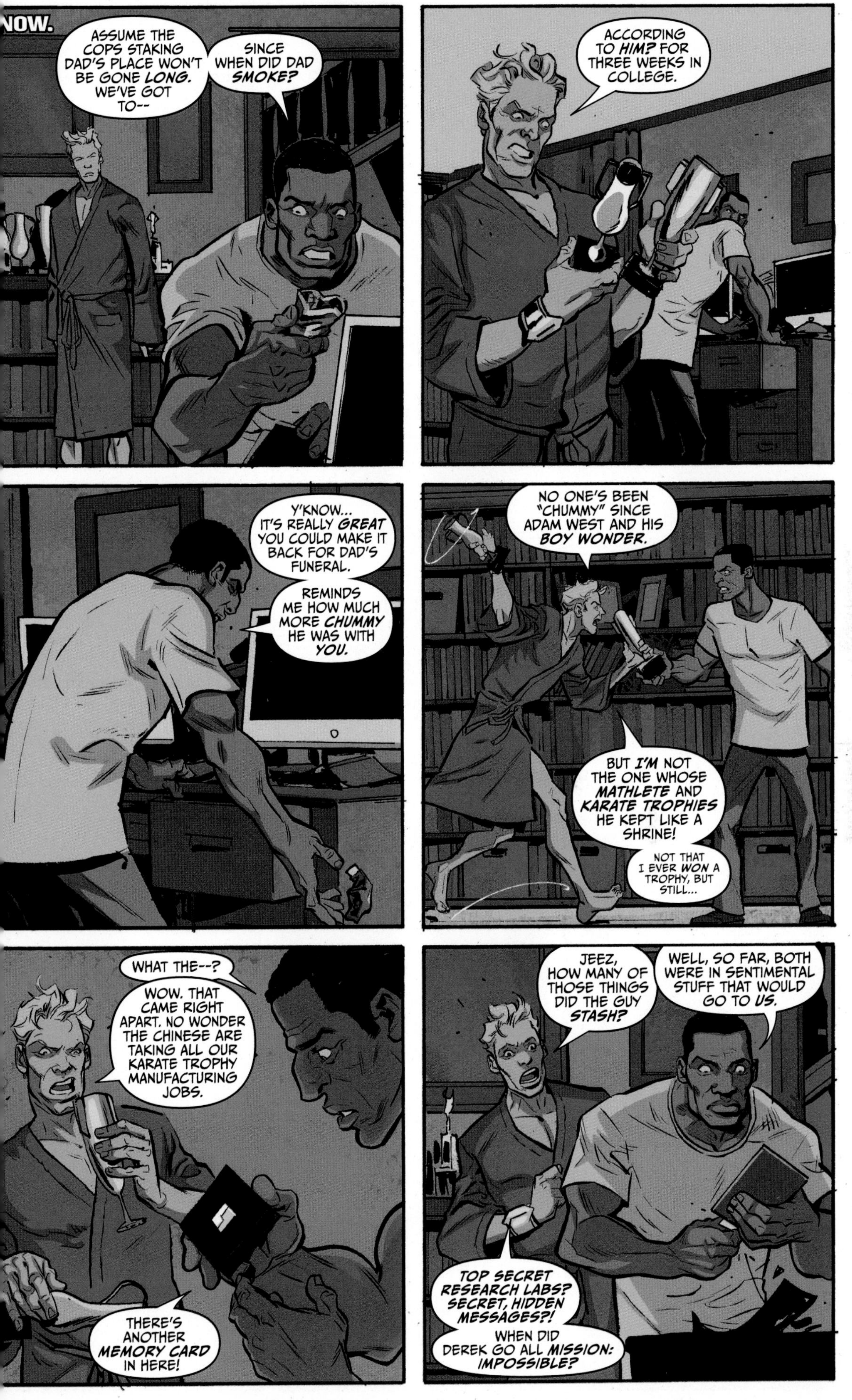
NOW.
ASSUME THE COPS STAKING DAD'S PLACE WON'T BE GONE LONG. WE'VE GOT TO--
SINCE WHEN DID DAD SMOKE?
ACCORDING TO HIM? FOR THREE WEEKS IN COLLEGE.
Y'KNOW... IT'S REALLY GREAT YOU COULD MAKE IT BACK FOR DAD'S FUNERAL.
REMINDS ME HOW MUCH MORE CHUMMY HE WAS WITH YOU.
NO ONE'S BEEN "CHUMMY" SINCE ADAM WEST AND HIS BOY WONDER.
BUT I'M NOT THE ONE WHOSE MATHLETE AND KARATE TROPHIES HE KEPT LIKE A SHRINE!
NOT THAT I EVER WON A TROPHY, BUT STILL...
WHAT THE--?
WOW. THAT CAME RIGHT APART. NO WONDER THE CHINESE ARE TAKING ALL OUR KARATE TROPHY MANUFACTURING JOBS.
THERE'S ANOTHER MEMORY CARD IN HERE!
JEEZ, HOW MANY OF THOSE THINGS DID THE GUY STASH?
WELL, SO FAR, BOTH WERE IN SENTIMENTAL STUFF THAT WOULD GO TO US.
TOP SECRET RESEARCH LABS? SECRET, HIDDEN MESSAGES?!
WHEN DID DEREK GO ALL MISSION: IMPOSSIBLE?

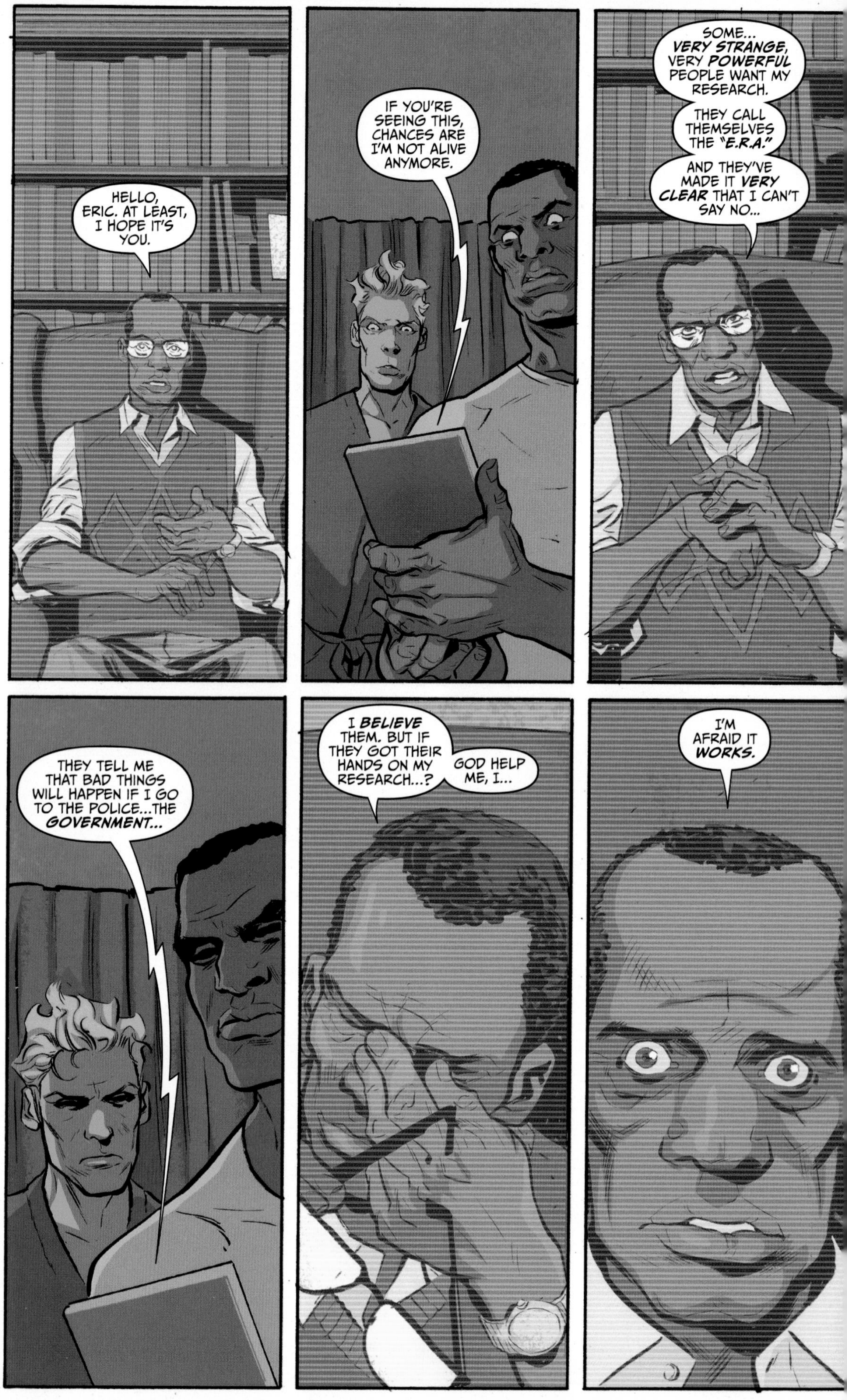
HELLO, ERIC. AT LEAST, I HOPE IT'S YOU.
IF YOU'RE SEEING THIS, CHANCES ARE I'M NOT ALIVE ANYMORE.
SOME... VERY STRANGE, VERY POWERFUL PEOPLE WANT MY RESEARCH.
THEY CALL THEMSELVES THE "E.R.A."
AND THEY'VE MADE IT VERY CLEAR THAT I CAN'T SAY NO...
THEY TELL ME THAT BAD THINGS WILL HAPPEN IF I GO TO THE POLICE...THE GOVERNMENT...
I BELIEVE THEM. BUT IF THEY GOT THEIR HANDS ON MY RESEARCH...?
GOD HELP ME, I...
I'M AFRAID IT WORKS.

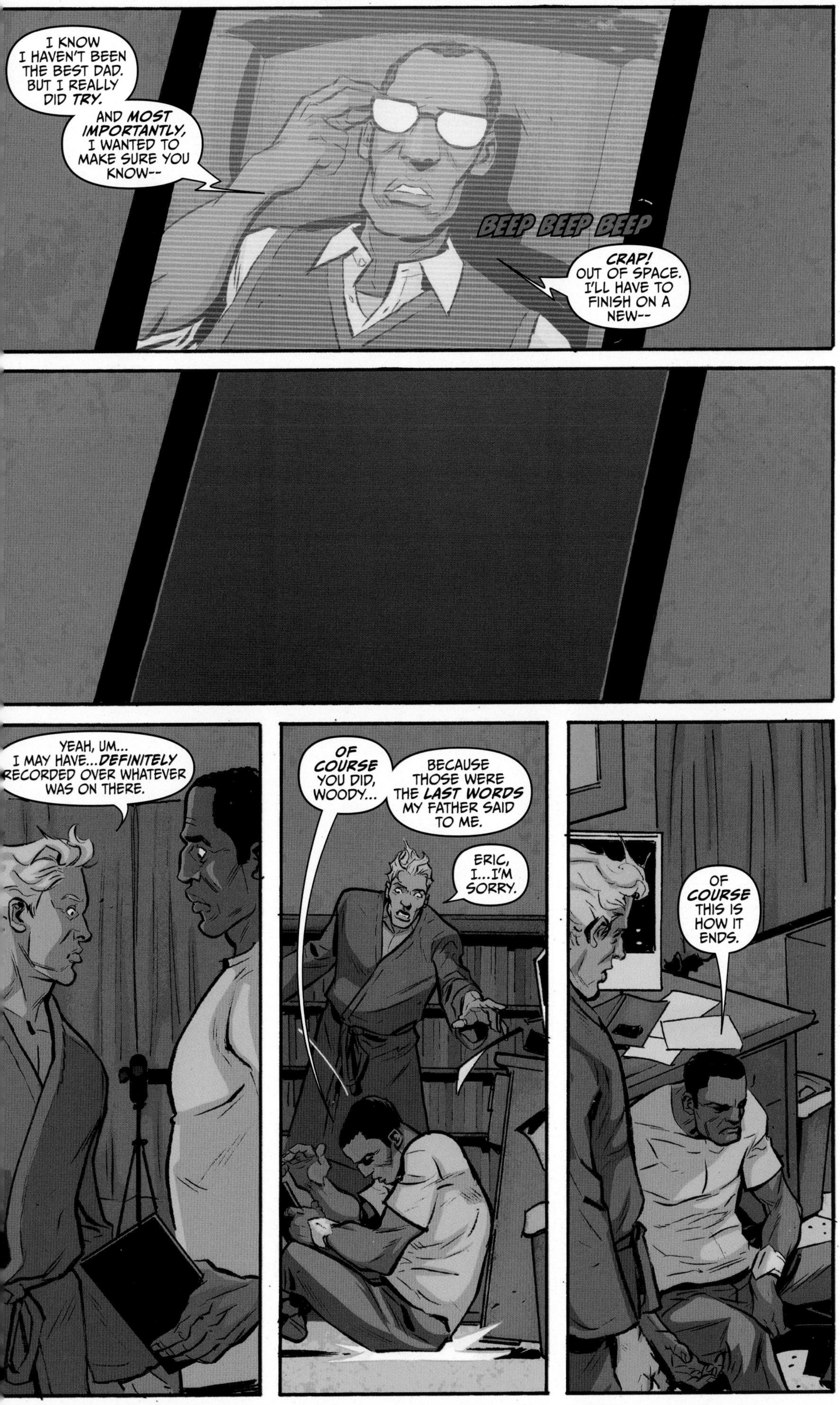
I KNOW I HAVEN'T BEEN THE BEST DAD. BUT I REALLY DID *TRY.*
AND ***MOST IMPORTANTLY,*** I WANTED TO MAKE SURE YOU KNOW--
BEEP BEEP BEEP
CRAP! OUT OF SPACE. I'LL HAVE TO FINISH ON A NEW--
YEAH, UM... I MAY HAVE...***DEFINITELY*** RECORDED OVER WHATEVER WAS ON THERE.
OF COURSE YOU DID, WOODY...
BECAUSE THOSE WERE THE ***LAST WORDS*** MY FATHER SAID TO ME.
ERIC, I...I'M SORRY.
OF ***COURSE*** THIS IS HOW IT ENDS.

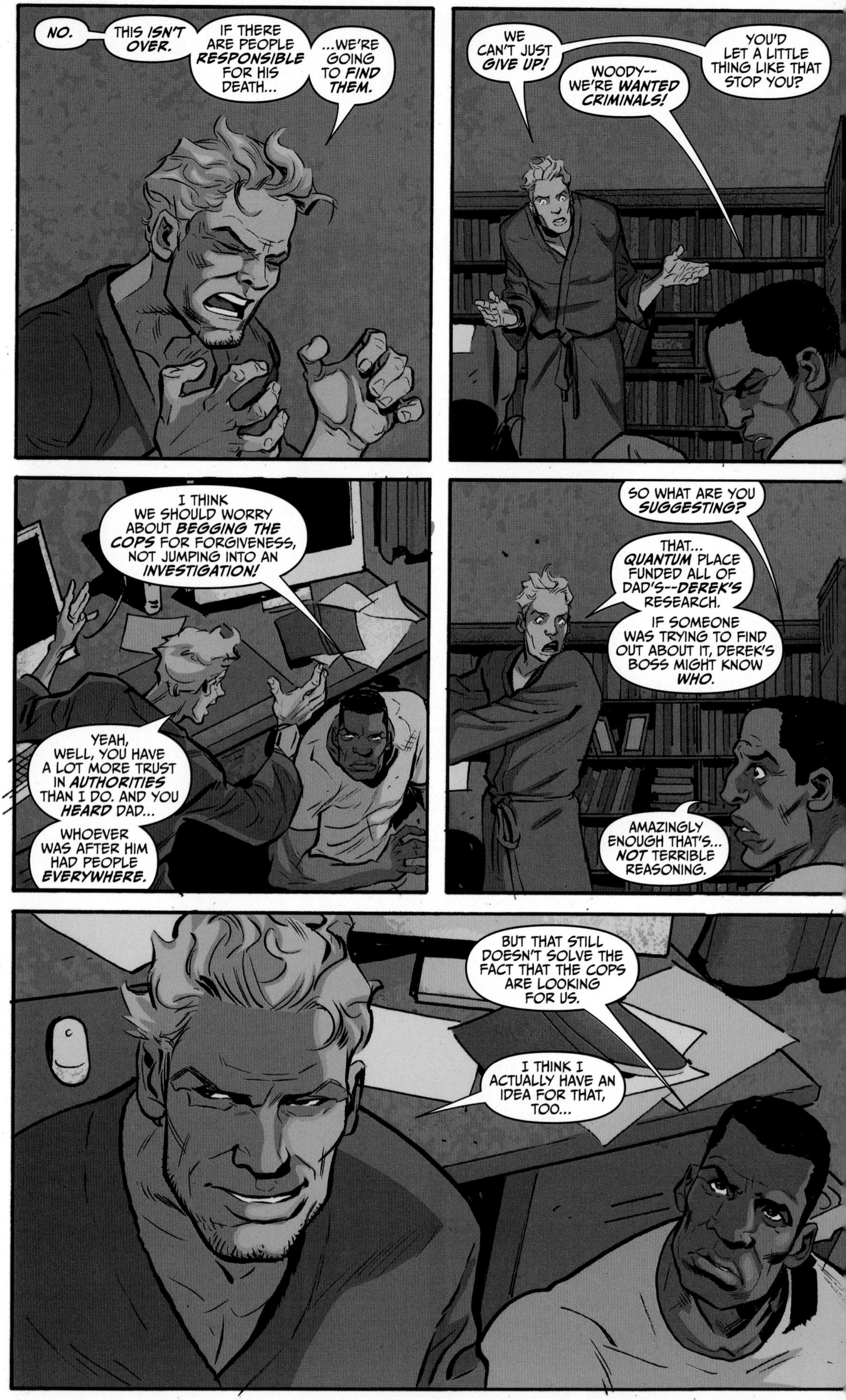

NO.
THIS ISN'T OVER.
IF THERE ARE PEOPLE RESPONSIBLE FOR HIS DEATH...
...WE'RE GOING TO FIND THEM.
WE CAN'T JUST GIVE UP!
WOODY-- WE'RE WANTED CRIMINALS!
YOU'D LET A LITTLE THING LIKE THAT STOP YOU?
I THINK WE SHOULD WORRY ABOUT BEGGING THE COPS FOR FORGIVENESS, NOT JUMPING INTO AN INVESTIGATION!
YEAH, WELL, YOU HAVE A LOT MORE TRUST IN AUTHORITIES THAN I DO. AND YOU HEARD DAD...
WHOEVER WAS AFTER HIM HAD PEOPLE EVERYWHERE.
SO WHAT ARE YOU SUGGESTING?
THAT... QUANTUM PLACE FUNDED ALL OF DAD'S--DEREK'S RESEARCH.
IF SOMEONE WAS TRYING TO FIND OUT ABOUT IT, DEREK'S BOSS MIGHT KNOW WHO.
AMAZINGLY ENOUGH THAT'S... NOT TERRIBLE REASONING.
BUT THAT STILL DOESN'T SOLVE THE FACT THAT THE COPS ARE LOOKING FOR US.
I THINK I ACTUALLY HAVE AN IDEA FOR THAT, TOO...

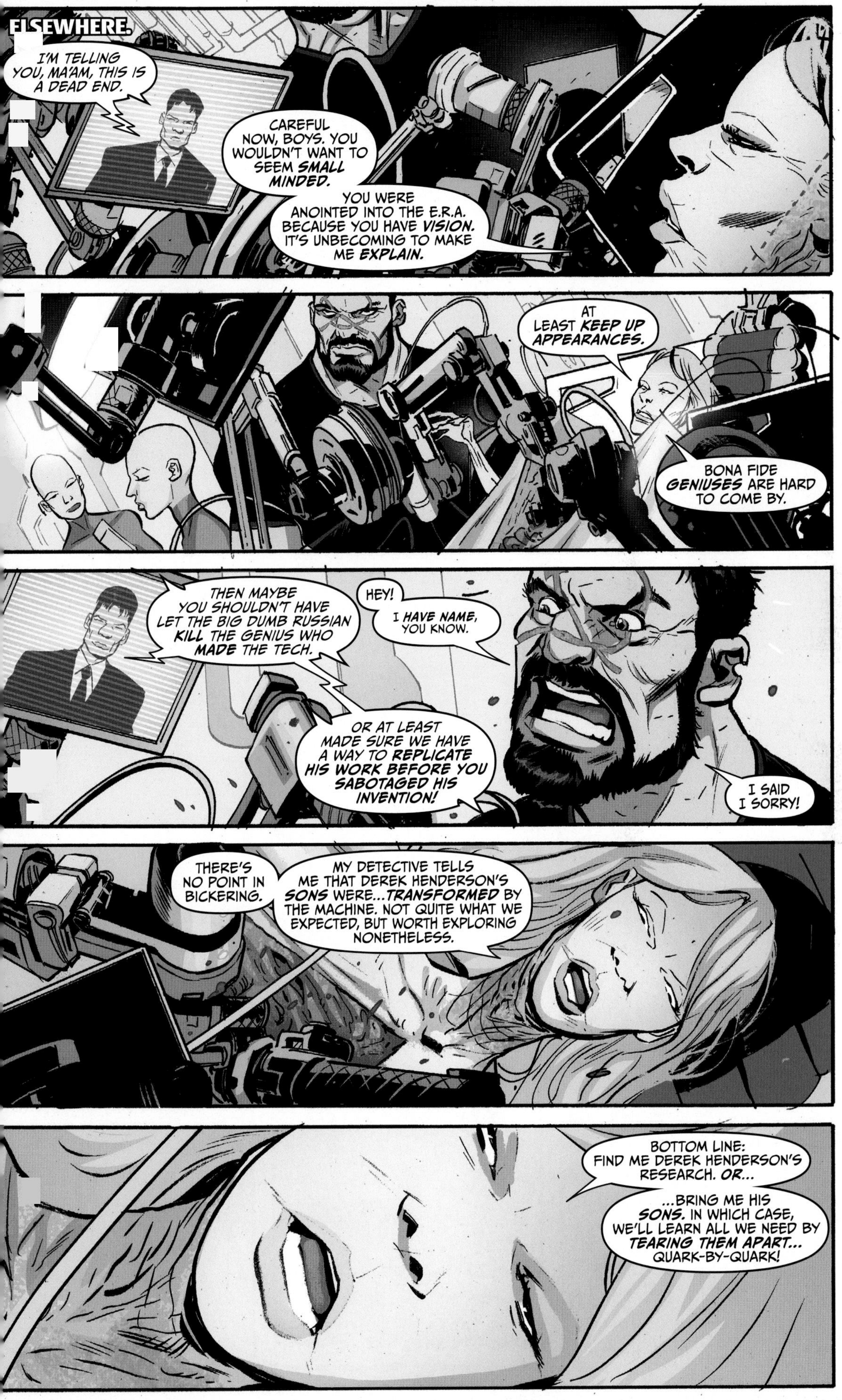
ELSEWHERE.
I'M TELLING YOU, MA'AM, THIS IS A DEAD END.
CAREFUL NOW, BOYS. YOU WOULDN'T WANT TO SEEM SMALL MINDED.
YOU WERE ANOINTED INTO THE E.R.A. BECAUSE YOU HAVE VISION. IT'S UNBECOMING TO MAKE ME EXPLAIN.
AT LEAST KEEP UP APPEARANCES.
BONA FIDE GENIUSES ARE HARD TO COME BY.
THEN MAYBE YOU SHOULDN'T HAVE LET THE BIG DUMB RUSSIAN KILL THE GENIUS WHO MADE THE TECH.
HEY!
I HAVE NAME, YOU KNOW.
OR AT LEAST MADE SURE WE HAVE A WAY TO REPLICATE HIS WORK BEFORE YOU SABOTAGED HIS INVENTION!
I SAID I SORRY!
THERE'S NO POINT IN BICKERING.
MY DETECTIVE TELLS ME THAT DEREK HENDERSON'S SONS WERE...TRANSFORMED BY THE MACHINE. NOT QUITE WHAT WE EXPECTED, BUT WORTH EXPLORING NONETHELESS.
BOTTOM LINE: FIND ME DEREK HENDERSON'S RESEARCH. OR...
...BRING ME HIS SONS. IN WHICH CASE, WE'LL LEARN ALL WE NEED BY TEARING THEM APART... QUARK-BY-QUARK!

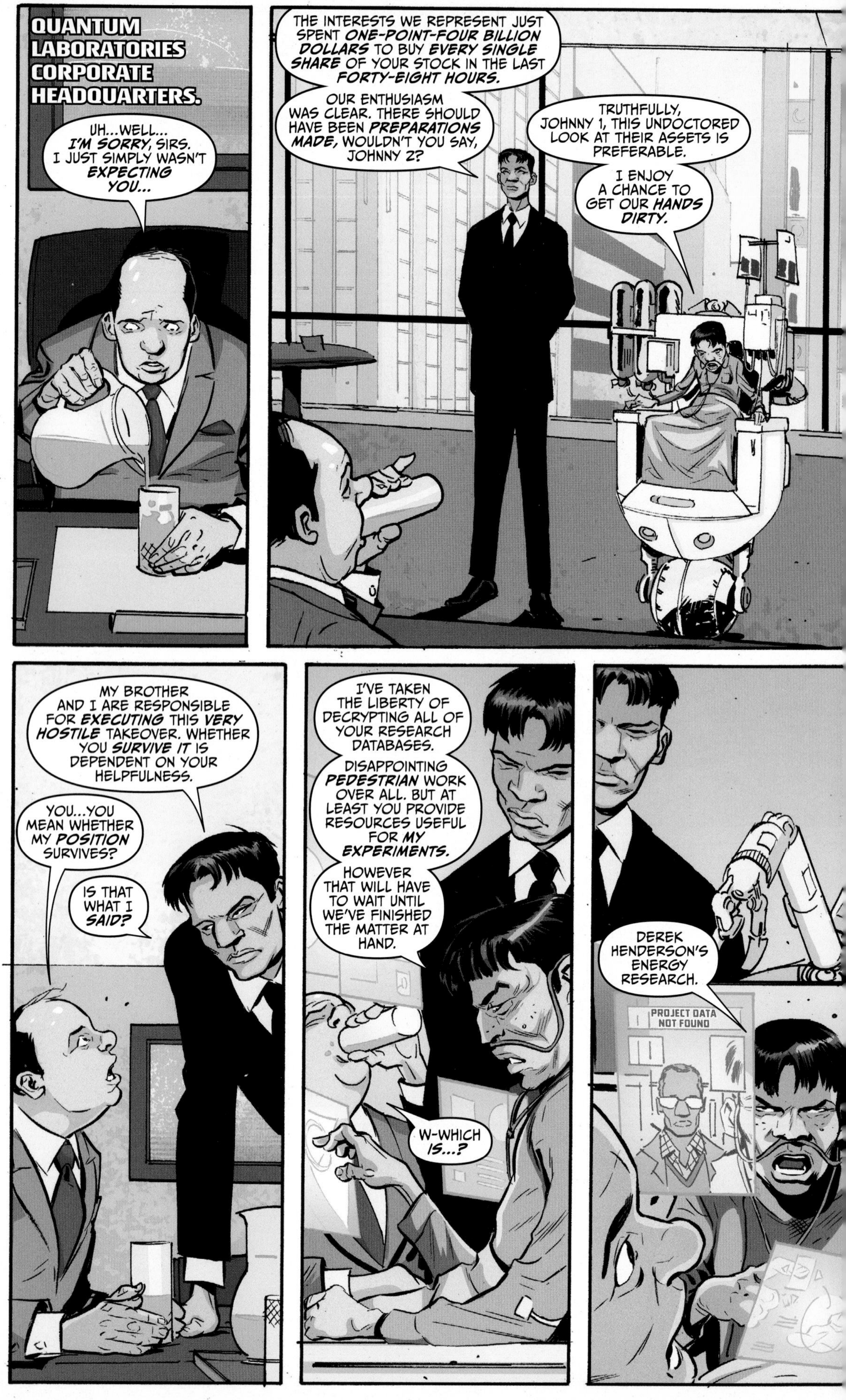
QUANTUM LABORATORIES CORPORATE HEADQUARTERS.
UH...WELL... I'M SORRY, SIRS. I JUST SIMPLY WASN'T EXPECTING YOU...
THE INTERESTS WE REPRESENT JUST SPENT ONE-POINT-FOUR BILLION DOLLARS TO BUY EVERY SINGLE SHARE OF YOUR STOCK IN THE LAST FORTY-EIGHT HOURS.
OUR ENTHUSIASM WAS CLEAR. THERE SHOULD HAVE BEEN PREPARATIONS MADE, WOULDN'T YOU SAY, JOHNNY 2?
TRUTHFULLY, JOHNNY 1, THIS UNDOCTORED LOOK AT THEIR ASSETS IS PREFERABLE.
I ENJOY A CHANCE TO GET OUR HANDS DIRTY.
MY BROTHER AND I ARE RESPONSIBLE FOR EXECUTING THIS VERY HOSTILE TAKEOVER. WHETHER YOU SURVIVE IT IS DEPENDENT ON YOUR HELPFULNESS.
YOU...YOU MEAN WHETHER MY POSITION SURVIVES?
IS THAT WHAT I SAID?
I'VE TAKEN THE LIBERTY OF DECRYPTING ALL OF YOUR RESEARCH DATABASES.
DISAPPOINTING PEDESTRIAN WORK OVER ALL. BUT AT LEAST YOU PROVIDE RESOURCES USEFUL FOR MY EXPERIMENTS.
HOWEVER THAT WILL HAVE TO WAIT UNTIL WE'VE FINISHED THE MATTER AT HAND.
W-WHICH IS...?
DEREK HENDERSON'S ENERGY RESEARCH.
PROJECT DATA NOT FOUND

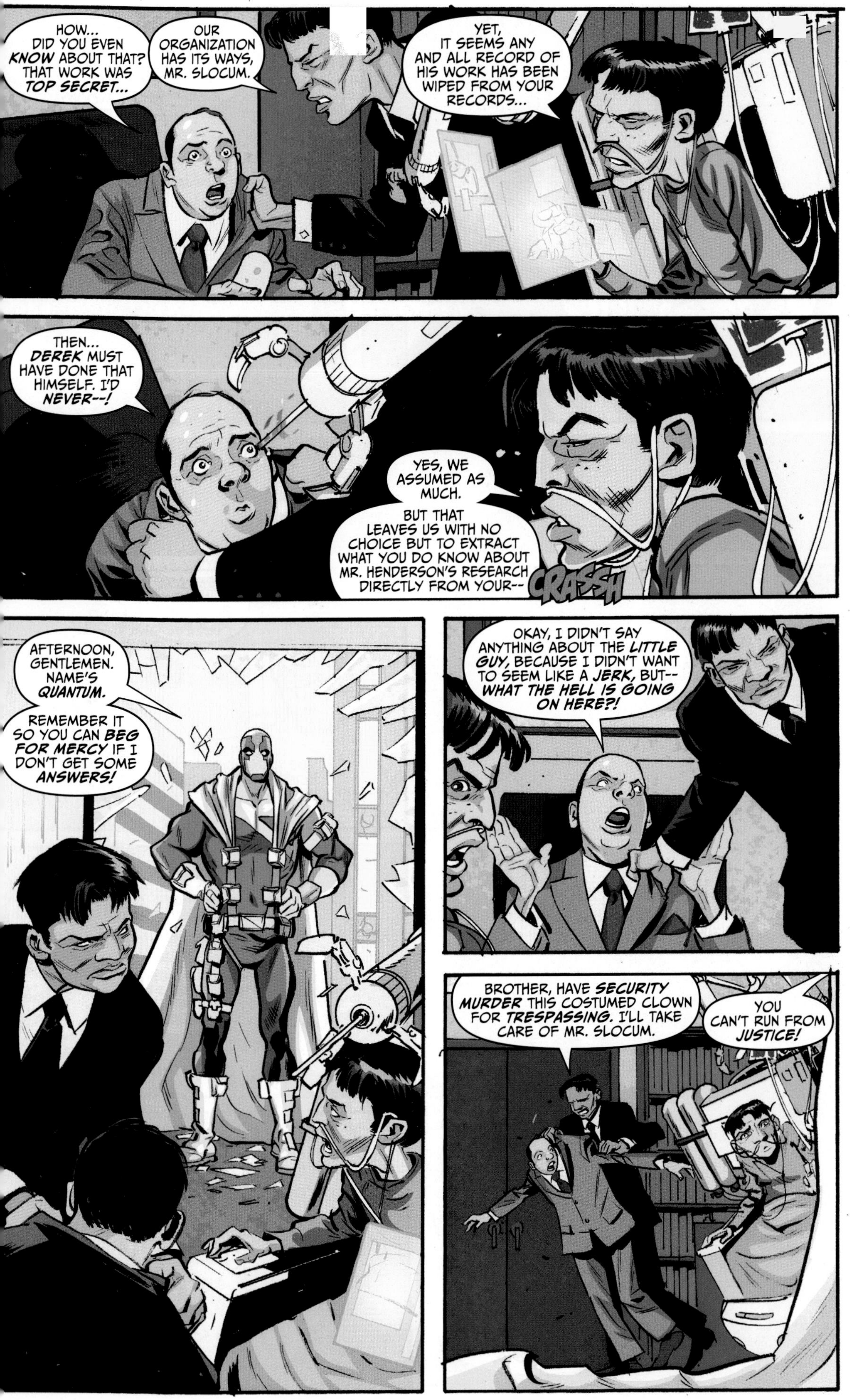
HOW... DID YOU EVEN KNOW ABOUT THAT? THAT WORK WAS TOP SECRET...
OUR ORGANIZATION HAS ITS WAYS, MR. SLOCUM.
YET, IT SEEMS ANY AND ALL RECORD OF HIS WORK HAS BEEN WIPED FROM YOUR RECORDS...
THEN... DEREK MUST HAVE DONE THAT HIMSELF. I'D NEVER--!
YES, WE ASSUMED AS MUCH.
BUT THAT LEAVES US WITH NO CHOICE BUT TO EXTRACT WHAT YOU DO KNOW ABOUT MR. HENDERSON'S RESEARCH DIRECTLY FROM YOUR--
CRASSH
AFTERNOON, GENTLEMEN. NAME'S QUANTUM.
REMEMBER IT SO YOU CAN BEG FOR MERCY IF I DON'T GET SOME ANSWERS!
OKAY, I DIDN'T SAY ANYTHING ABOUT THE LITTLE GUY, BECAUSE I DIDN'T WANT TO SEEM LIKE A JERK, BUT-- WHAT THE HELL IS GOING ON HERE?!
BROTHER, HAVE SECURITY MURDER THIS COSTUMED CLOWN FOR TRESPASSING. I'LL TAKE CARE OF MR. SLOCUM.
YOU CAN'T RUN FROM JUSTICE!

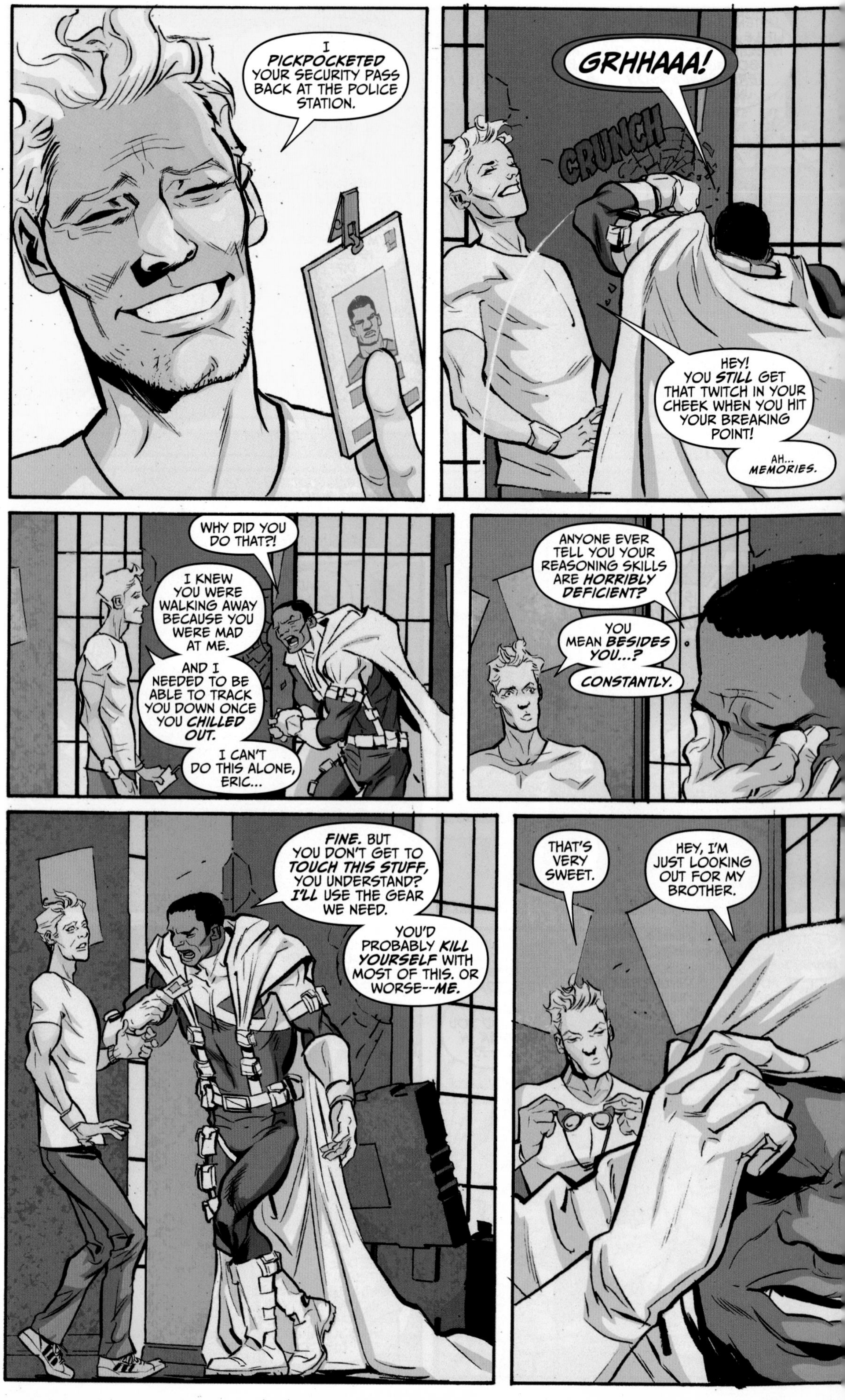
I PICKPOCKETED YOUR SECURITY PASS BACK AT THE POLICE STATION.
GRHHAAA!
CRUNCH
HEY! YOU STILL GET THAT TWITCH IN YOUR CHEEK WHEN YOU HIT YOUR BREAKING POINT!
AH... MEMORIES.
WHY DID YOU DO THAT?!
I KNEW YOU WERE WALKING AWAY BECAUSE YOU WERE MAD AT ME.
AND I NEEDED TO BE ABLE TO TRACK YOU DOWN ONCE YOU CHILLED OUT.
I CAN'T DO THIS ALONE, ERIC...
ANYONE EVER TELL YOU YOUR REASONING SKILLS ARE HORRIBLY DEFICIENT?
YOU MEAN BESIDES YOU...?
CONSTANTLY.
FINE. BUT YOU DON'T GET TO TOUCH THIS STUFF, YOU UNDERSTAND? I'LL USE THE GEAR WE NEED.
YOU'D PROBABLY KILL YOURSELF WITH MOST OF THIS. OR WORSE--ME.
THAT'S VERY SWEET.
HEY, I'M JUST LOOKING OUT FOR MY BROTHER.

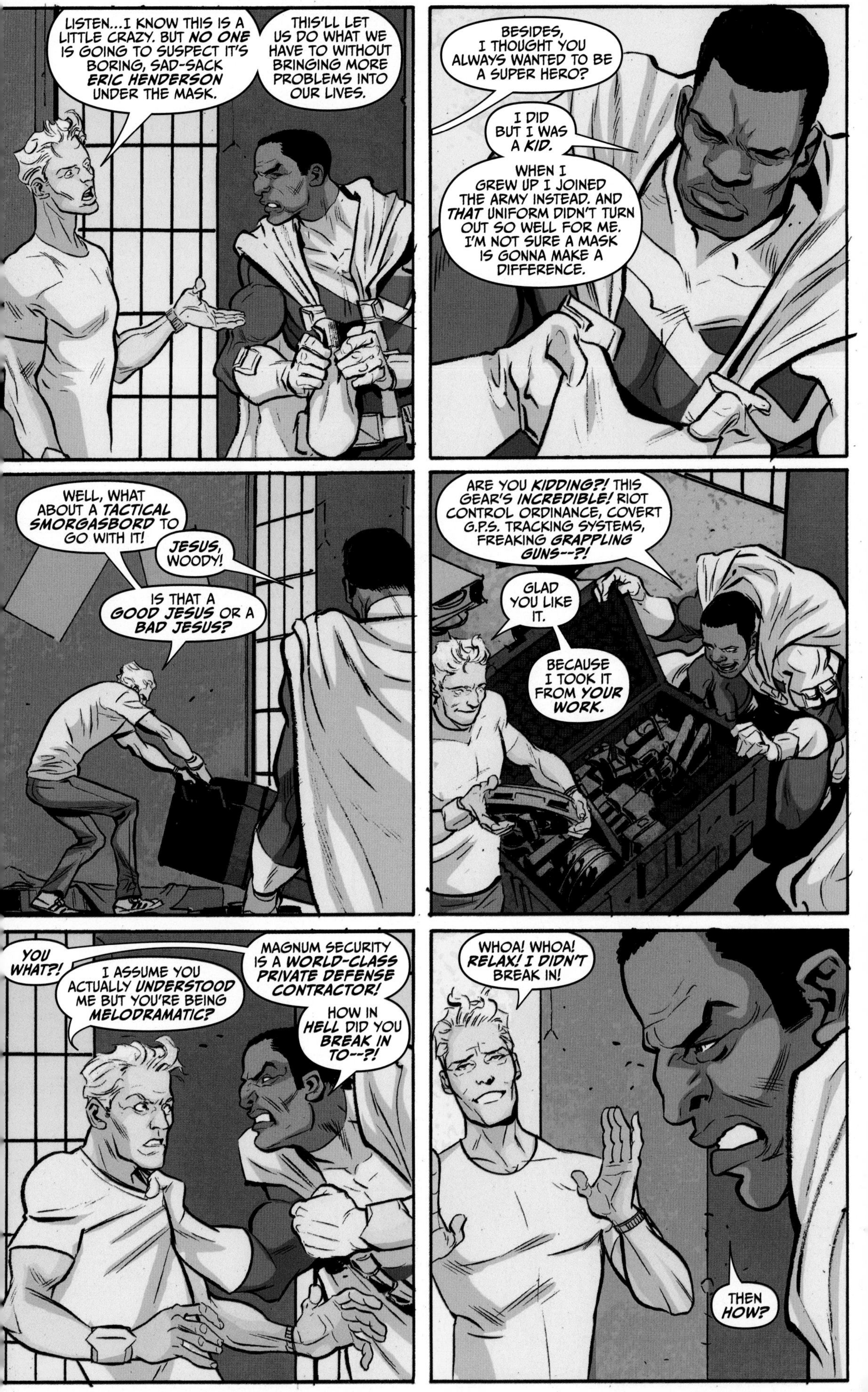
LISTEN...I KNOW THIS IS A LITTLE CRAZY. BUT NO ONE IS GOING TO SUSPECT IT'S BORING, SAD-SACK ERIC HENDERSON UNDER THE MASK.
THIS'LL LET US DO WHAT WE HAVE TO WITHOUT BRINGING MORE PROBLEMS INTO OUR LIVES.
BESIDES, I THOUGHT YOU ALWAYS WANTED TO BE A SUPER HERO?
I DID BUT I WAS A KID.
WHEN I GREW UP I JOINED THE ARMY INSTEAD. AND THAT UNIFORM DIDN'T TURN OUT SO WELL FOR ME. I'M NOT SURE A MASK IS GONNA MAKE A DIFFERENCE.
WELL, WHAT ABOUT A TACTICAL SMORGASBORD TO GO WITH IT!
JESUS, WOODY!
IS THAT A GOOD JESUS OR A BAD JESUS?
ARE YOU KIDDING?! THIS GEAR'S INCREDIBLE! RIOT CONTROL ORDINANCE, COVERT G.P.S. TRACKING SYSTEMS, FREAKING GRAPPLING GUNS--?!
GLAD YOU LIKE IT.
BECAUSE I TOOK IT FROM YOUR WORK.
YOU WHAT?!
MAGNUM SECURITY IS A WORLD-CLASS PRIVATE DEFENSE CONTRACTOR!
I ASSUME YOU ACTUALLY UNDERSTOOD ME BUT YOU'RE BEING MELODRAMATIC?
HOW IN HELL DID YOU BREAK IN TO--?!
WHOA! WHOA! RELAX! I DIDN'T BREAK IN!
THEN HOW?

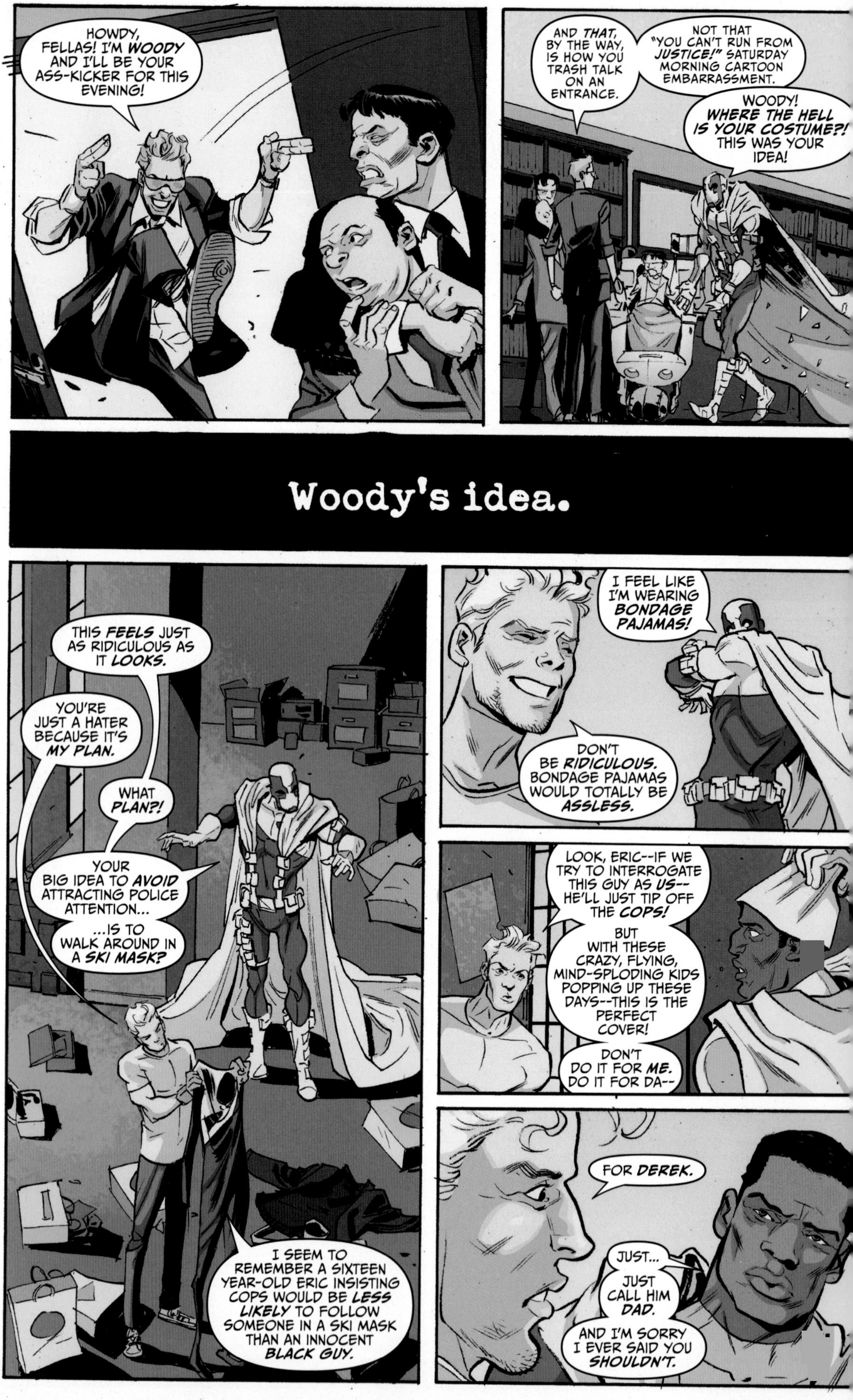
HOWDY, FELLAS! I'M WOODY AND I'LL BE YOUR ASS-KICKER FOR THIS EVENING!
AND THAT, BY THE WAY, IS HOW YOU TRASH TALK ON AN ENTRANCE.
NOT THAT "YOU CAN'T RUN FROM JUSTICE!" SATURDAY MORNING CARTOON EMBARRASSMENT.
WOODY! WHERE THE HELL IS YOUR COSTUME?! THIS WAS YOUR IDEA!
Woody's idea.
THIS FEELS JUST AS RIDICULOUS AS IT LOOKS.
YOU'RE JUST A HATER BECAUSE IT'S MY PLAN.
WHAT PLAN?!
YOUR BIG IDEA TO AVOID ATTRACTING POLICE ATTENTION...
...IS TO WALK AROUND IN A SKI MASK?
I SEEM TO REMEMBER A SIXTEEN YEAR-OLD ERIC INSISTING COPS WOULD BE LESS LIKELY TO FOLLOW SOMEONE IN A SKI MASK THAN AN INNOCENT BLACK GUY.
I FEEL LIKE I'M WEARING BONDAGE PAJAMAS!
DON'T BE RIDICULOUS. BONDAGE PAJAMAS WOULD TOTALLY BE ASSLESS.
LOOK, ERIC--IF WE TRY TO INTERROGATE THIS GUY AS US--HE'LL JUST TIP OFF THE COPS!
BUT WITH THESE CRAZY, FLYING, MIND-SPLODING KIDS POPPING UP THESE DAYS--THIS IS THE PERFECT COVER!
DON'T DO IT FOR ME. DO IT FOR DA--
FOR DEREK.
JUST...
JUST CALL HIM DAD.
AND I'M SORRY I EVER SAID YOU SHOULDN'T.

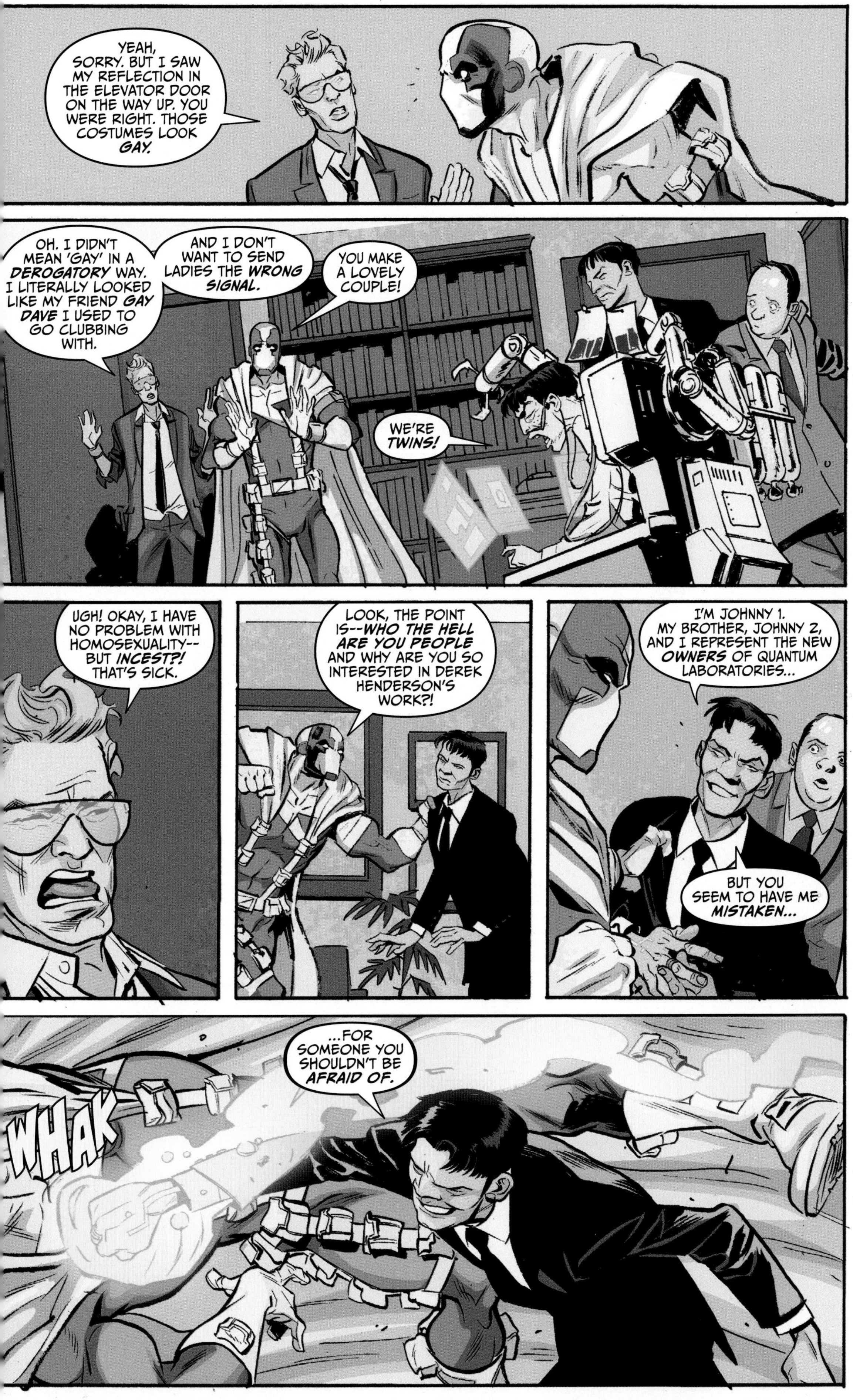
YEAH, SORRY. BUT I SAW MY REFLECTION IN THE ELEVATOR DOOR ON THE WAY UP. YOU WERE RIGHT. THOSE COSTUMES LOOK GAY.
OH. I DIDN'T MEAN 'GAY' IN A DEROGATORY WAY. I LITERALLY LOOKED LIKE MY FRIEND GAY DAVE I USED TO GO CLUBBING WITH.
AND I DON'T WANT TO SEND LADIES THE WRONG SIGNAL.
YOU MAKE A LOVELY COUPLE!
WE'RE TWINS!
UGH! OKAY, I HAVE NO PROBLEM WITH HOMOSEXUALITY--BUT INCEST?! THAT'S SICK.
LOOK, THE POINT IS--WHO THE HELL ARE YOU PEOPLE AND WHY ARE YOU SO INTERESTED IN DEREK HENDERSON'S WORK?!
I'M JOHNNY 1. MY BROTHER, JOHNNY 2, AND I REPRESENT THE NEW OWNERS OF QUANTUM LABORATORIES...
BUT YOU SEEM TO HAVE ME MISTAKEN...
...FOR SOMEONE YOU SHOULDN'T BE AFRAID OF.
WHAK

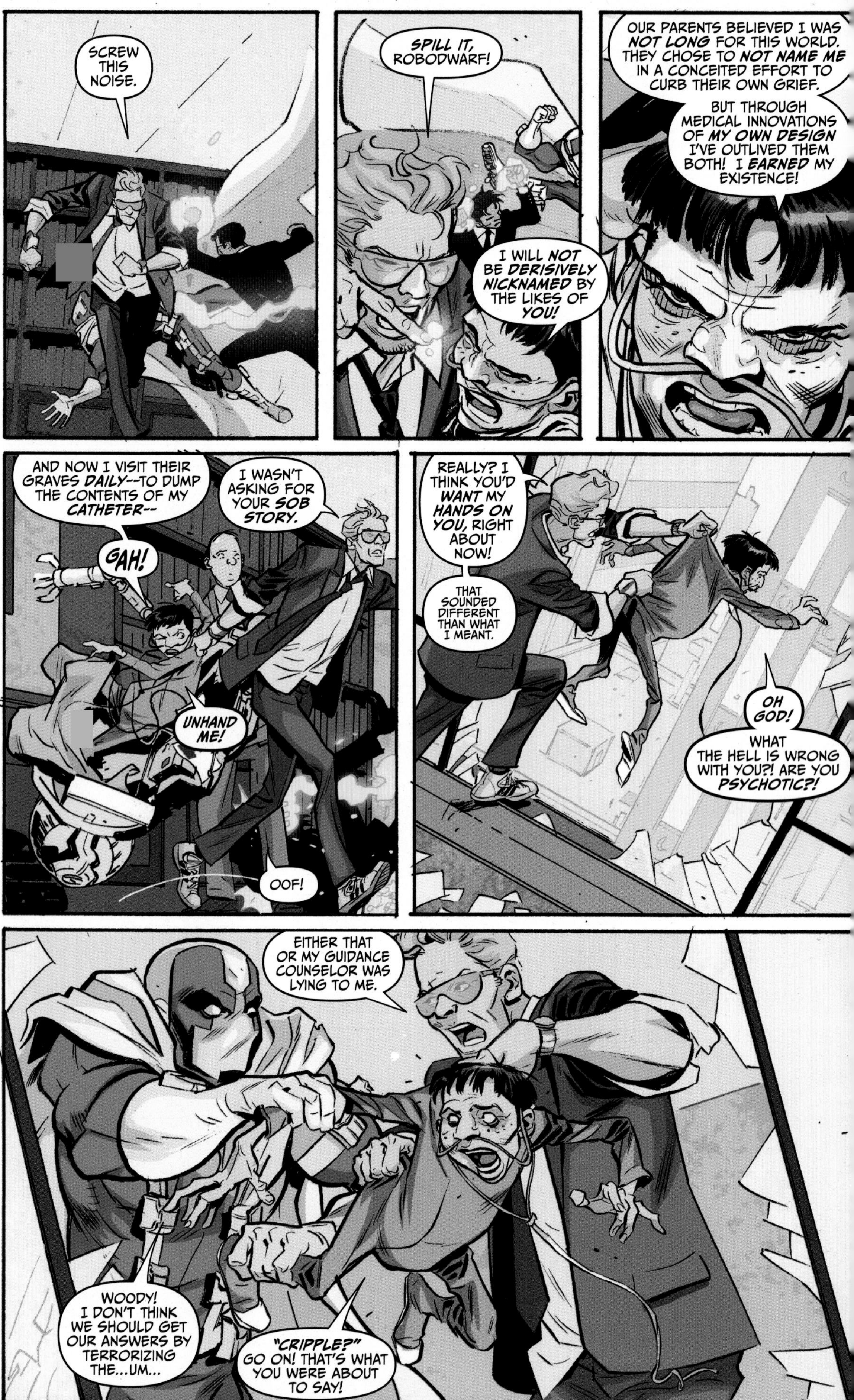
SCREW THIS NOISE.
SPILL IT, ROBODWARF!
I WILL NOT BE DERISIVELY NICKNAMED BY THE LIKES OF YOU!
OUR PARENTS BELIEVED I WAS NOT LONG FOR THIS WORLD. THEY CHOSE TO NOT NAME ME IN A CONCEITED EFFORT TO CURB THEIR OWN GRIEF.
BUT THROUGH MEDICAL INNOVATIONS OF MY OWN DESIGN I'VE OUTLIVED THEM BOTH! I EARNED MY EXISTENCE!
AND NOW I VISIT THEIR GRAVES DAILY--TO DUMP THE CONTENTS OF MY CATHETER--
I WASN'T ASKING FOR YOUR SOB STORY.
GAH!
UNHAND ME!
OOF!
REALLY? I THINK YOU'D WANT MY HANDS ON YOU, RIGHT ABOUT NOW!
THAT SOUNDED DIFFERENT THAN WHAT I MEANT.
OH GOD!
WHAT THE HELL IS WRONG WITH YOU?! ARE YOU PSYCHOTIC?!
EITHER THAT OR MY GUIDANCE COUNSELOR WAS LYING TO ME.
WOODY! I DON'T THINK WE SHOULD GET OUR ANSWERS BY TERRORIZING THE...UM...
"CRIPPLE?" GO ON! THAT'S WHAT YOU WERE ABOUT TO SAY!

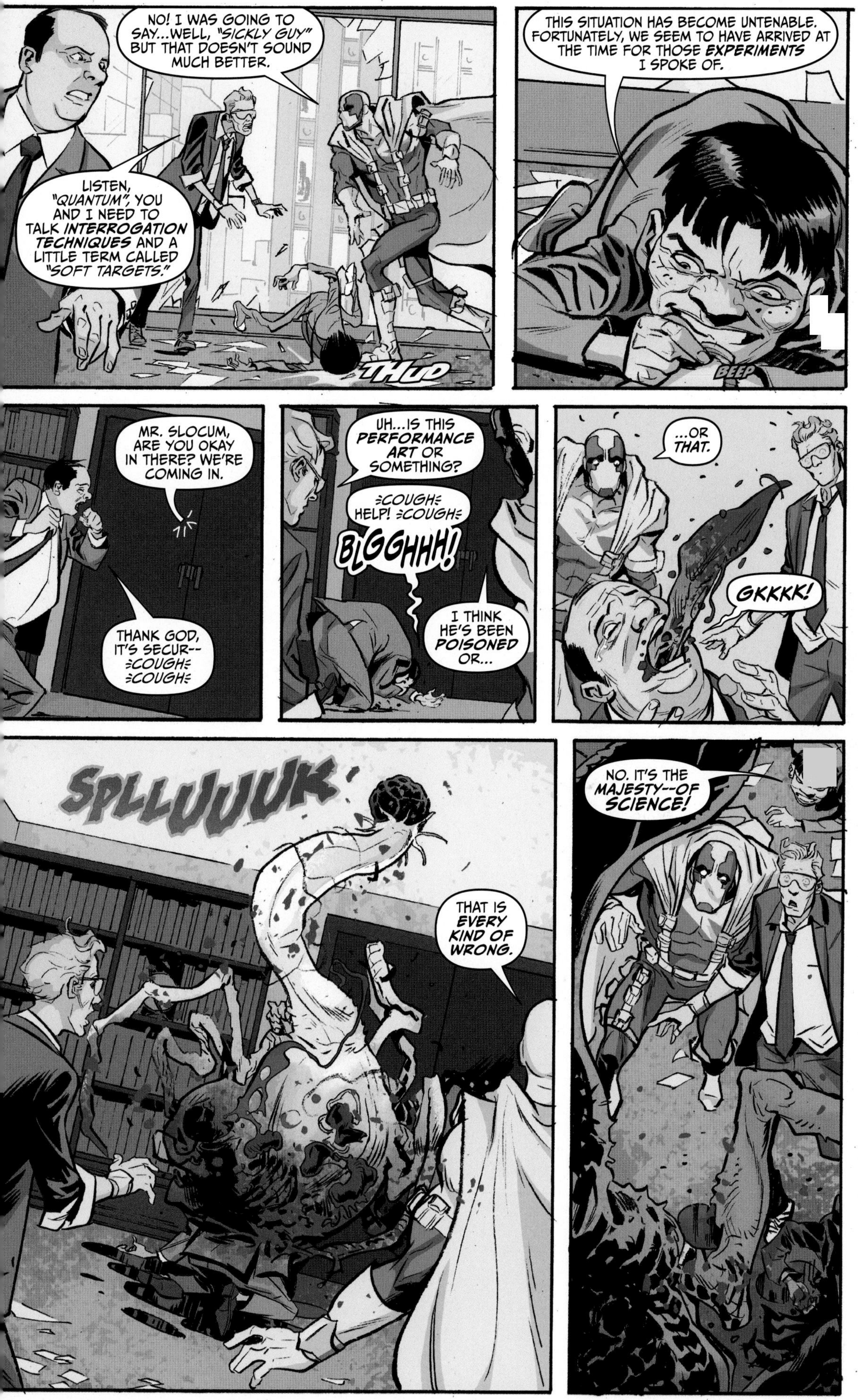
NO! I WAS GOING TO SAY...WELL, "SICKLY GUY" BUT THAT DOESN'T SOUND MUCH BETTER.
LISTEN, "QUANTUM", YOU AND I NEED TO TALK INTERROGATION TECHNIQUES AND A LITTLE TERM CALLED "SOFT TARGETS."
THUD
THIS SITUATION HAS BECOME UNTENABLE. FORTUNATELY, WE SEEM TO HAVE ARRIVED AT THE TIME FOR THOSE EXPERIMENTS I SPOKE OF.
BEEP
MR. SLOCUM, ARE YOU OKAY IN THERE? WE'RE COMING IN.
THANK GOD, IT'S SECUR-- COUGH COUGH
UH...IS THIS PERFORMANCE ART OR SOMETHING?
COUGH HELP! COUGH
BLGGHHH!
I THINK HE'S BEEN POISONED OR...
...OR THAT.
GKKKK!
SPLLUUUUK
THAT IS EVERY KIND OF WRONG.
NO. IT'S THE MAJESTY--OF SCIENCE!

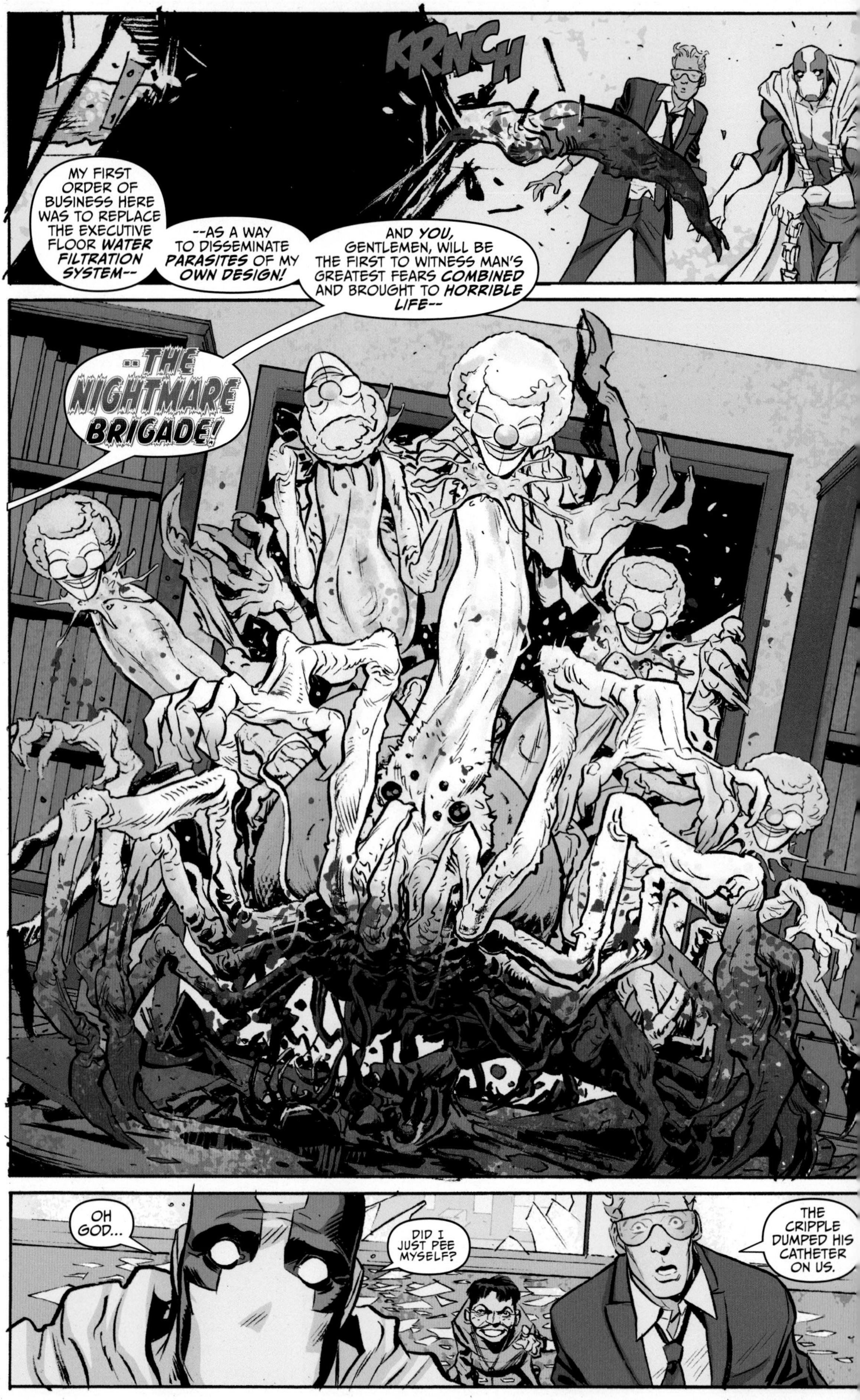
KRNCH
MY FIRST ORDER OF BUSINESS HERE WAS TO REPLACE THE EXECUTIVE FLOOR WATER FILTRATION SYSTEM--
--AS A WAY TO DISSEMINATE PARASITES OF MY OWN DESIGN!
AND YOU, GENTLEMEN, WILL BE THE FIRST TO WITNESS MAN'S GREATEST FEARS COMBINED AND BROUGHT TO HORRIBLE LIFE--
--THE NIGHTMARE BRIGADE!
OH GOD...
DID I JUST PEE MYSELF?
THE CRIPPLE DUMPED HIS CATHETER ON US.

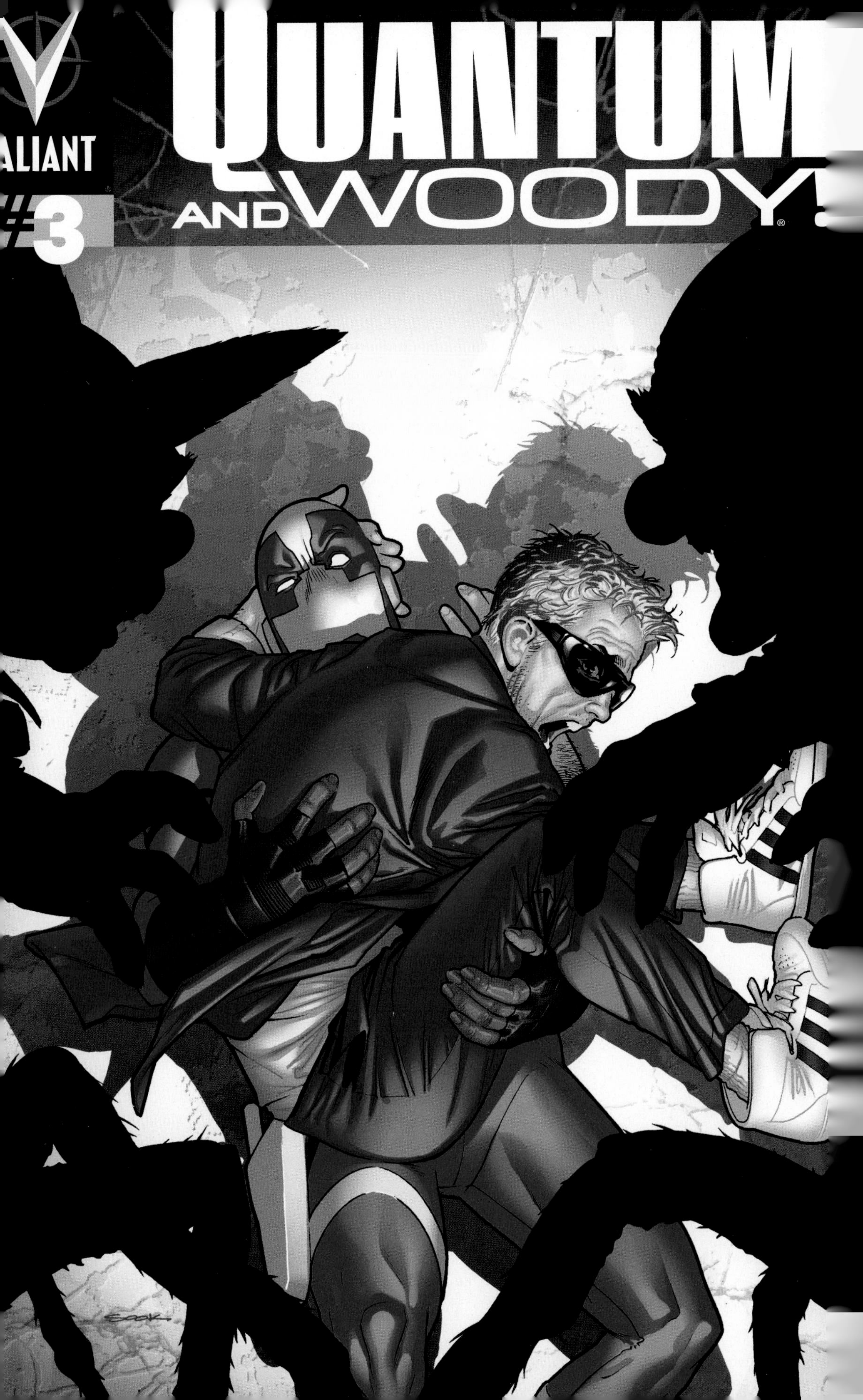
ALIANT
#3
QUANTUM
AND WOODY!

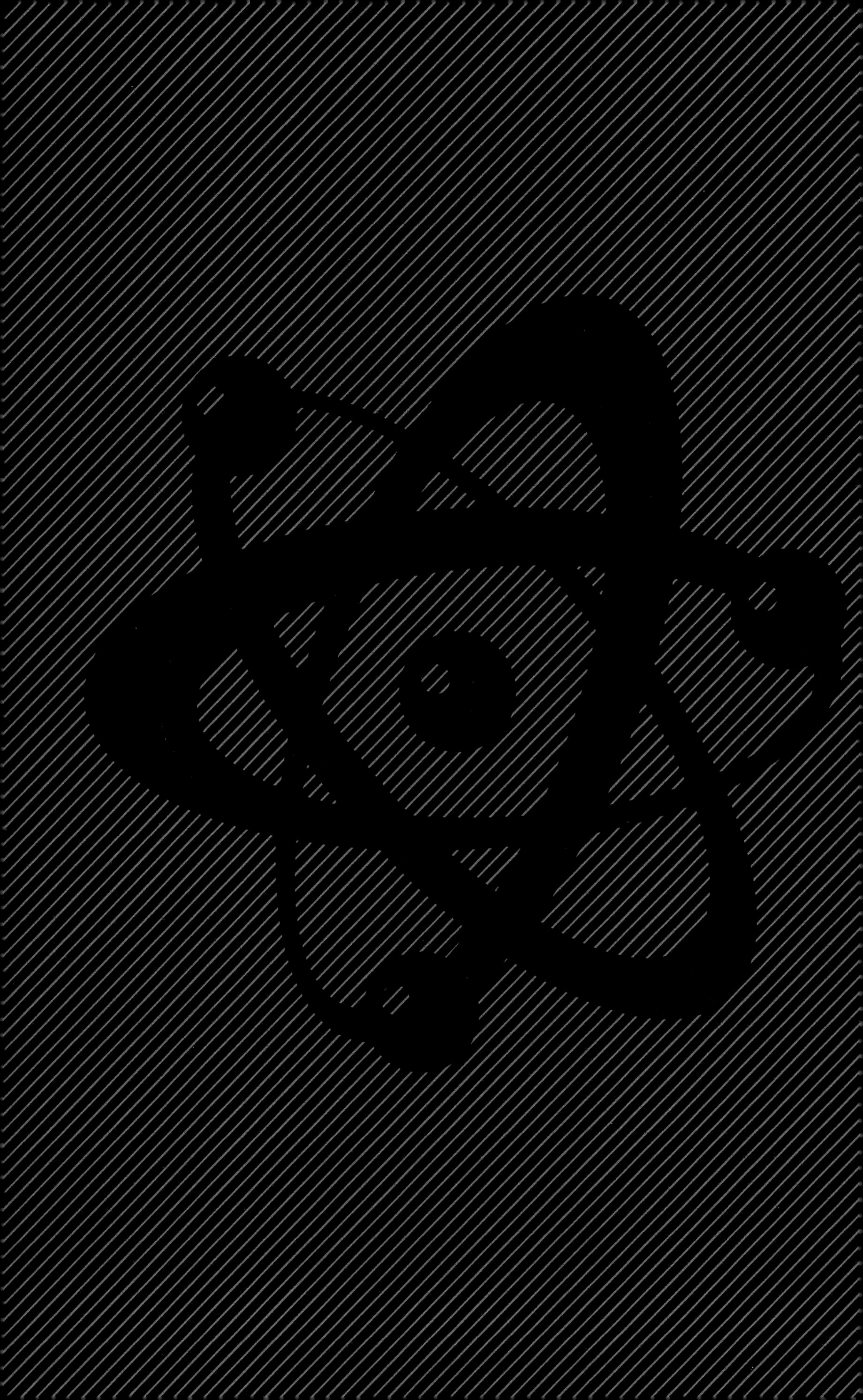

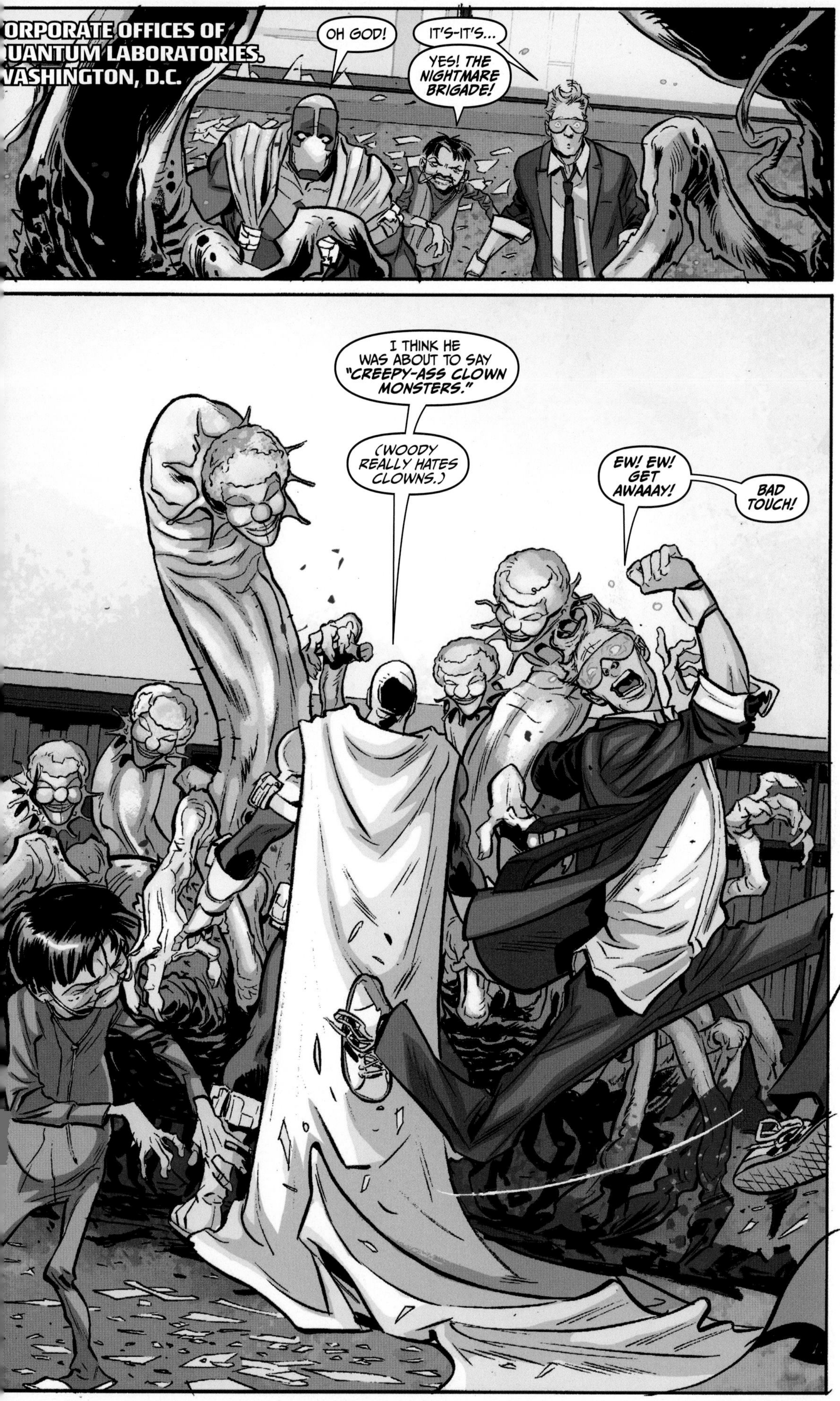
ORPORATE OFFICES OF
UANTUM LABORATORIES.
VASHINGTON, D.C.
OH GOD!
IT'S-IT'S...
YES! THE NIGHTMARE BRIGADE!
I THINK HE WAS ABOUT TO SAY "CREEPY-ASS CLOWN MONSTERS."
(WOODY REALLY HATES CLOWNS.)
EW! EW! GET AWAAAY!
BAD TOUCH!

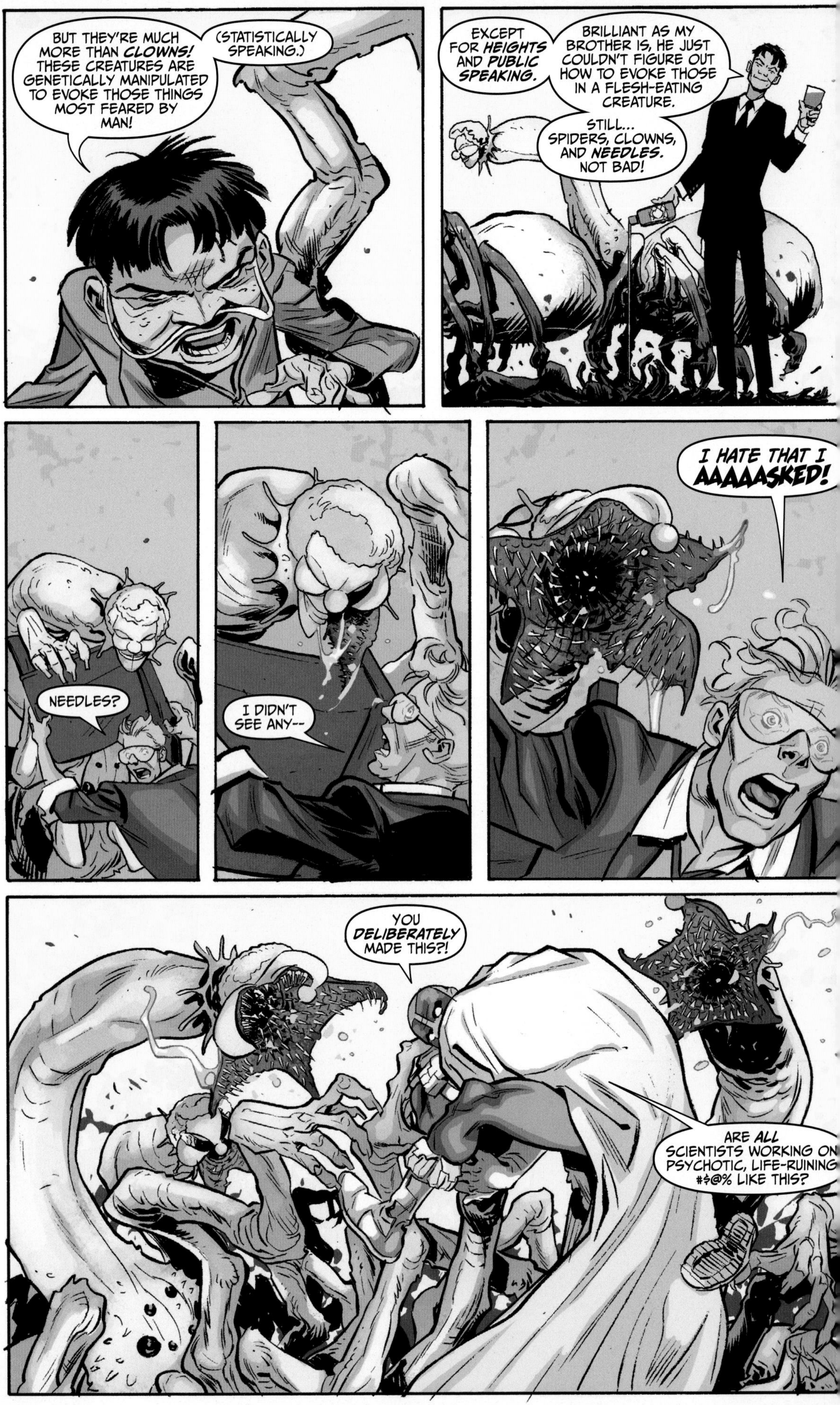

BUT THEY'RE MUCH MORE THAN CLOWNS! THESE CREATURES ARE GENETICALLY MANIPULATED TO EVOKE THOSE THINGS MOST FEARED BY MAN!
(STATISTICALLY SPEAKING.)
EXCEPT FOR HEIGHTS AND PUBLIC SPEAKING.
BRILLIANT AS MY BROTHER IS, HE JUST COULDN'T FIGURE OUT HOW TO EVOKE THOSE IN A FLESH-EATING CREATURE.
STILL... SPIDERS, CLOWNS, AND NEEDLES. NOT BAD!
NEEDLES?
I DIDN'T SEE ANY--
I HATE THAT I AAAAASKED!
YOU DELIBERATELY MADE THIS?!
ARE ALL SCIENTISTS WORKING ON PSYCHOTIC, LIFE-RUINING #$@% LIKE THIS?

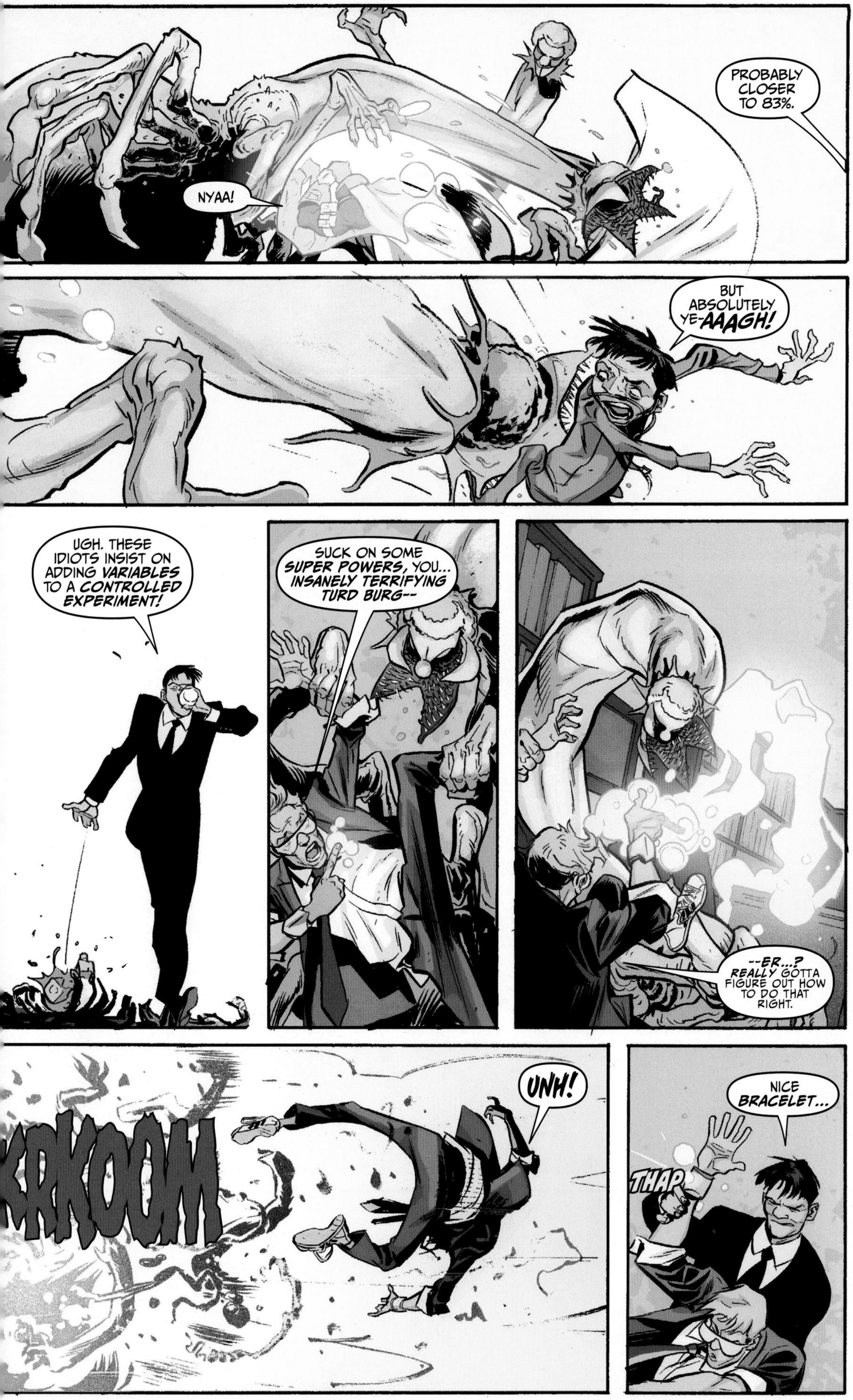

PROBABLY CLOSER TO 83%.
NYAA!
BUT ABSOLUTELY YE-AAAGH!
UGH. THESE IDIOTS INSIST ON ADDING VARIABLES TO A CONTROLLED EXPERIMENT!
SUCK ON SOME SUPER POWERS, YOU... INSANELY TERRIFYING TURD BURG--
--ER...? REALLY GOTTA FIGURE OUT HOW TO DO THAT RIGHT.
KRKOOM
UNH!
NICE BRACELET...
THAP

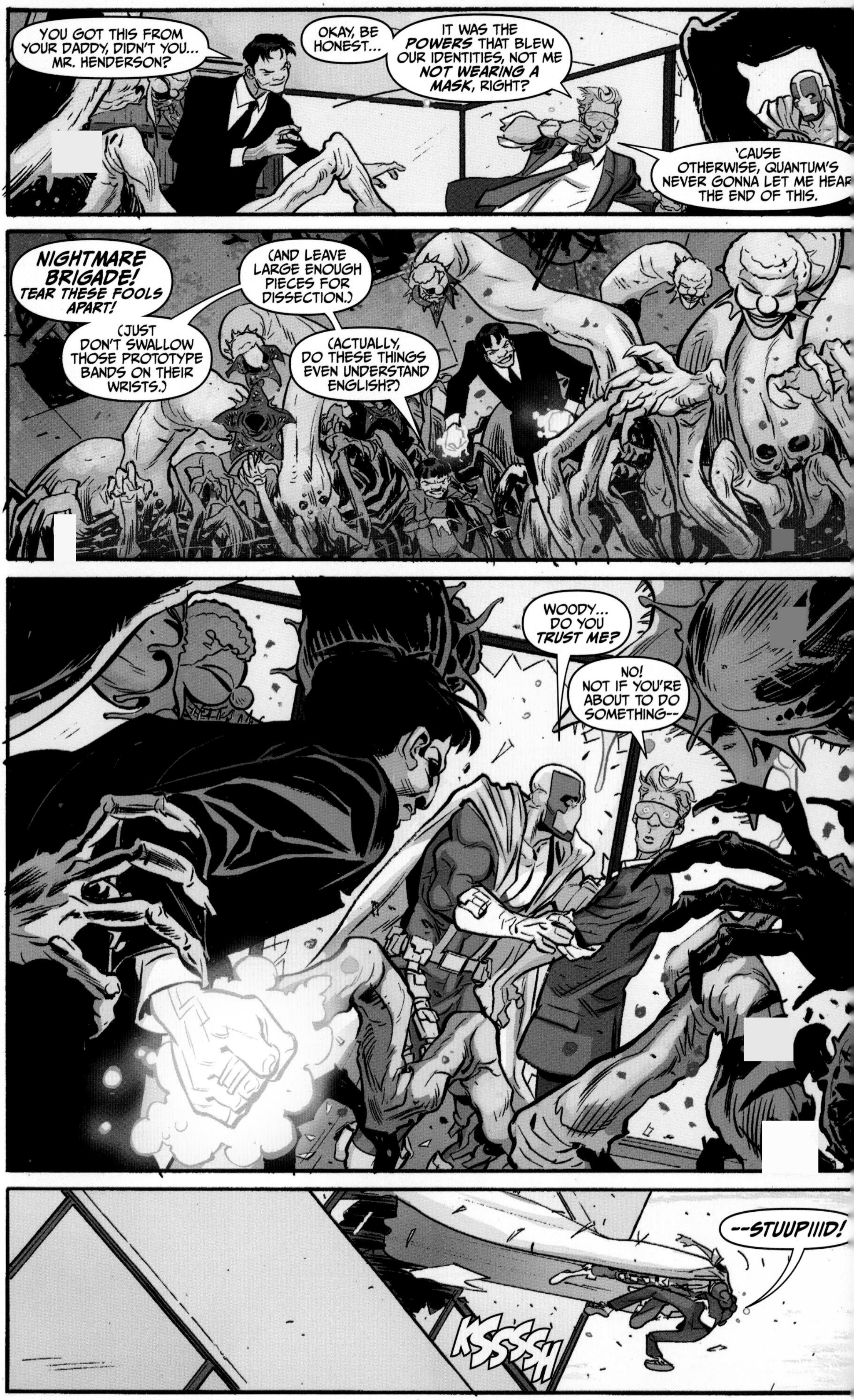
YOU GOT THIS FROM YOUR DADDY, DIDN'T YOU... MR. HENDERSON?
OKAY, BE HONEST...
IT WAS THE POWERS THAT BLEW OUR IDENTITIES, NOT ME NOT WEARING A MASK, RIGHT?
'CAUSE OTHERWISE, QUANTUM'S NEVER GONNA LET ME HEAR THE END OF THIS.
NIGHTMARE BRIGADE! TEAR THESE FOOLS APART!
(JUST DON'T SWALLOW THOSE PROTOTYPE BANDS ON THEIR WRISTS.)
(AND LEAVE LARGE ENOUGH PIECES FOR DISSECTION.)
(ACTUALLY, DO THESE THINGS EVEN UNDERSTAND ENGLISH?)
WOODY... DO YOU TRUST ME?
NO! NOT IF YOU'RE ABOUT TO DO SOMETHING--
--STUUPIIID!
KSSSH

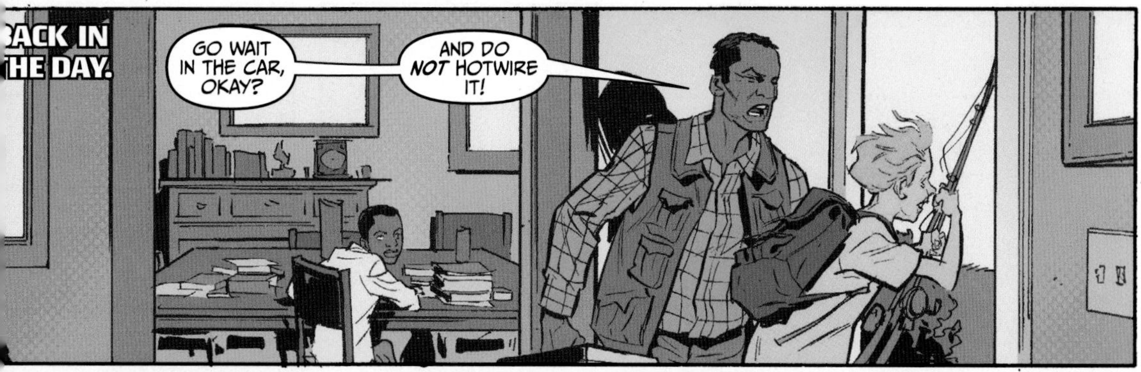
ACK IN
HE DAY.
GO WAIT IN THE CAR, OKAY?
AND DO NOT HOTWIRE IT!

Fishing for Validation.

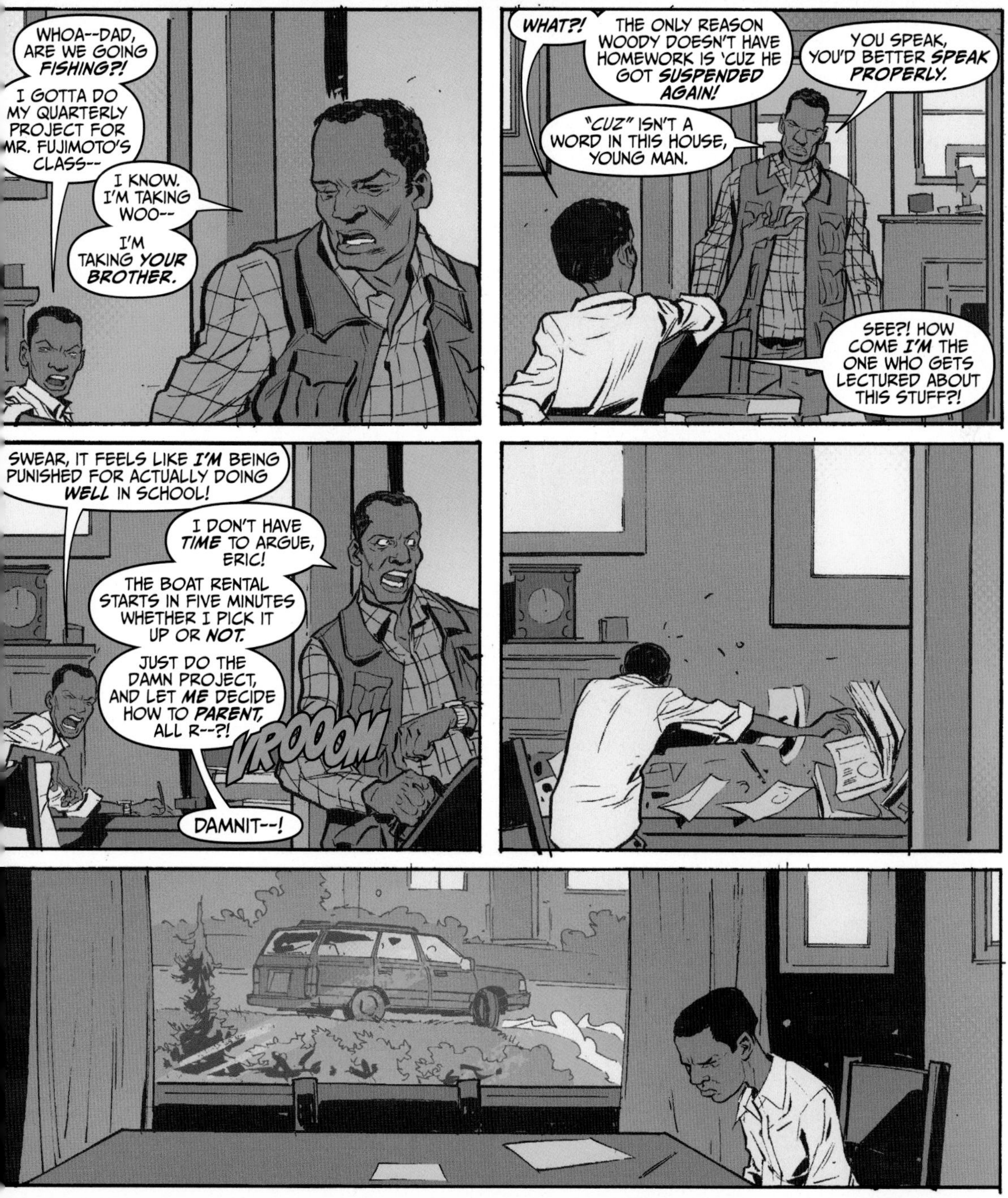
WHOA--DAD, ARE WE GOING FISHING?!
I GOTTA DO MY QUARTERLY PROJECT FOR MR. FUJIMOTO'S CLASS--
I KNOW. I'M TAKING WOO--
I'M TAKING YOUR BROTHER.
WHAT?!
THE ONLY REASON WOODY DOESN'T HAVE HOMEWORK IS 'CUZ HE GOT SUSPENDED AGAIN!
"CUZ" ISN'T A WORD IN THIS HOUSE, YOUNG MAN.
YOU SPEAK, YOU'D BETTER SPEAK PROPERLY.
SEE?! HOW COME I'M THE ONE WHO GETS LECTURED ABOUT THIS STUFF?!
SWEAR, IT FEELS LIKE I'M BEING PUNISHED FOR ACTUALLY DOING WELL IN SCHOOL!
I DON'T HAVE TIME TO ARGUE, ERIC!
THE BOAT RENTAL STARTS IN FIVE MINUTES WHETHER I PICK IT UP OR NOT.
JUST DO THE DAMN PROJECT, AND LET ME DECIDE HOW TO PARENT, ALL R--?!
VROOOM
DAMNIT--!

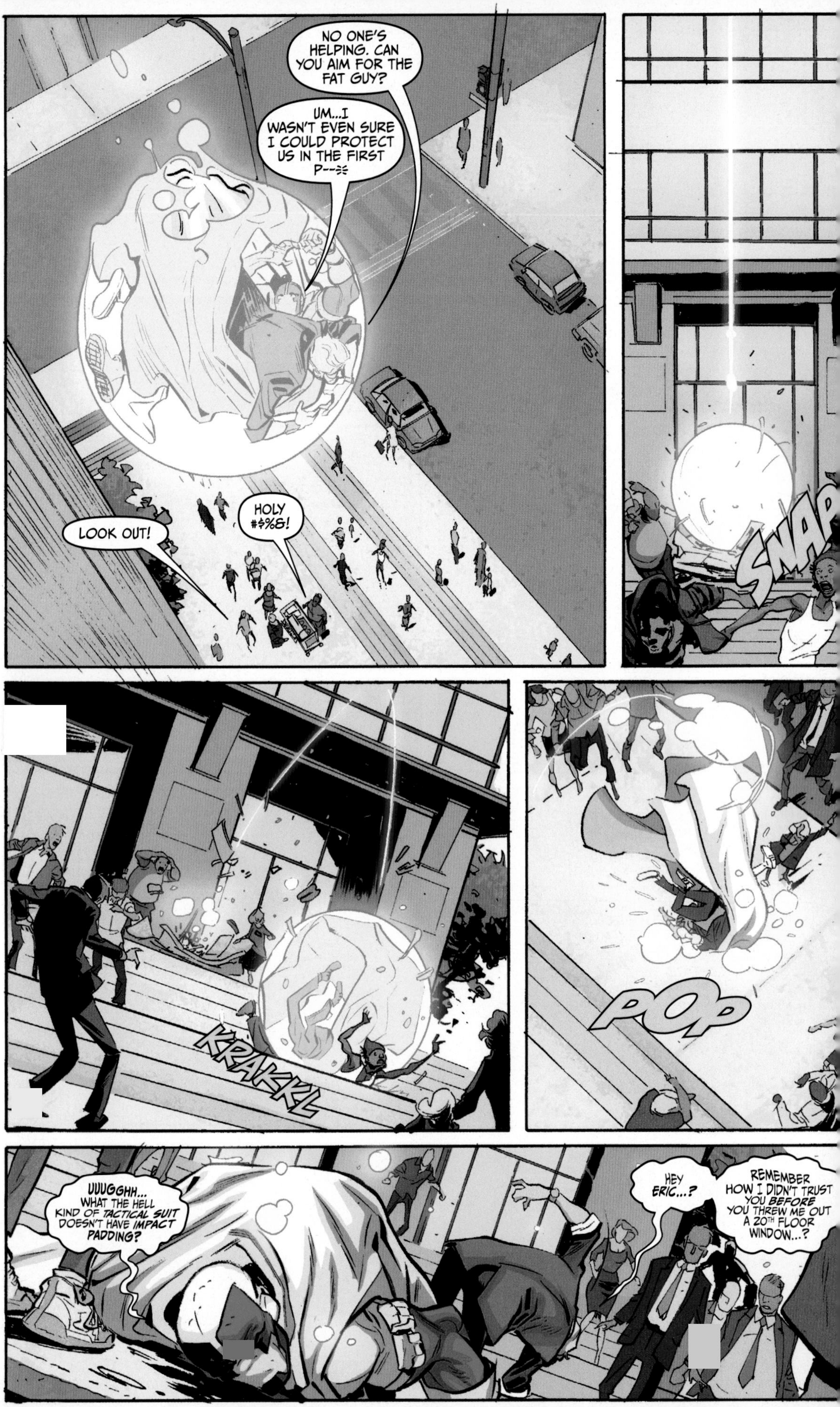
NO ONE'S HELPING. CAN YOU AIM FOR THE FAT GUY?
UM...I WASN'T EVEN SURE I COULD PROTECT US IN THE FIRST P--
HOLY #$%&!
LOOK OUT!
SNAP
KRAKKL
POP
UUUGGHH... WHAT THE HELL KIND OF TACTICAL SUIT DOESN'T HAVE IMPACT PADDING?
HEY ERIC...?
REMEMBER HOW I DIDN'T TRUST YOU BEFORE YOU THREW ME OUT A 20TH FLOOR WINDOW...?

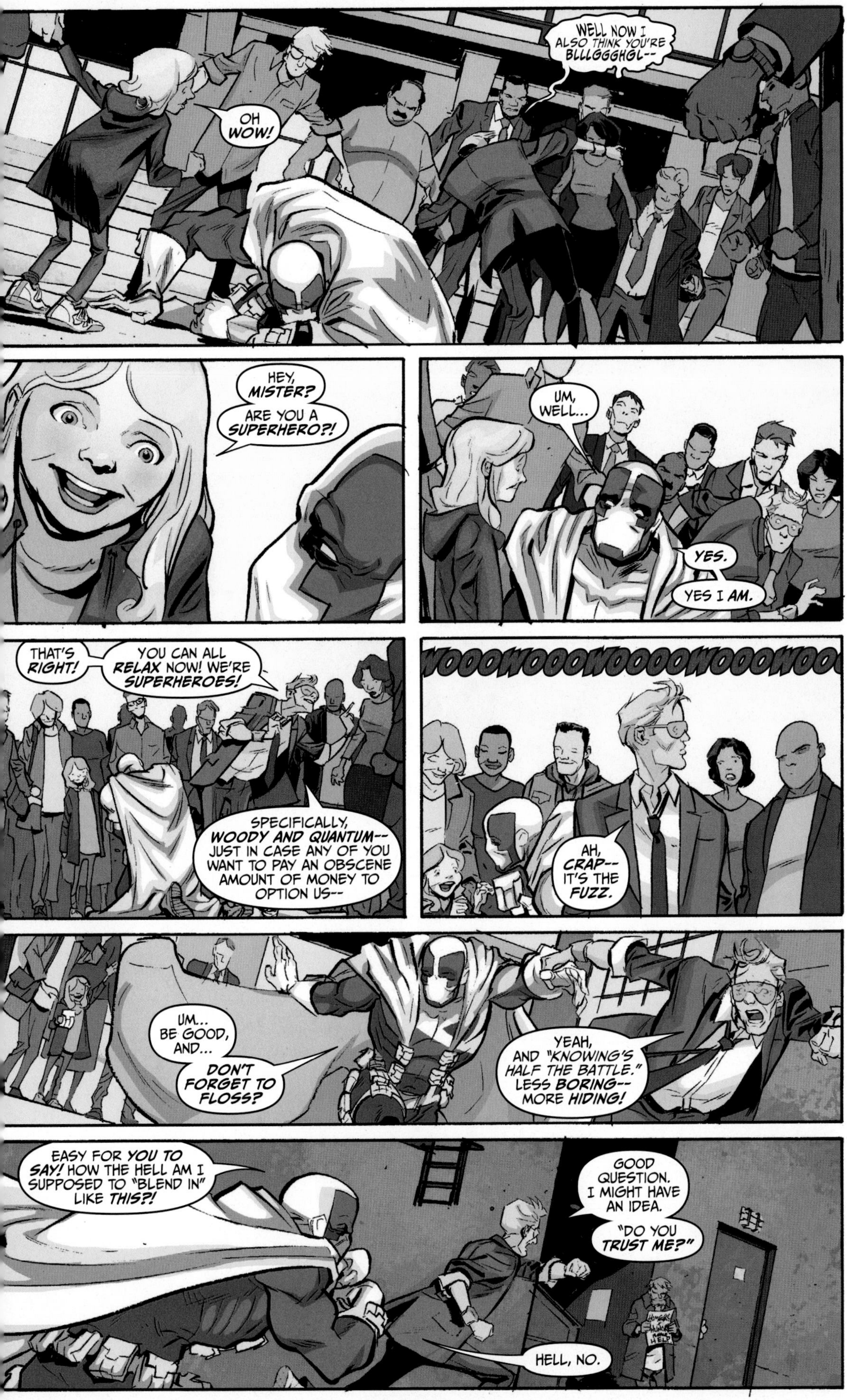
WELL NOW I ALSO THINK YOU'RE BLLLGGGHGL--
OH WOW!
HEY, MISTER?
ARE YOU A SUPERHERO?!
UM, WELL...
YES.
YES I AM.
THAT'S RIGHT!
YOU CAN ALL RELAX NOW! WE'RE SUPERHEROES!
SPECIFICALLY, WOODY AND QUANTUM-- JUST IN CASE ANY OF YOU WANT TO PAY AN OBSCENE AMOUNT OF MONEY TO OPTION US--
WOOOWOOOWOOOOWOOOWOOO
AH, CRAP-- IT'S THE FUZZ.
UM... BE GOOD, AND...
DON'T FORGET TO FLOSS?
YEAH, AND "KNOWING'S HALF THE BATTLE." LESS BORING-- MORE HIDING!
EASY FOR YOU TO SAY! HOW THE HELL AM I SUPPOSED TO "BLEND IN" LIKE THIS?!
GOOD QUESTION. I MIGHT HAVE AN IDEA.
"DO YOU TRUST ME?"
HELL, NO.

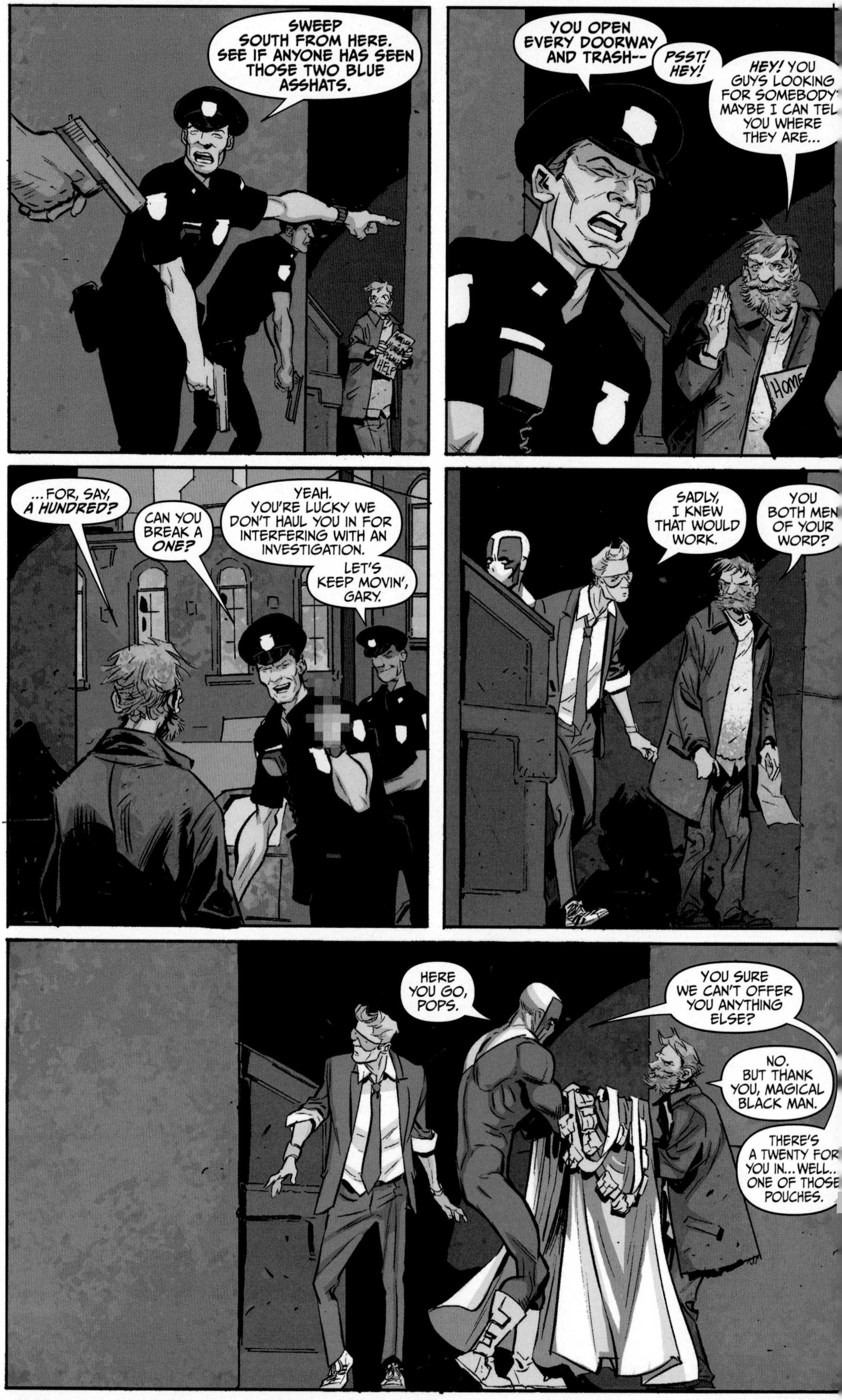
SWEEP SOUTH FROM HERE. SEE IF ANYONE HAS SEEN THOSE TWO BLUE ASSHATS.
YOU OPEN EVERY DOORWAY AND TRASH--
PSST! HEY!
HEY! YOU GUYS LOOKING FOR SOMEBODY? MAYBE I CAN TEL YOU WHERE THEY ARE...
...FOR, SAY, A HUNDRED?
CAN YOU BREAK A ONE?
YEAH. YOU'RE LUCKY WE DON'T HAUL YOU IN FOR INTERFERING WITH AN INVESTIGATION.
LET'S KEEP MOVIN', GARY.
SADLY, I KNEW THAT WOULD WORK.
YOU BOTH MEN OF YOUR WORD?
HERE YOU GO, POPS.
YOU SURE WE CAN'T OFFER YOU ANYTHING ELSE?
NO. BUT THANK YOU, MAGICAL BLACK MAN.
THERE'S A TWENTY FOR YOU IN...WELL... ONE OF THOSE POUCHES.

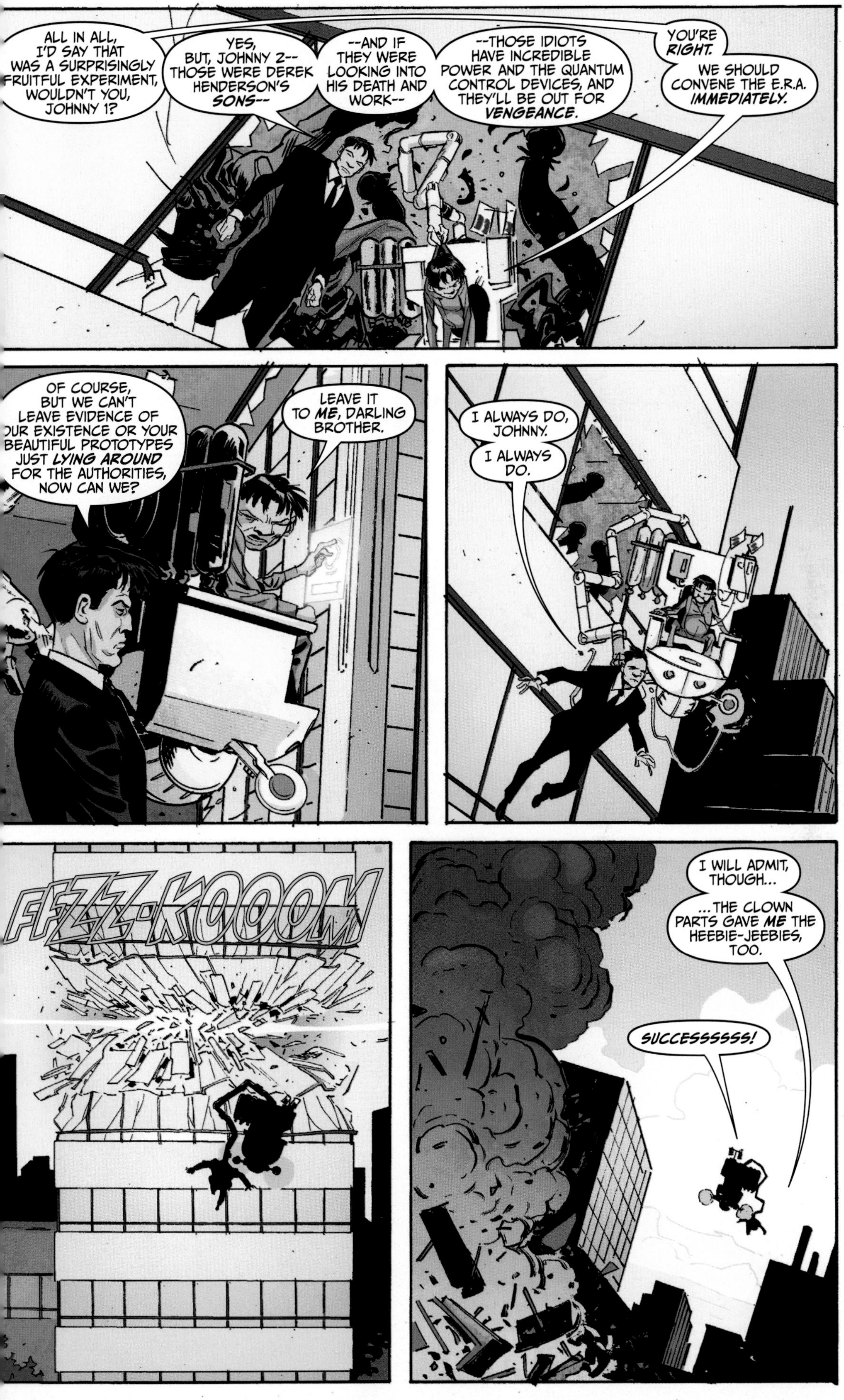
ALL IN ALL, I'D SAY THAT WAS A SURPRISINGLY FRUITFUL EXPERIMENT, WOULDN'T YOU, JOHNNY 1?
YES, BUT, JOHNNY 2-- THOSE WERE DEREK HENDERSON'S SONS--
--AND IF THEY WERE LOOKING INTO HIS DEATH AND WORK--
--THOSE IDIOTS HAVE INCREDIBLE POWER AND THE QUANTUM CONTROL DEVICES, AND THEY'LL BE OUT FOR VENGEANCE.
YOU'RE RIGHT.
WE SHOULD CONVENE THE E.R.A. IMMEDIATELY.
OF COURSE, BUT WE CAN'T LEAVE EVIDENCE OF OUR EXISTENCE OR YOUR BEAUTIFUL PROTOTYPES JUST LYING AROUND FOR THE AUTHORITIES, NOW CAN WE?
LEAVE IT TO ME, DARLING BROTHER.
I ALWAYS DO, JOHNNY.
I ALWAYS DO.
FFZZ-KOOOOM
I WILL ADMIT, THOUGH...
...THE CLOWN PARTS GAVE ME THE HEEBIE-JEEBIES, TOO.
SUCCESSSSSS!

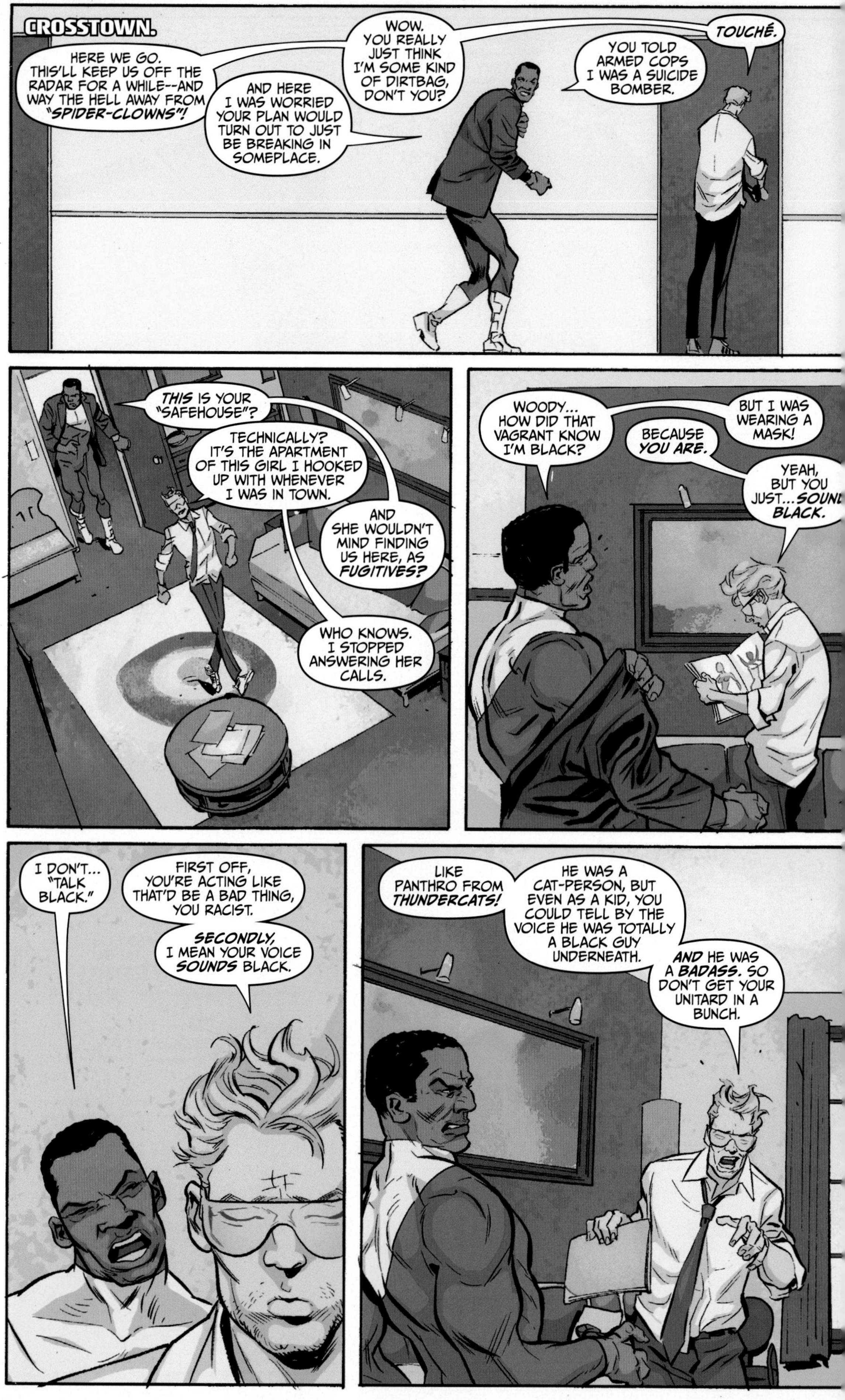
CROSSTOWN.
HERE WE GO. THIS'LL KEEP US OFF THE RADAR FOR A WHILE--AND WAY THE HELL AWAY FROM "SPIDER-CLOWNS"!
AND HERE I WAS WORRIED YOUR PLAN WOULD TURN OUT TO JUST BE BREAKING IN SOMEPLACE.
WOW. YOU REALLY JUST THINK I'M SOME KIND OF DIRTBAG, DON'T YOU?
YOU TOLD ARMED COPS I WAS A SUICIDE BOMBER.
TOUCHÉ.
THIS IS YOUR "SAFEHOUSE"?
TECHNICALLY? IT'S THE APARTMENT OF THIS GIRL I HOOKED UP WITH WHENEVER I WAS IN TOWN.
AND SHE WOULDN'T MIND FINDING US HERE, AS FUGITIVES?
WHO KNOWS. I STOPPED ANSWERING HER CALLS.
WOODY... HOW DID THAT VAGRANT KNOW I'M BLACK?
BECAUSE YOU ARE.
BUT I WAS WEARING A MASK!
YEAH, BUT YOU JUST...SOUND BLACK.
I DON'T... "TALK BLACK."
FIRST OFF, YOU'RE ACTING LIKE THAT'D BE A BAD THING, YOU RACIST.
SECONDLY, I MEAN YOUR VOICE SOUNDS BLACK.
LIKE PANTHRO FROM THUNDERCATS!
HE WAS A CAT-PERSON, BUT EVEN AS A KID, YOU COULD TELL BY THE VOICE HE WAS TOTALLY A BLACK GUY UNDERNEATH.
AND HE WAS A BADASS. SO DON'T GET YOUR UNITARD IN A BUNCH.

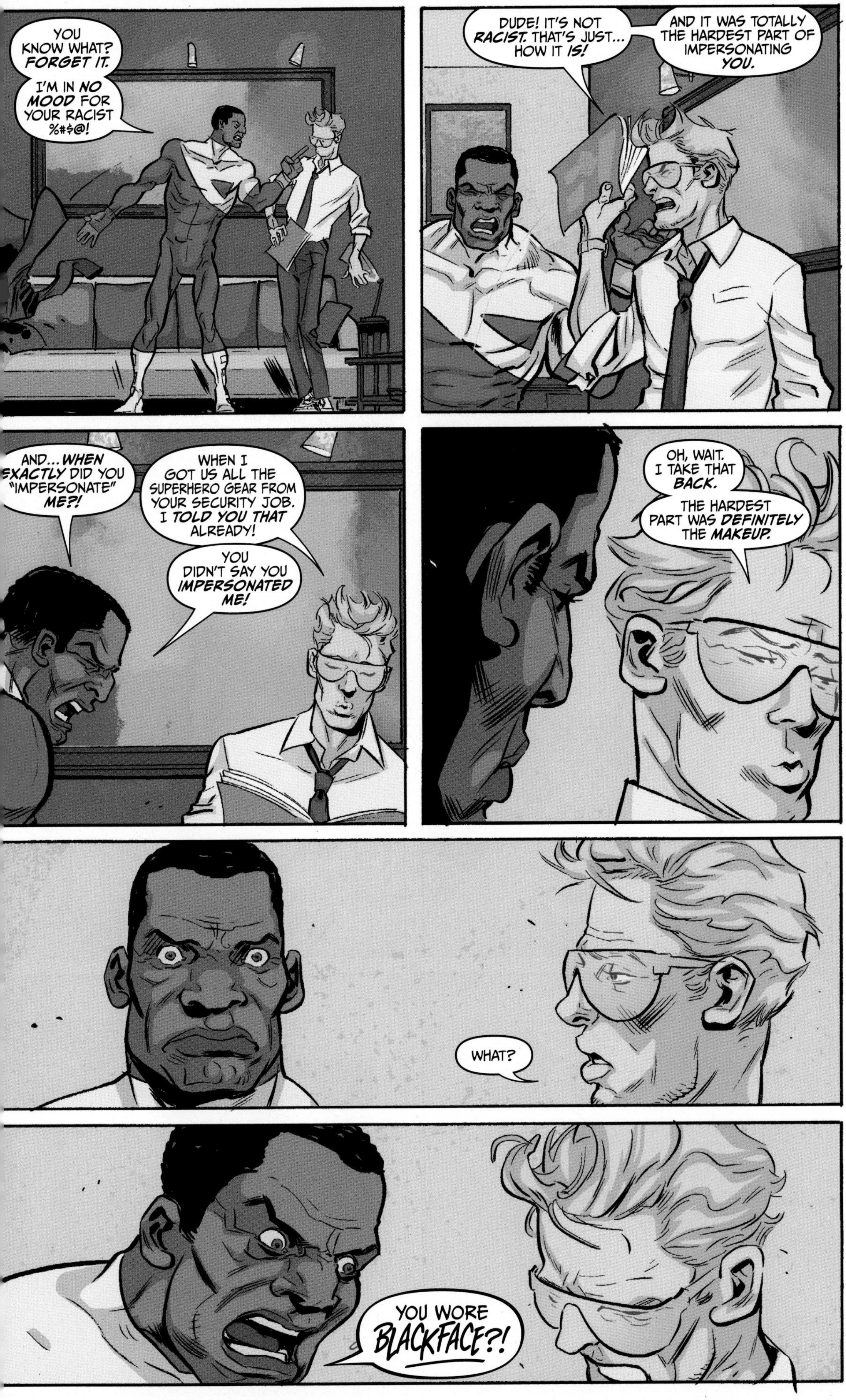
YOU KNOW WHAT? FORGET IT.
I'M IN NO MOOD FOR YOUR RACIST %#$@!
DUDE! IT'S NOT RACIST. THAT'S JUST... HOW IT IS!
AND IT WAS TOTALLY THE HARDEST PART OF IMPERSONATING YOU.
AND... WHEN EXACTLY DID YOU "IMPERSONATE" ME?!
WHEN I GOT US ALL THE SUPERHERO GEAR FROM YOUR SECURITY JOB. I TOLD YOU THAT ALREADY!
YOU DIDN'T SAY YOU IMPERSONATED ME!
OH, WAIT. I TAKE THAT BACK.
THE HARDEST PART WAS DEFINITELY THE MAKEUP.
WHAT?
YOU WORE BLACKFACE?!

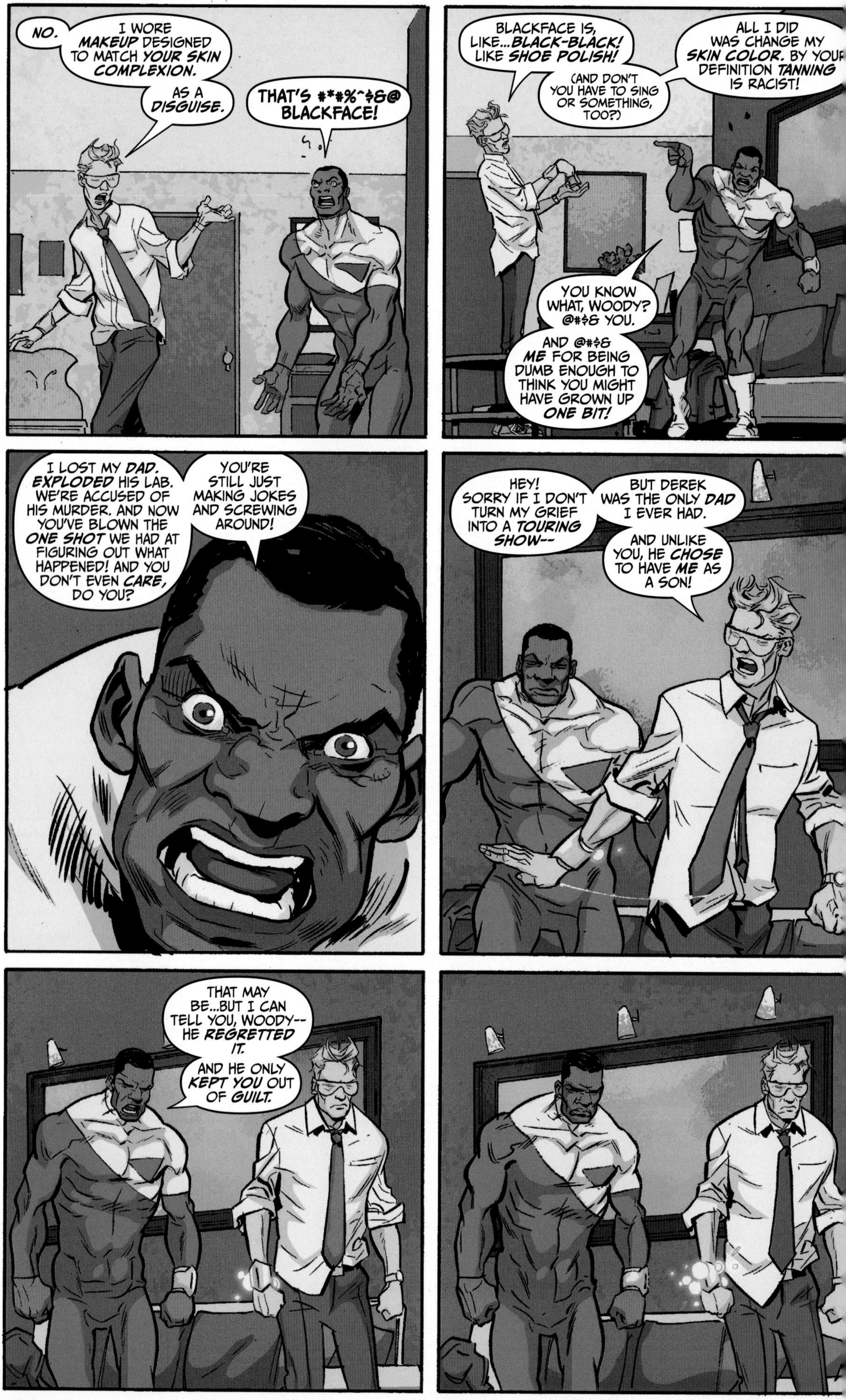
NO.
I WORE MAKEUP DESIGNED TO MATCH YOUR SKIN COMPLEXION.
AS A DISGUISE.
THAT'S #*#%^$&@ BLACKFACE!
BLACKFACE IS, LIKE...BLACK-BLACK! LIKE SHOE POLISH!
(AND DON'T YOU HAVE TO SING OR SOMETHING, TOO?)
ALL I DID WAS CHANGE MY SKIN COLOR. BY YOUR DEFINITION TANNING IS RACIST!
YOU KNOW WHAT, WOODY? @#$& YOU.
AND @#$& ME FOR BEING DUMB ENOUGH TO THINK YOU MIGHT HAVE GROWN UP ONE BIT!
I LOST MY DAD. EXPLODED HIS LAB. WE'RE ACCUSED OF HIS MURDER. AND NOW YOU'VE BLOWN THE ONE SHOT WE HAD AT FIGURING OUT WHAT HAPPENED! AND YOU DON'T EVEN CARE, DO YOU?
YOU'RE STILL JUST MAKING JOKES AND SCREWING AROUND!
HEY! SORRY IF I DON'T TURN MY GRIEF INTO A TOURING SHOW--
BUT DEREK WAS THE ONLY DAD I EVER HAD.
AND UNLIKE YOU, HE CHOSE TO HAVE ME AS A SON!
THAT MAY BE...BUT I CAN TELL YOU, WOODY-- HE REGRETTED IT.
AND HE ONLY KEPT YOU OUT OF GUILT.

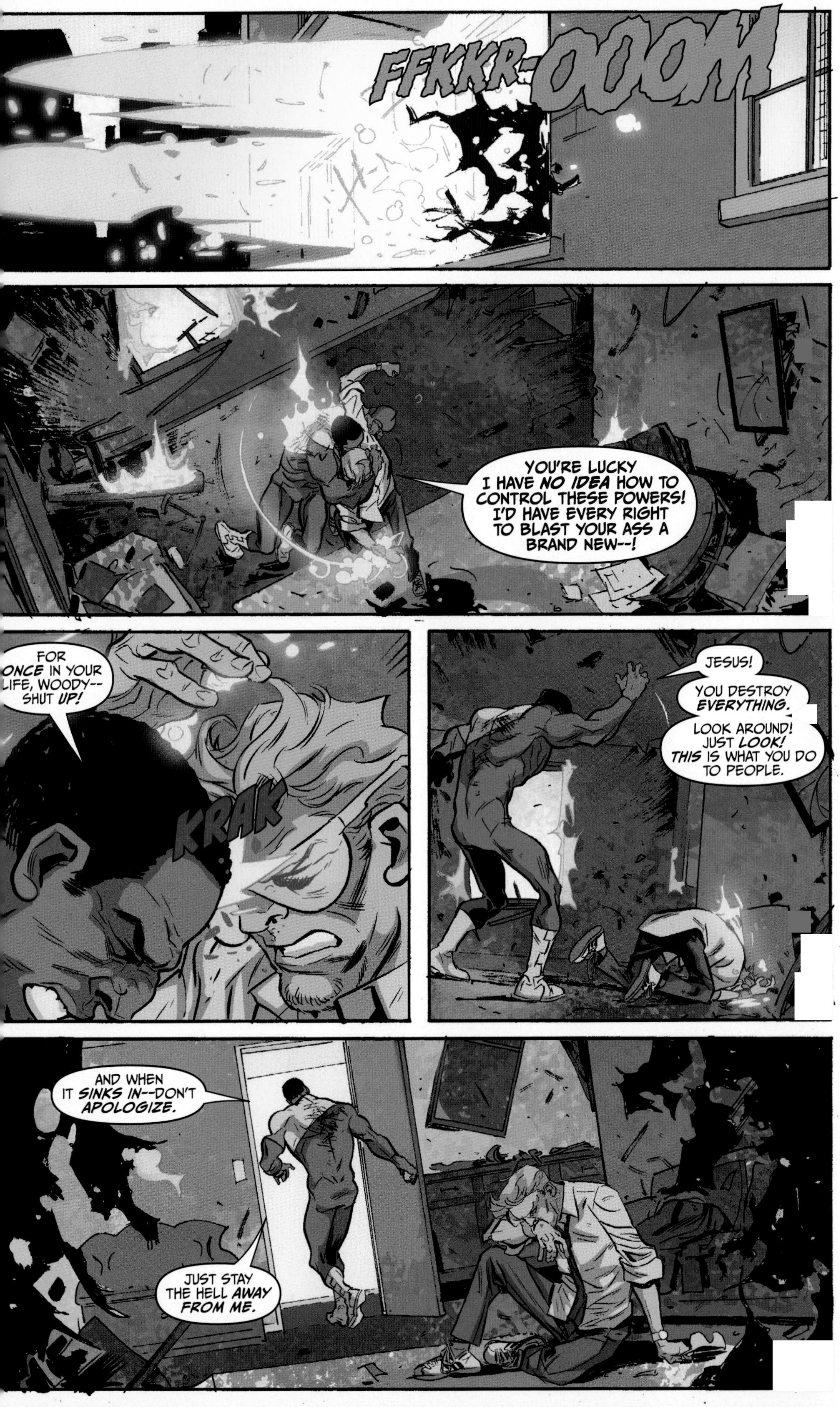
FFKKR-OOOM
YOU'RE LUCKY I HAVE NO IDEA HOW TO CONTROL THESE POWERS! I'D HAVE EVERY RIGHT TO BLAST YOUR ASS A BRAND NEW--!
FOR ONCE IN YOUR LIFE, WOODY-- SHUT UP!
KRAK
JESUS!
YOU DESTROY EVERYTHING.
LOOK AROUND! JUST LOOK! THIS IS WHAT YOU DO TO PEOPLE.
AND WHEN IT SINKS IN--DON'T APOLOGIZE.
JUST STAY THE HELL AWAY FROM ME.

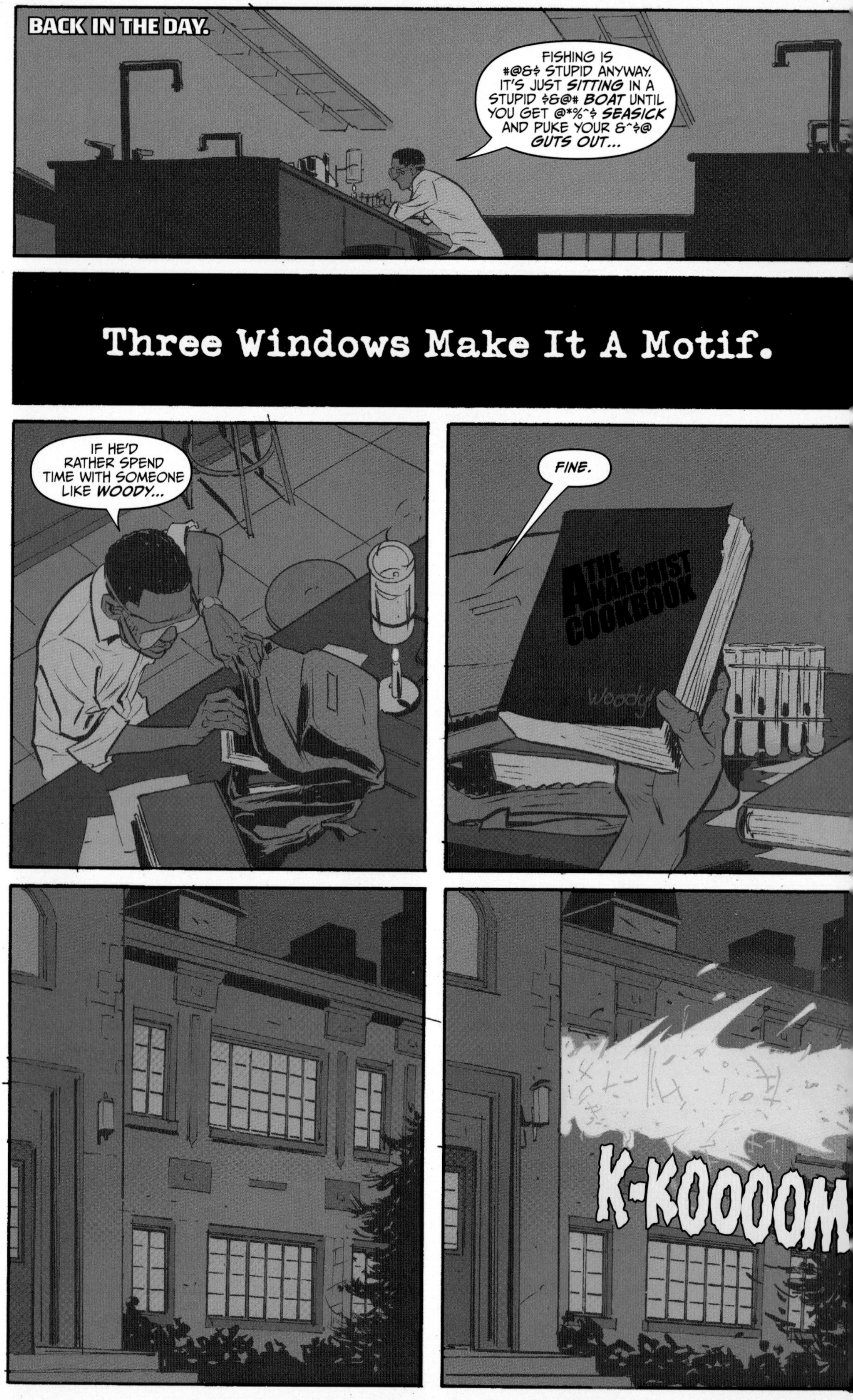
BACK IN THE DAY.
FISHING IS #@&$ STUPID ANYWAY. IT'S JUST SITTING IN A STUPID $&@# BOAT UNTIL YOU GET @*%^$ SEASICK AND PUKE YOUR &^$@ GUTS OUT...
Three Windows Make It A Motif.
IF HE'D RATHER SPEND TIME WITH SOMEONE LIKE WOODY...
FINE.
THE ANARCHIST COOKBOOK
Woody!
K-KOOOOM

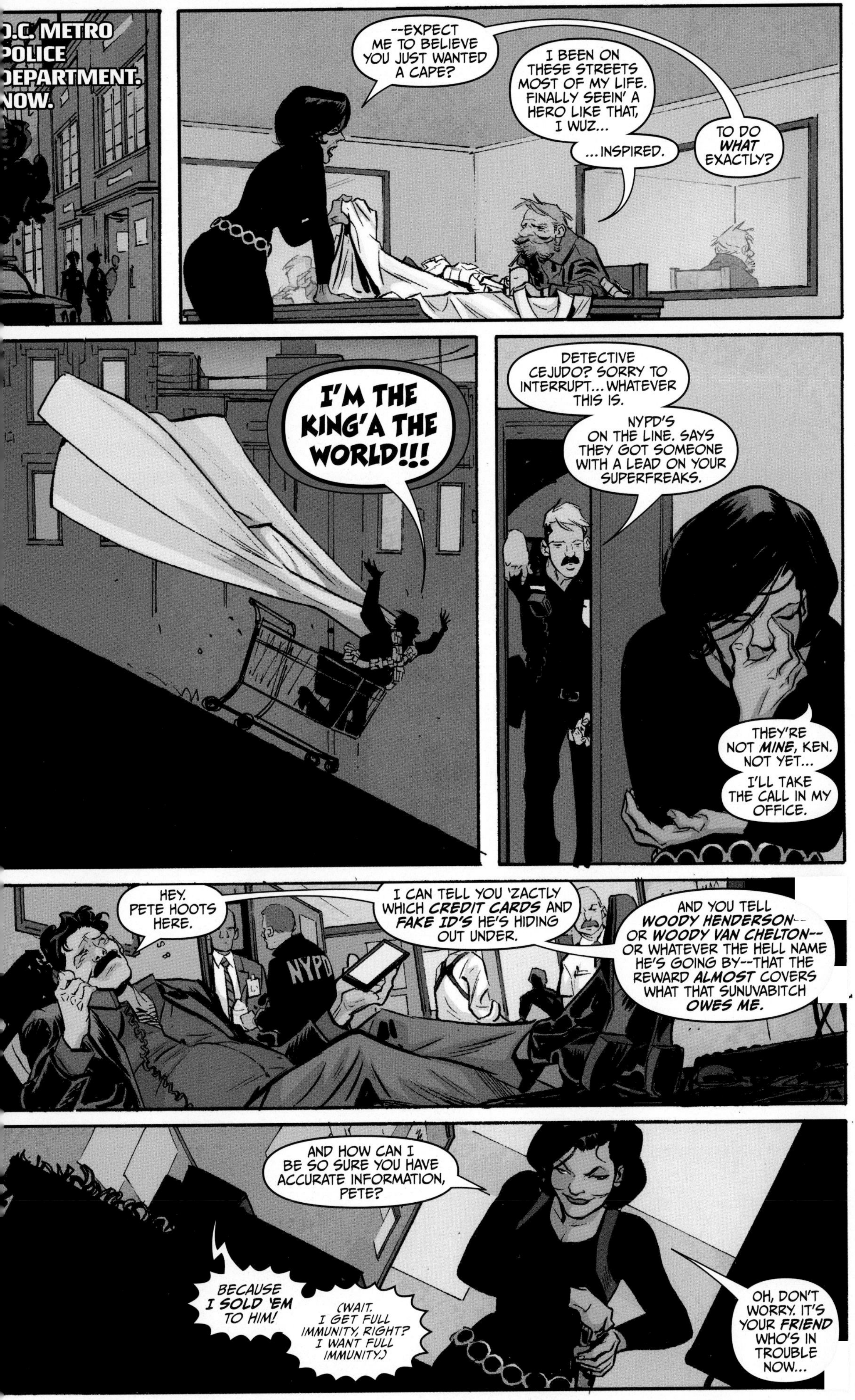
D.C. METRO POLICE DEPARTMENT. NOW.
--EXPECT ME TO BELIEVE YOU JUST WANTED A CAPE?
I BEEN ON THESE STREETS MOST OF MY LIFE. FINALLY SEEIN' A HERO LIKE THAT, I WUZ...
...INSPIRED.
TO DO WHAT EXACTLY?
I'M THE KING'A THE WORLD!!!
DETECTIVE CEJUDO? SORRY TO INTERRUPT... WHATEVER THIS IS.
NYPD'S ON THE LINE. SAYS THEY GOT SOMEONE WITH A LEAD ON YOUR SUPERFREAKS.
THEY'RE NOT MINE, KEN. NOT YET...
I'LL TAKE THE CALL IN MY OFFICE.
HEY. PETE HOOTS HERE.
I CAN TELL YOU 'ZACTLY WHICH CREDIT CARDS AND FAKE ID'S HE'S HIDING OUT UNDER.
AND YOU TELL WOODY HENDERSON-- OR WOODY VAN CHELTON-- OR WHATEVER THE HELL NAME HE'S GOING BY--THAT THE REWARD ALMOST COVERS WHAT THAT SUNUVABITCH OWES ME.
NYPD
AND HOW CAN I BE SO SURE YOU HAVE ACCURATE INFORMATION, PETE?
BECAUSE I SOLD 'EM TO HIM!
(WAIT. I GET FULL IMMUNITY, RIGHT? I WANT FULL IMMUNITY.)
OH, DON'T WORRY. IT'S YOUR FRIEND WHO'S IN TROUBLE NOW...

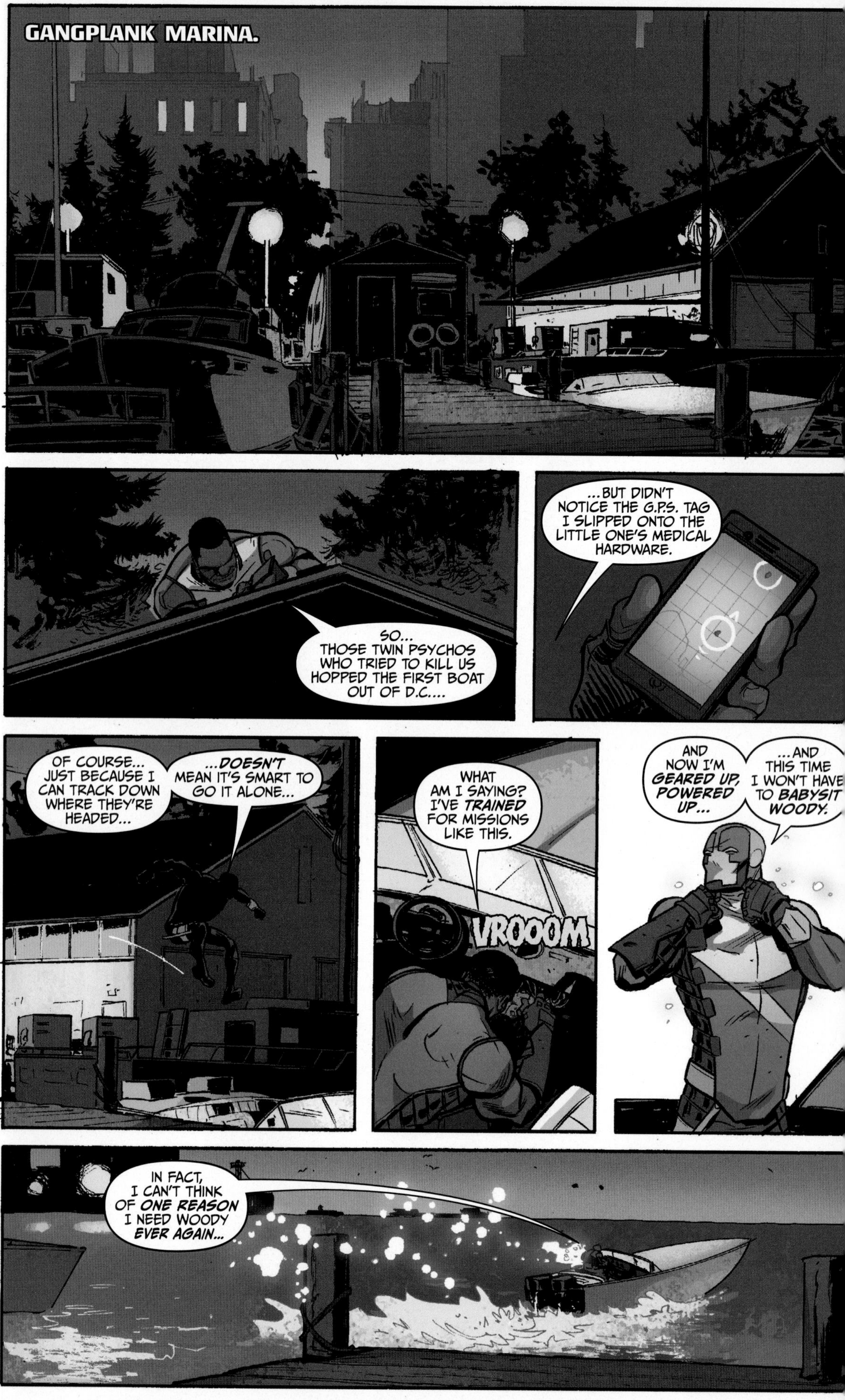
GANGPLANK MARINA.
SO... THOSE TWIN PSYCHOS WHO TRIED TO KILL US HOPPED THE FIRST BOAT OUT OF D.C....
...BUT DIDN'T NOTICE THE G.P.S. TAG I SLIPPED ONTO THE LITTLE ONE'S MEDICAL HARDWARE.
OF COURSE... JUST BECAUSE I CAN TRACK DOWN WHERE THEY'RE HEADED...
...DOESN'T MEAN IT'S SMART TO GO IT ALONE...
WHAT AM I SAYING? I'VE TRAINED FOR MISSIONS LIKE THIS.
VROOOM
AND NOW I'M GEARED UP, POWERED UP...
...AND THIS TIME I WON'T HAVE TO BABYSIT WOODY.
IN FACT, I CAN'T THINK OF ONE REASON I NEED WOODY EVER AGAIN...

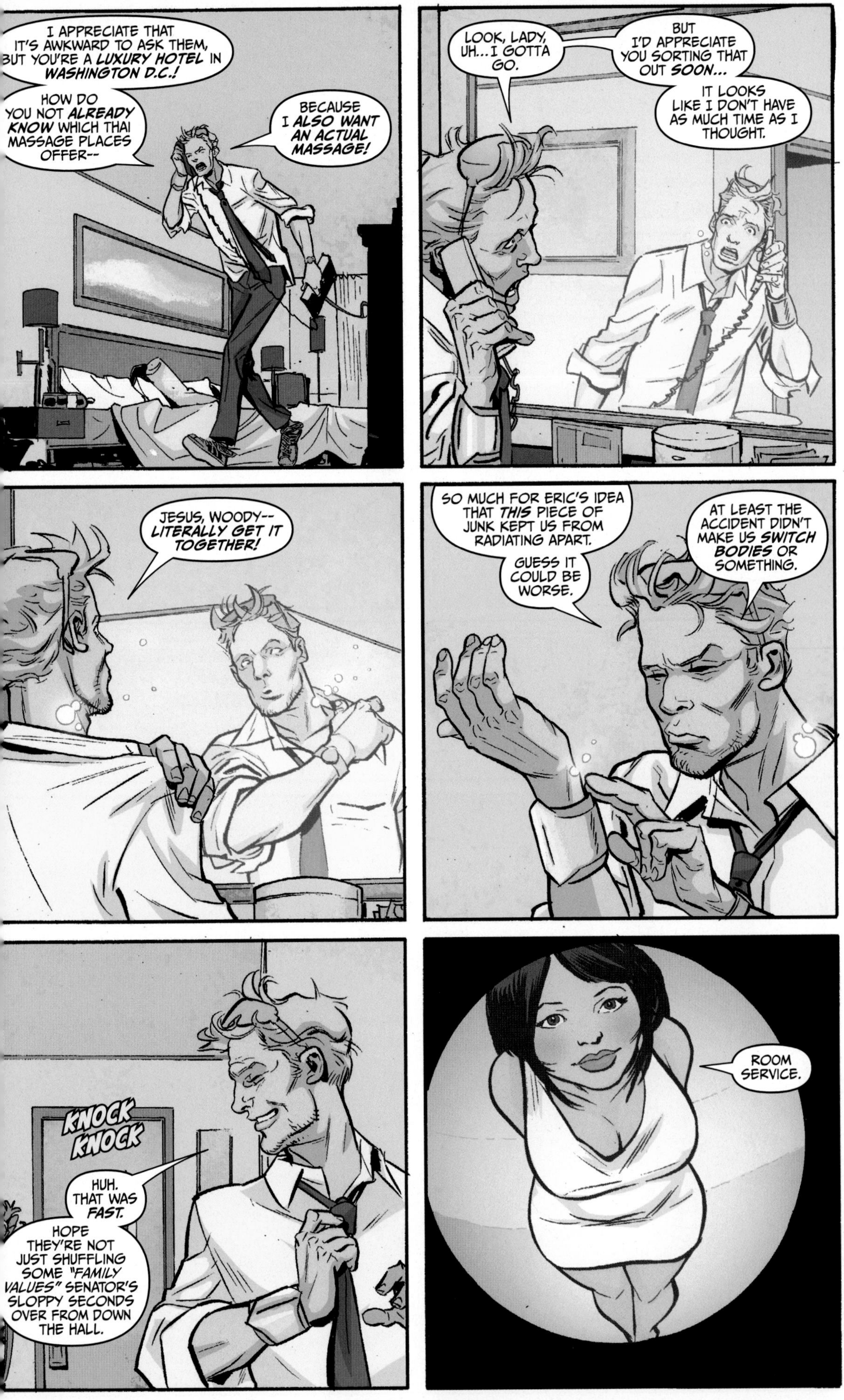
I APPRECIATE THAT IT'S AWKWARD TO ASK THEM, BUT YOU'RE A LUXURY HOTEL IN WASHINGTON D.C.!
HOW DO YOU NOT ALREADY KNOW WHICH THAI MASSAGE PLACES OFFER--
BECAUSE I ALSO WANT AN ACTUAL MASSAGE!
LOOK, LADY, UH...I GOTTA GO.
BUT I'D APPRECIATE YOU SORTING THAT OUT SOON...
IT LOOKS LIKE I DON'T HAVE AS MUCH TIME AS I THOUGHT.
JESUS, WOODY-- LITERALLY GET IT TOGETHER!
SO MUCH FOR ERIC'S IDEA THAT THIS PIECE OF JUNK KEPT US FROM RADIATING APART.
GUESS IT COULD BE WORSE.
AT LEAST THE ACCIDENT DIDN'T MAKE US SWITCH BODIES OR SOMETHING.
KNOCK KNOCK
HUH. THAT WAS FAST.
HOPE THEY'RE NOT JUST SHUFFLING SOME "FAMILY VALUES" SENATOR'S SLOPPY SECONDS OVER FROM DOWN THE HALL.
ROOM SERVICE.

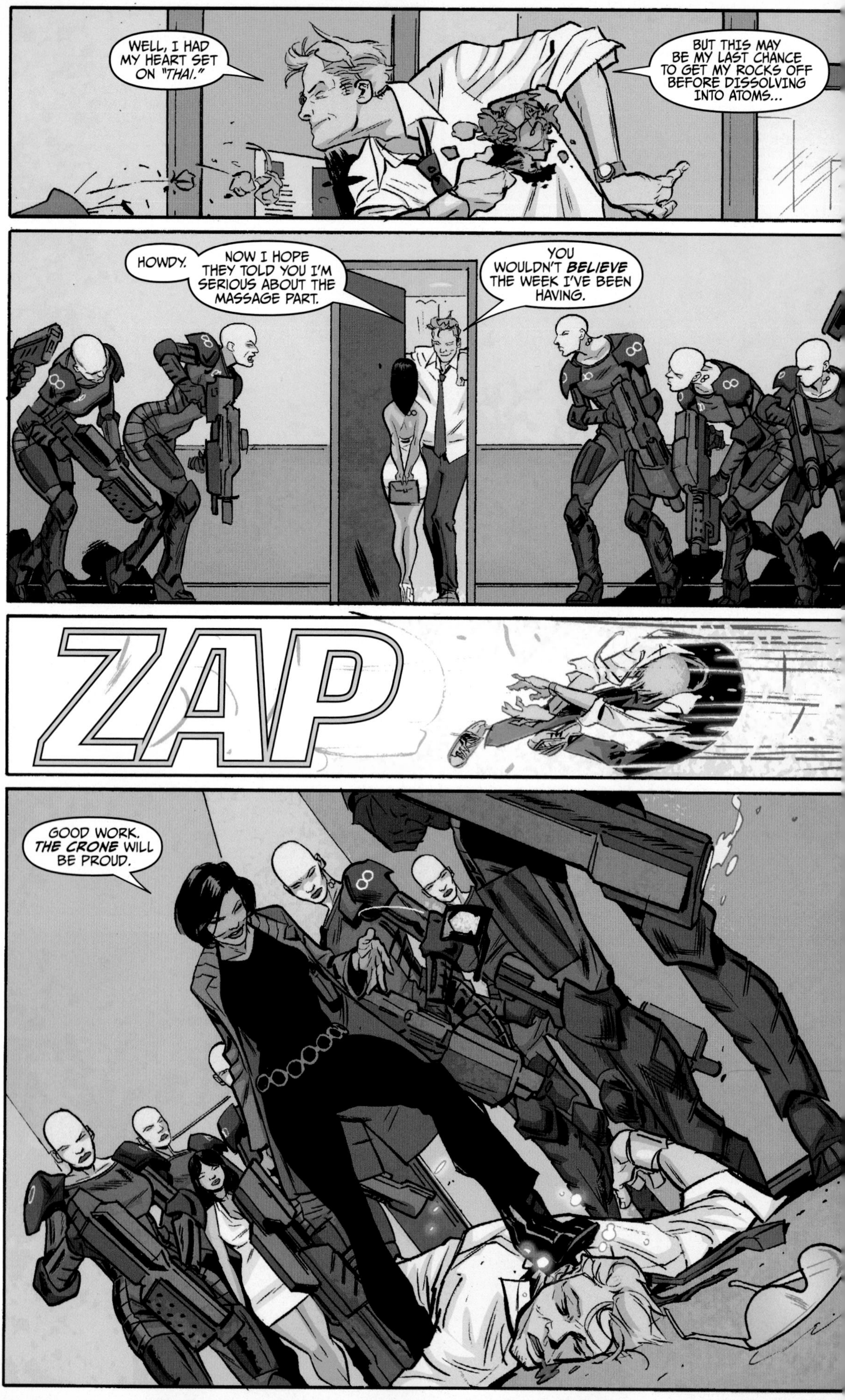
WELL, I HAD MY HEART SET ON "THAI."
BUT THIS MAY BE MY LAST CHANCE TO GET MY ROCKS OFF BEFORE DISSOLVING INTO ATOMS...
HOWDY.
NOW I HOPE THEY TOLD YOU I'M SERIOUS ABOUT THE MASSAGE PART.
YOU WOULDN'T BELIEVE THE WEEK I'VE BEEN HAVING.
ZAP
GOOD WORK. THE CRONE WILL BE PROUD.

In International Waters, No One Can Hear You Scream...

THANK YOU ALL FOR WAITING.

A WOMAN MY AGE NEEDS TIME TO PUT ON HER FACE.

...And There's Gonna Be Some Screaming.

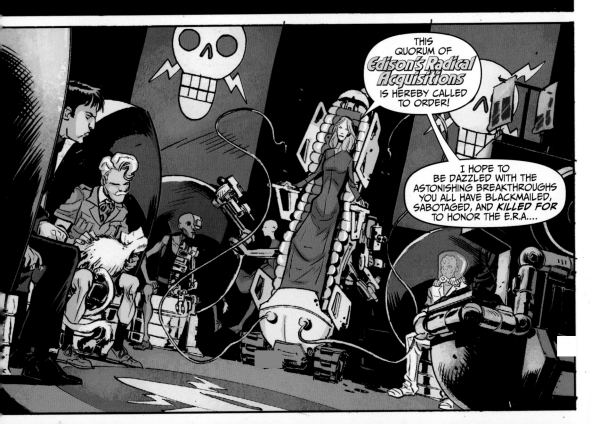

THIS QUORUM OF *Edison's Radical Acquisitions* IS HEREBY CALLED TO ORDER!

I HOPE TO BE DAZZLED WITH THE ASTONISHING BREAKTHROUGHS YOU ALL HAVE BLACKMAILED, SABOTAGED, AND *KILLED FOR* TO HONOR THE E.R.A....

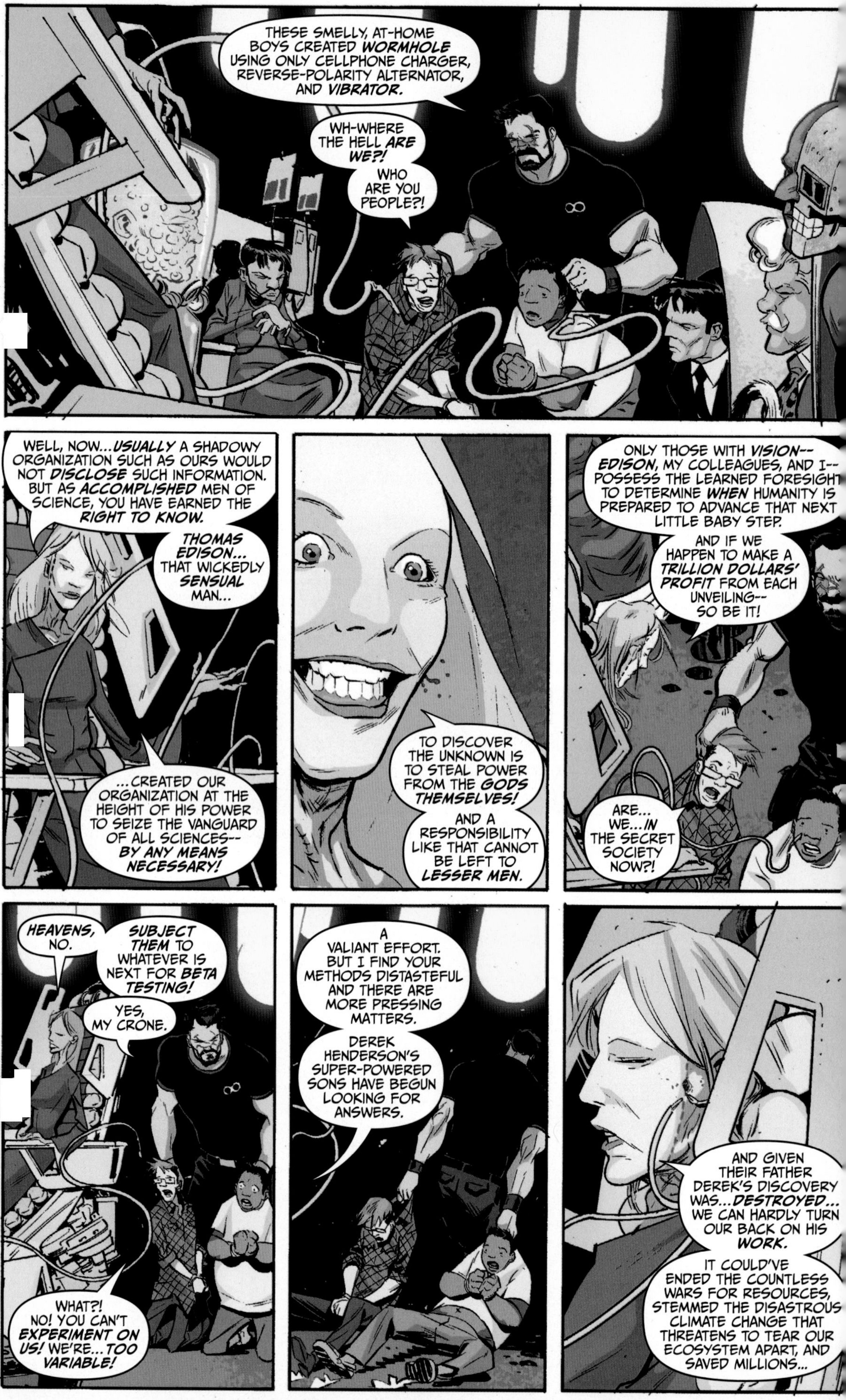
THESE SMELLY, AT-HOME BOYS CREATED WORMHOLE USING ONLY CELLPHONE CHARGER, REVERSE-POLARITY ALTERNATOR, AND VIBRATOR.
WH-WHERE THE HELL ARE WE?!
WHO ARE YOU PEOPLE?!
WELL, NOW...USUALLY A SHADOWY ORGANIZATION SUCH AS OURS WOULD NOT DISCLOSE SUCH INFORMATION. BUT AS ACCOMPLISHED MEN OF SCIENCE, YOU HAVE EARNED THE RIGHT TO KNOW.
THOMAS EDISON... THAT WICKEDLY SENSUAL MAN...
...CREATED OUR ORGANIZATION AT THE HEIGHT OF HIS POWER TO SEIZE THE VANGUARD OF ALL SCIENCES--BY ANY MEANS NECESSARY!
TO DISCOVER THE UNKNOWN IS TO STEAL POWER FROM THE GODS THEMSELVES!
AND A RESPONSIBILITY LIKE THAT CANNOT BE LEFT TO LESSER MEN.
ONLY THOSE WITH VISION--EDISON, MY COLLEAGUES, AND I--POSSESS THE LEARNED FORESIGHT TO DETERMINE WHEN HUMANITY IS PREPARED TO ADVANCE THAT NEXT LITTLE BABY STEP.
AND IF WE HAPPEN TO MAKE A TRILLION DOLLARS' PROFIT FROM EACH UNVEILING--SO BE IT!
ARE... WE...IN THE SECRET SOCIETY NOW?!
HEAVENS, NO.
SUBJECT THEM TO WHATEVER IS NEXT FOR BETA TESTING!
YES, MY CRONE.
WHAT?! NO! YOU CAN'T EXPERIMENT ON US! WE'RE...TOO VARIABLE!
A VALIANT EFFORT. BUT I FIND YOUR METHODS DISTASTEFUL AND THERE ARE MORE PRESSING MATTERS.
DEREK HENDERSON'S SUPER-POWERED SONS HAVE BEGUN LOOKING FOR ANSWERS.
AND GIVEN THEIR FATHER DEREK'S DISCOVERY WAS...DESTROYED... WE CAN HARDLY TURN OUR BACK ON HIS WORK.
IT COULD'VE ENDED THE COUNTLESS WARS FOR RESOURCES, STEMMED THE DISASTROUS CLIMATE CHANGE THAT THREATENS TO TEAR OUR ECOSYSTEM APART, AND SAVED MILLIONS...

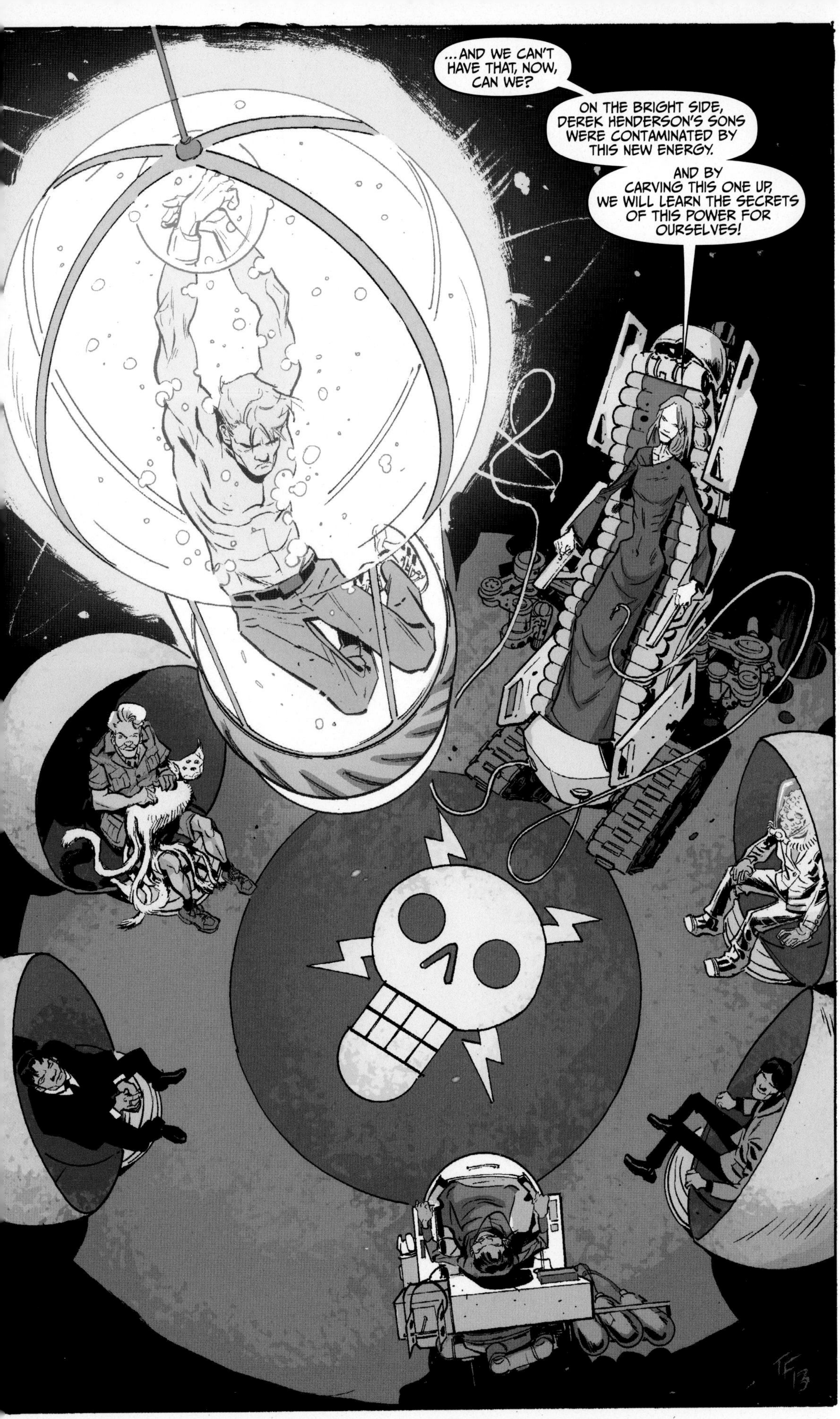
...AND WE CAN'T HAVE THAT, NOW, CAN WE?
ON THE BRIGHT SIDE, DEREK HENDERSON'S SONS WERE CONTAMINATED BY THIS NEW ENERGY.
AND BY CARVING THIS ONE UP, WE WILL LEARN THE SECRETS OF THIS POWER FOR OURSELVES!
TF 13

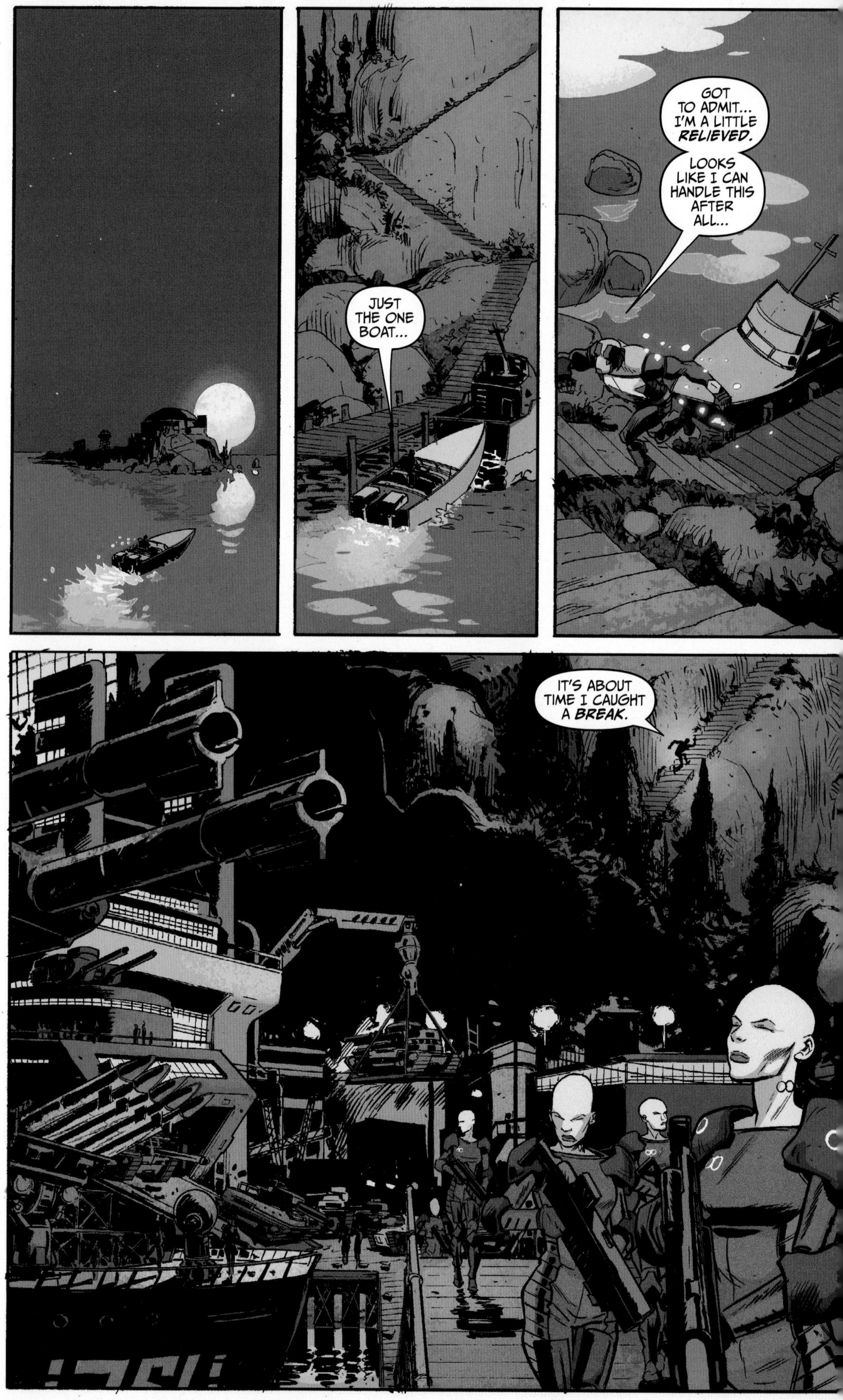
JUST THE ONE BOAT...
GOT TO ADMIT... I'M A LITTLE RELIEVED.
LOOKS LIKE I CAN HANDLE THIS AFTER ALL...
IT'S ABOUT TIME I CAUGHT A BREAK.

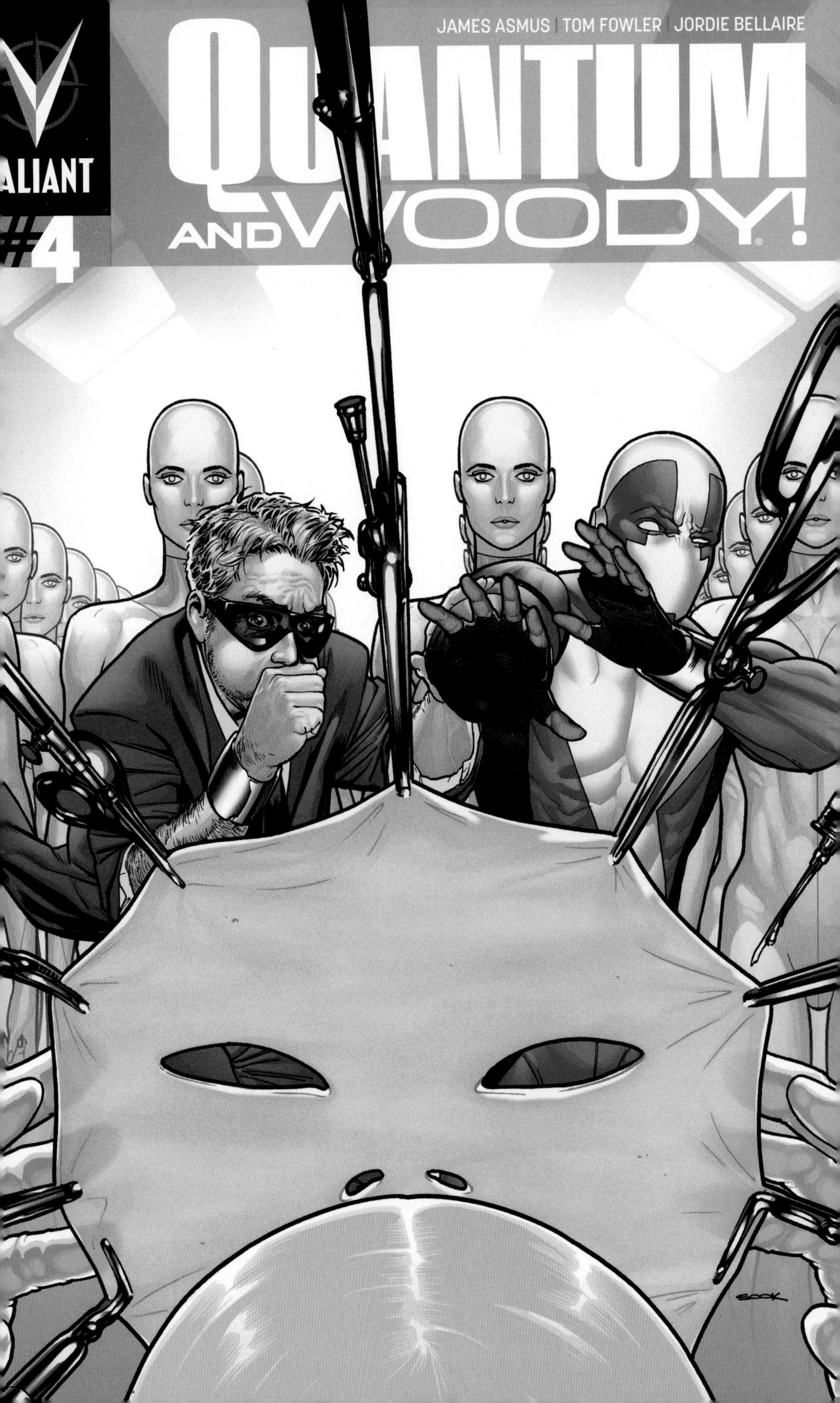

VALIANT
#4
JAMES ASMUS | TOM FOWLER | JORDIE BELLAIRE
QUANTUM AND WOODY!

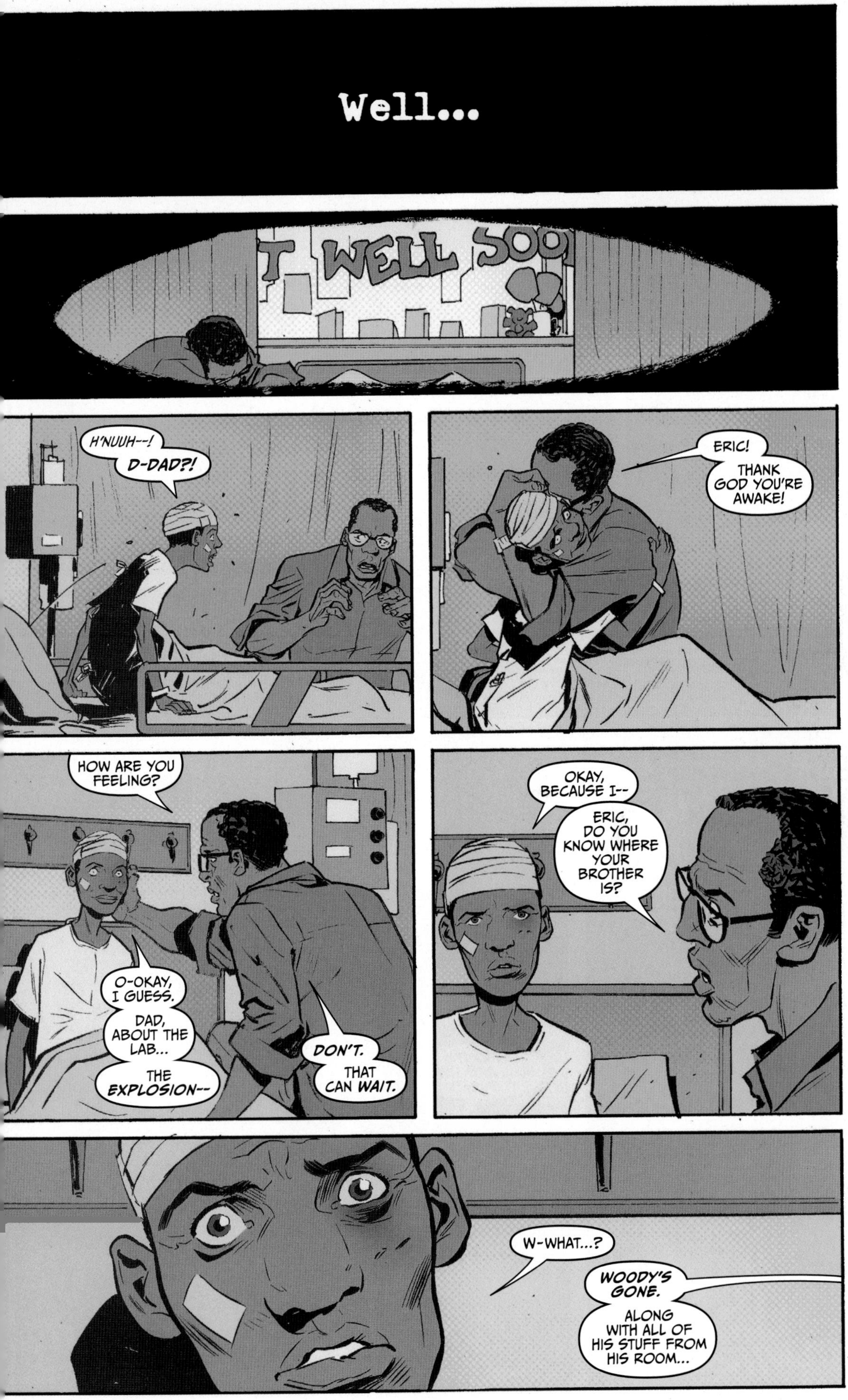

Well...
T WELL SOO
H'NUUH--! D-DAD?!
ERIC! THANK GOD YOU'RE AWAKE!
HOW ARE YOU FEELING?
O-OKAY, I GUESS.
DAD, ABOUT THE LAB...
THE EXPLOSION--
DON'T. THAT CAN WAIT.
OKAY, BECAUSE I--
ERIC, DO YOU KNOW WHERE YOUR BROTHER IS?
W-WHAT...?
WOODY'S GONE.
ALONG WITH ALL OF HIS STUFF FROM HIS ROOM...

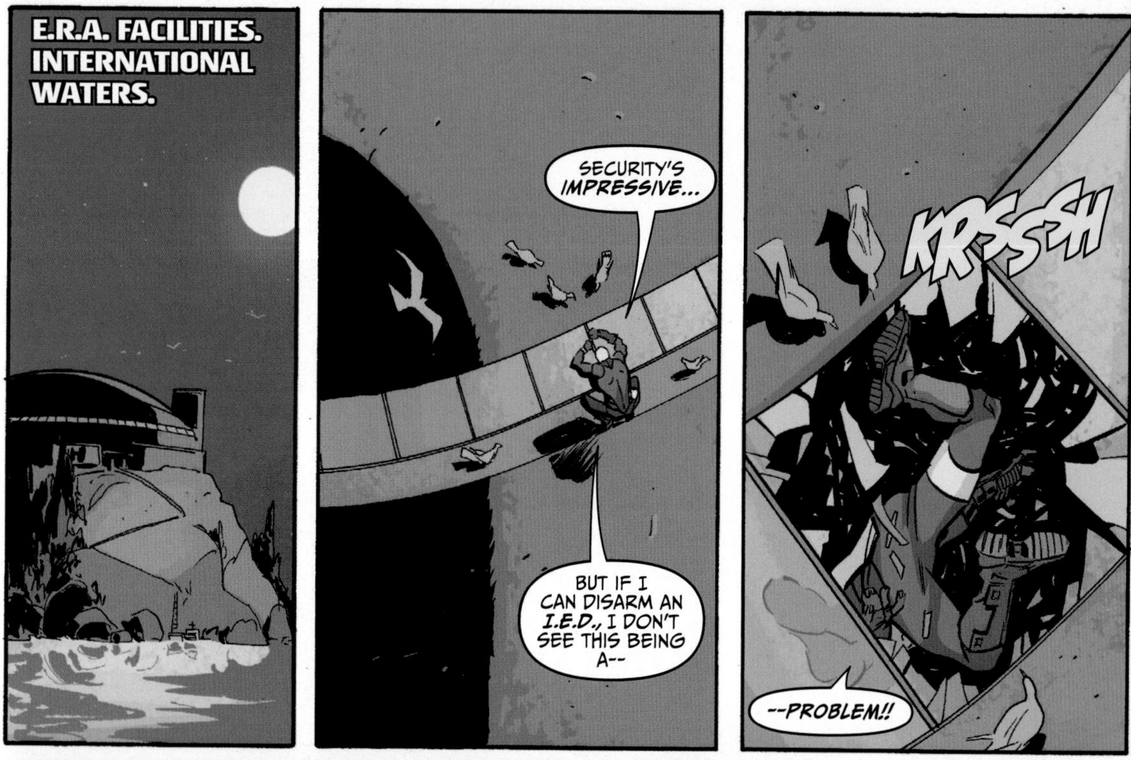
E.R.A. FACILITIES. INTERNATIONAL WATERS.
SECURITY'S IMPRESSIVE...
BUT IF I CAN DISARM AN I.E.D., I DON'T SEE THIS BEING A--
KRSSSH
--PROBLEM!!

Those seagulls are judging him.

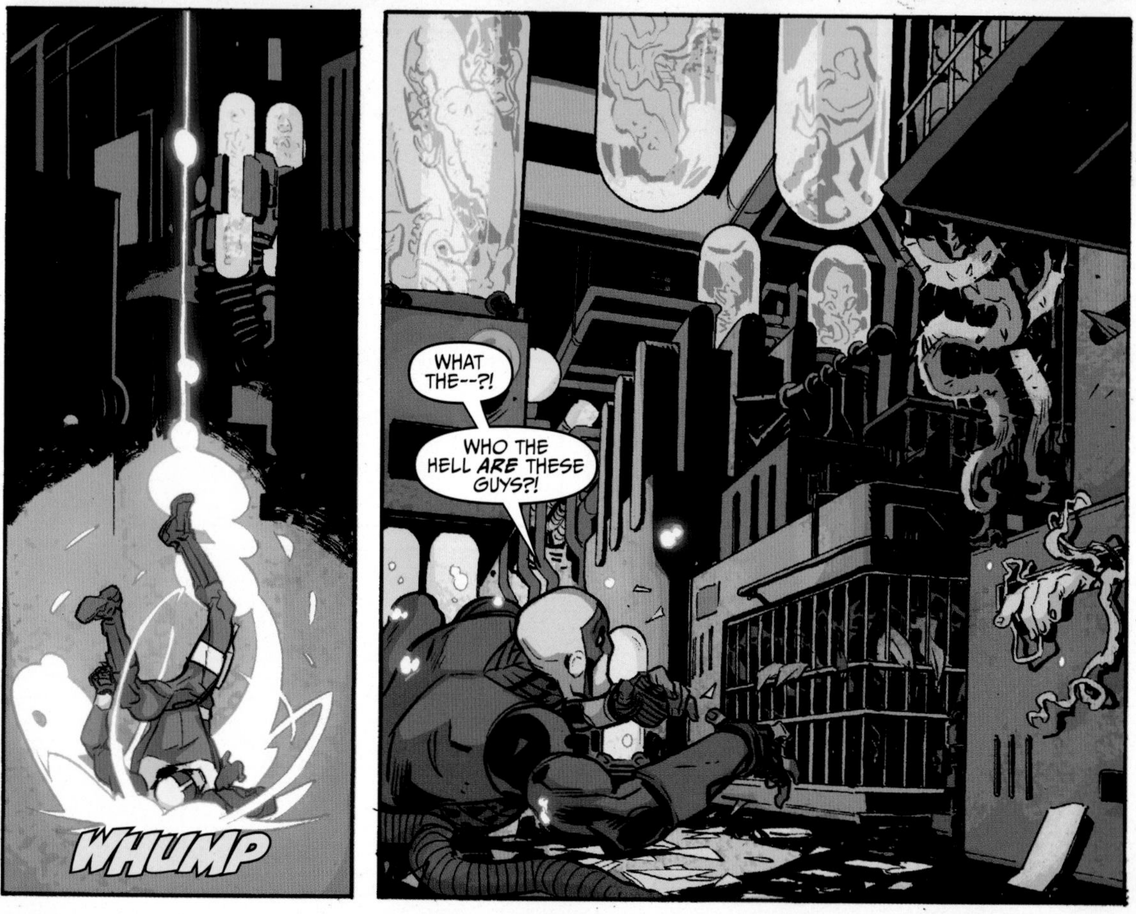
WHUMP
WHAT THE--?!
WHO THE HELL ARE THESE GUYS?!

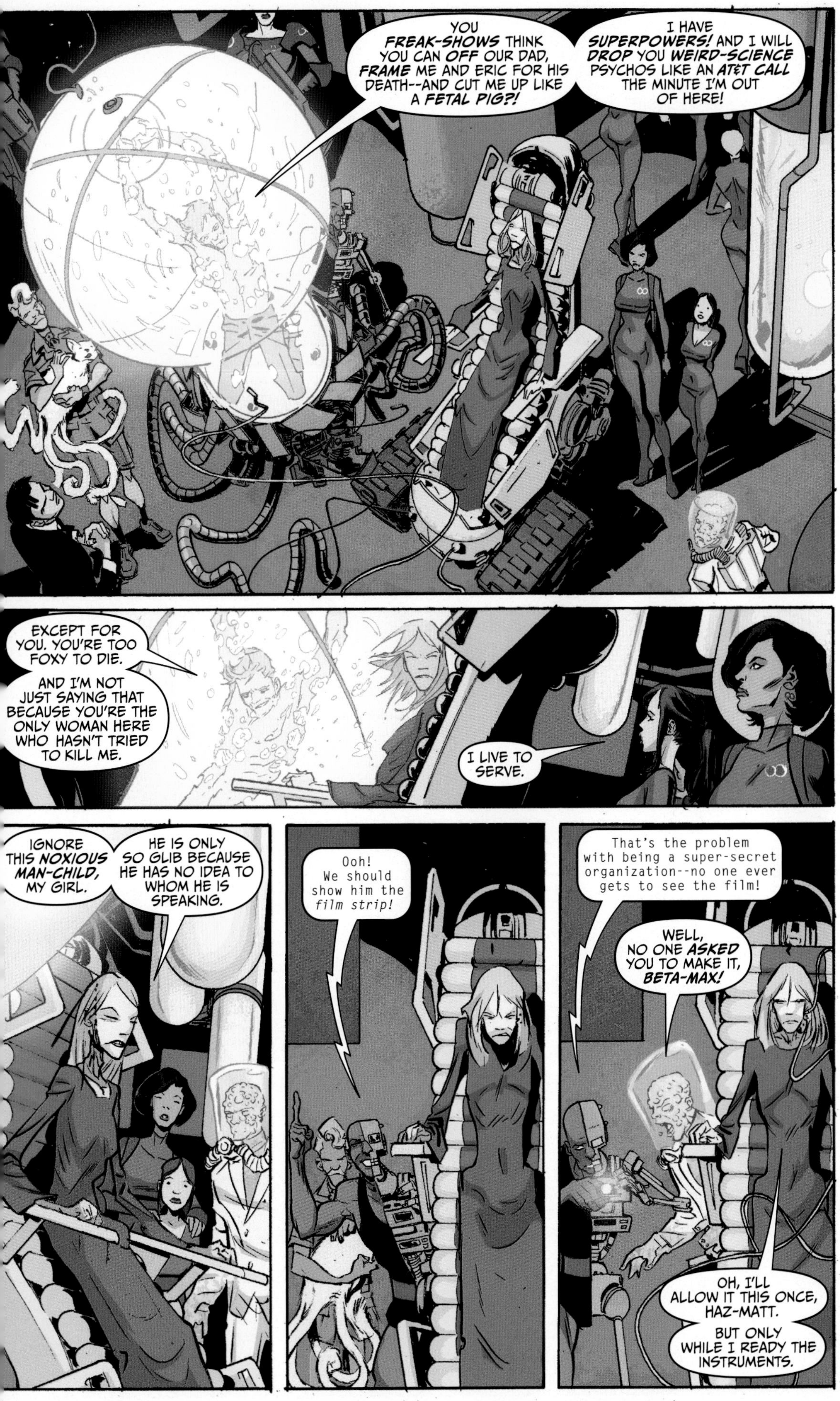

YOU FREAK-SHOWS THINK YOU CAN OFF OUR DAD, FRAME ME AND ERIC FOR HIS DEATH--AND CUT ME UP LIKE A FETAL PIG?!
I HAVE SUPERPOWERS! AND I WILL DROP YOU WEIRD-SCIENCE PSYCHOS LIKE AN AT&T CALL THE MINUTE I'M OUT OF HERE!
EXCEPT FOR YOU. YOU'RE TOO FOXY TO DIE.
AND I'M NOT JUST SAYING THAT BECAUSE YOU'RE THE ONLY WOMAN HERE WHO HASN'T TRIED TO KILL ME.
I LIVE TO SERVE.
IGNORE THIS NOXIOUS MAN-CHILD, MY GIRL.
HE IS ONLY SO GLIB BECAUSE HE HAS NO IDEA TO WHOM HE IS SPEAKING.
Ooh! We should show him the film strip!
That's the problem with being a super-secret organization--no one ever gets to see the film!
WELL, NO ONE ASKED YOU TO MAKE IT, BETA-MAX!
OH, I'LL ALLOW IT THIS ONCE, HAZ-MATT.
BUT ONLY WHILE I READY THE INSTRUMENTS.

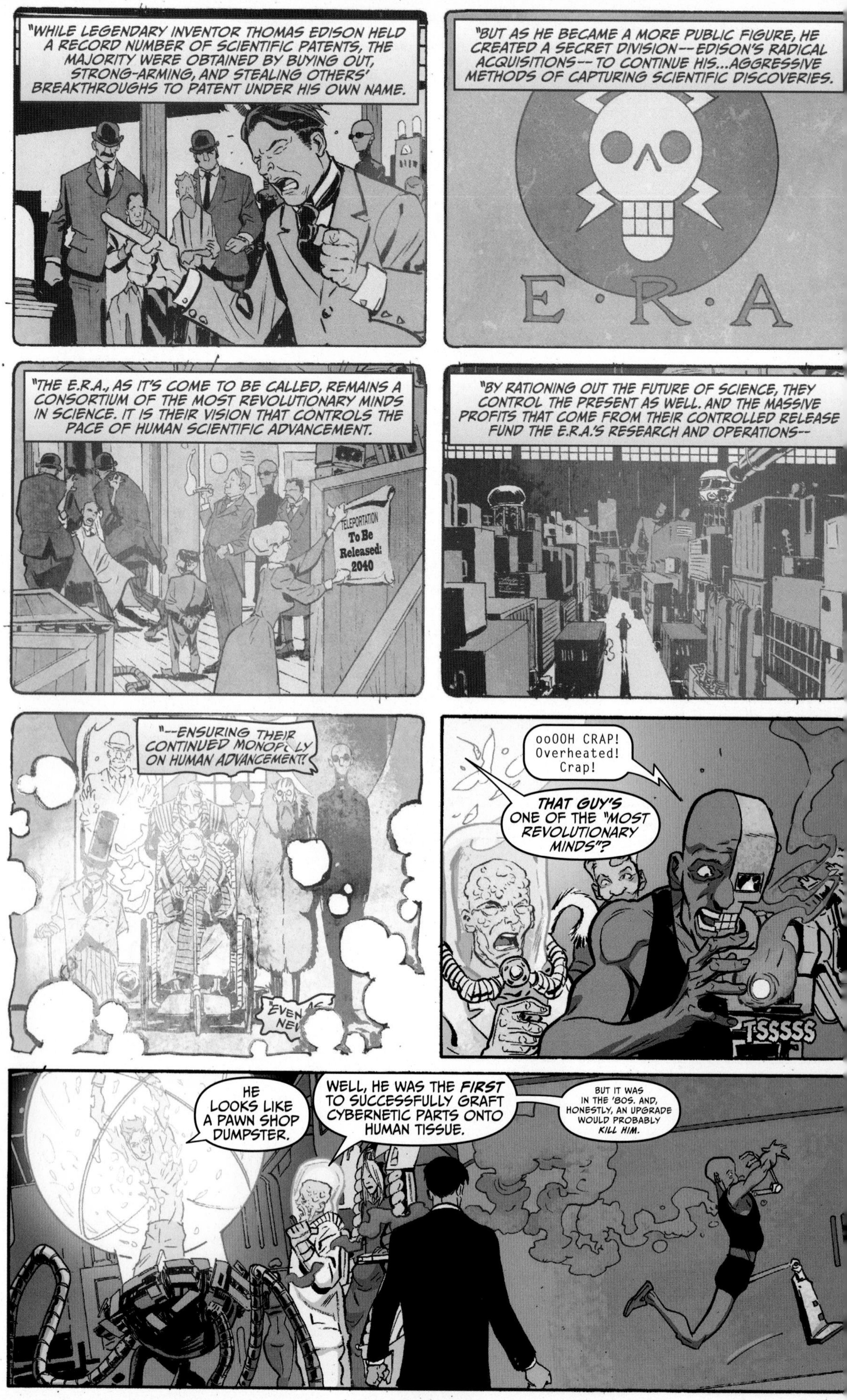
"WHILE LEGENDARY INVENTOR THOMAS EDISON HELD A RECORD NUMBER OF SCIENTIFIC PATENTS, THE MAJORITY WERE OBTAINED BY BUYING OUT, STRONG-ARMING, AND STEALING OTHERS' BREAKTHROUGHS TO PATENT UNDER HIS OWN NAME.
"BUT AS HE BECAME A MORE PUBLIC FIGURE, HE CREATED A SECRET DIVISION-- EDISON'S RADICAL ACQUISITIONS-- TO CONTINUE HIS... AGGRESSIVE METHODS OF CAPTURING SCIENTIFIC DISCOVERIES.
E.R.A
"THE E.R.A., AS IT'S COME TO BE CALLED, REMAINS A CONSORTIUM OF THE MOST REVOLUTIONARY MINDS IN SCIENCE. IT IS THEIR VISION THAT CONTROLS THE PACE OF HUMAN SCIENTIFIC ADVANCEMENT.
TELEPORTATION To Be Released: 2040
"BY RATIONING OUT THE FUTURE OF SCIENCE, THEY CONTROL THE PRESENT AS WELL. AND THE MASSIVE PROFITS THAT COME FROM THEIR CONTROLLED RELEASE FUND THE E.R.A.'S RESEARCH AND OPERATIONS--
"--ENSURING THEIR CONTINUED MONOPOLY ON HUMAN ADVANCEMENT?!
ooOOH CRAP! Overheated! Crap!
THAT GUY'S ONE OF THE "MOST REVOLUTIONARY MINDS"?
TSSSSS
HE LOOKS LIKE A PAWN SHOP DUMPSTER.
WELL, HE WAS THE FIRST TO SUCCESSFULLY GRAFT CYBERNETIC PARTS ONTO HUMAN TISSUE.
BUT IT WAS IN THE '80S. AND, HONESTLY, AN UPGRADE WOULD PROBABLY KILL HIM.

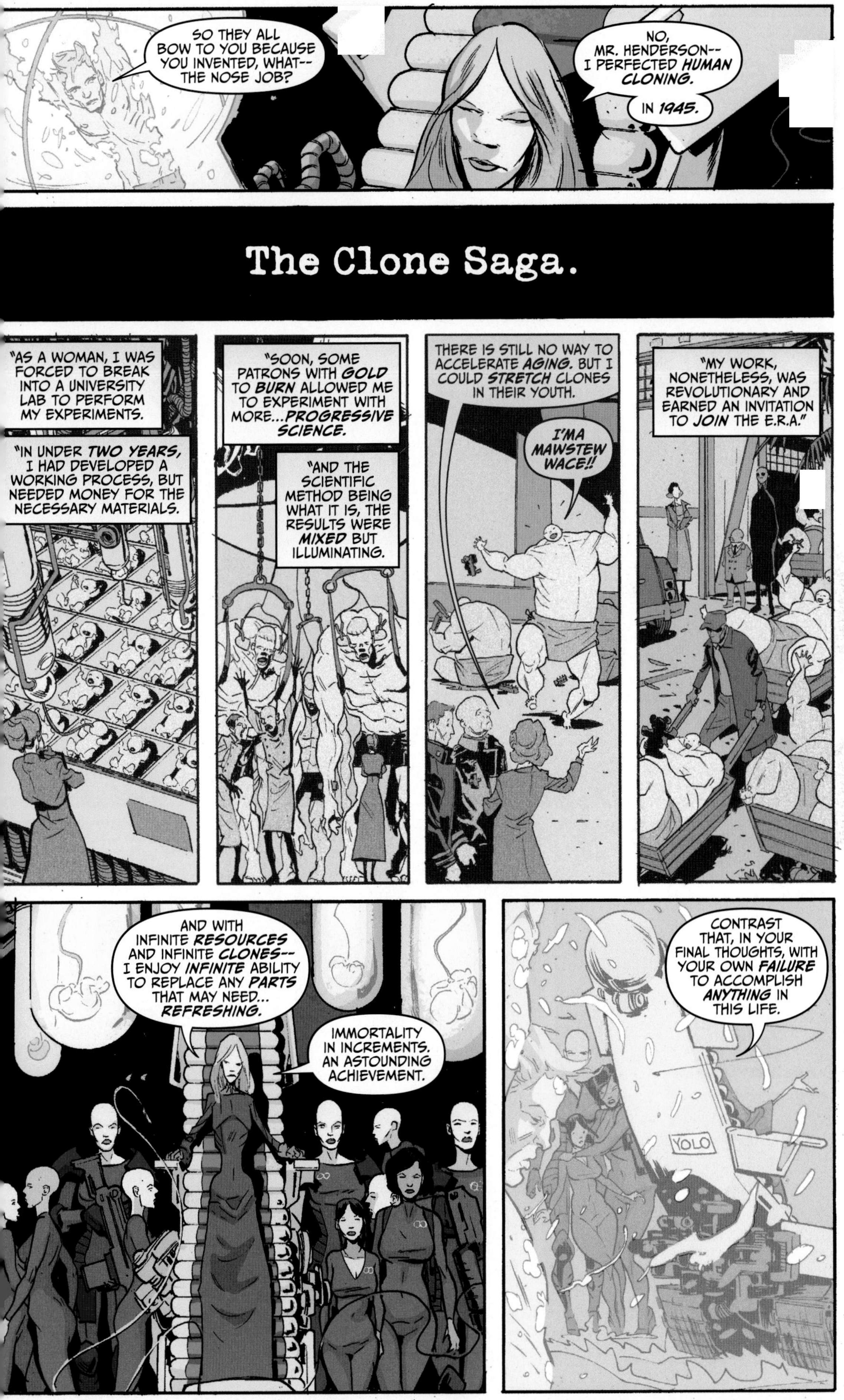
SO THEY ALL BOW TO YOU BECAUSE YOU INVENTED, WHAT-- THE NOSE JOB?
NO, MR. HENDERSON-- I PERFECTED HUMAN CLONING.
IN 1945.
The Clone Saga.
"AS A WOMAN, I WAS FORCED TO BREAK INTO A UNIVERSITY LAB TO PERFORM MY EXPERIMENTS.
"IN UNDER TWO YEARS, I HAD DEVELOPED A WORKING PROCESS, BUT NEEDED MONEY FOR THE NECESSARY MATERIALS.
"SOON, SOME PATRONS WITH GOLD TO BURN ALLOWED ME TO EXPERIMENT WITH MORE...PROGRESSIVE SCIENCE.
"AND THE SCIENTIFIC METHOD BEING WHAT IT IS, THE RESULTS WERE MIXED BUT ILLUMINATING.
THERE IS STILL NO WAY TO ACCELERATE AGING. BUT I COULD STRETCH CLONES IN THEIR YOUTH.
I'MA MAWSTEW WACE!!
"MY WORK, NONETHELESS, WAS REVOLUTIONARY AND EARNED AN INVITATION TO JOIN THE E.R.A."
AND WITH INFINITE RESOURCES AND INFINITE CLONES-- I ENJOY INFINITE ABILITY TO REPLACE ANY PARTS THAT MAY NEED... REFRESHING.
IMMORTALITY IN INCREMENTS. AN ASTOUNDING ACHIEVEMENT.
CONTRAST THAT, IN YOUR FINAL THOUGHTS, WITH YOUR OWN FAILURE TO ACCOMPLISH ANYTHING IN THIS LIFE.
YOLO

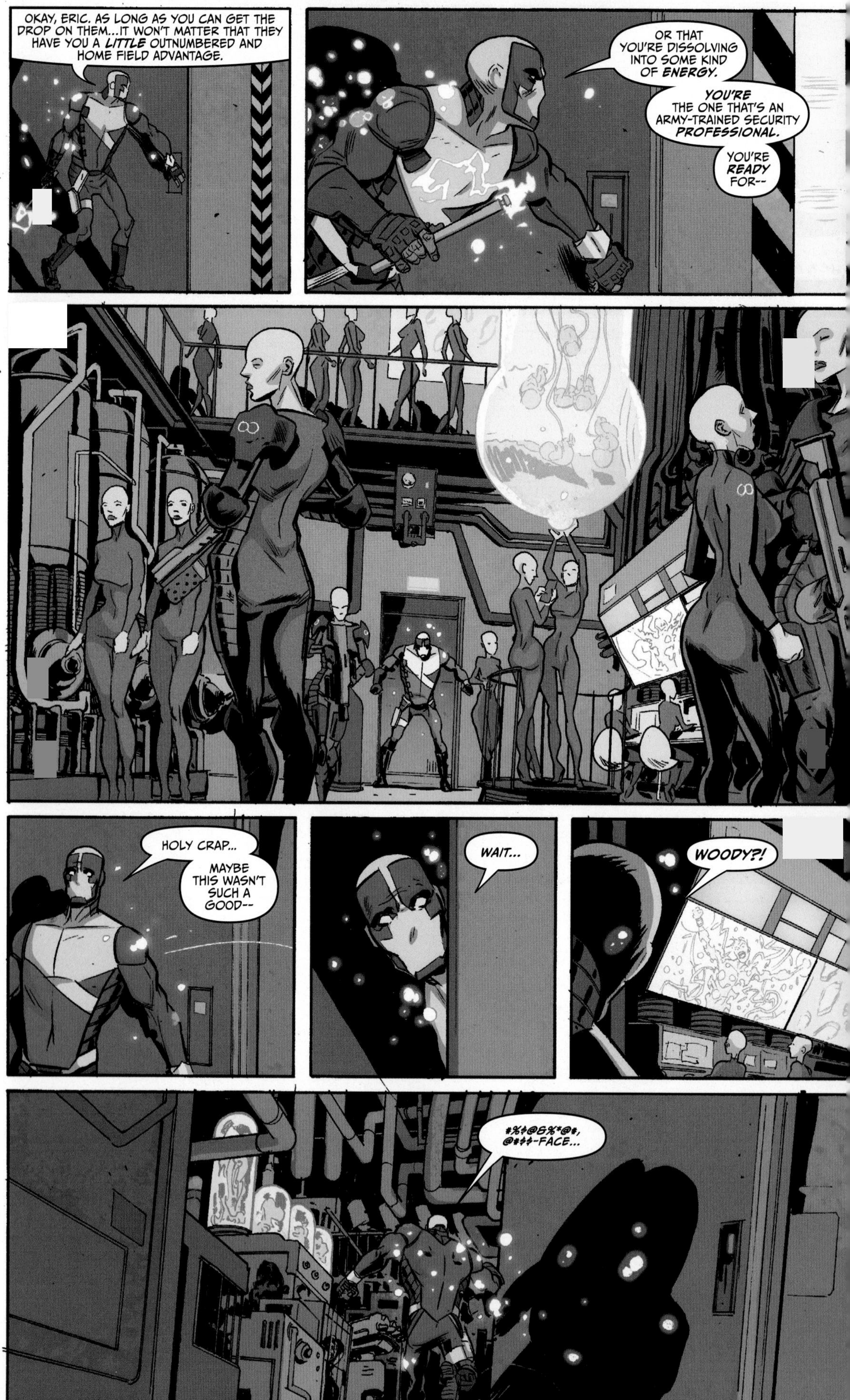

OKAY, ERIC. AS LONG AS YOU CAN GET THE DROP ON THEM...IT WON'T MATTER THAT THEY HAVE YOU A LITTLE OUTNUMBERED AND HOME FIELD ADVANTAGE.
OR THAT YOU'RE DISSOLVING INTO SOME KIND OF ENERGY.
YOU'RE THE ONE THAT'S AN ARMY-TRAINED SECURITY PROFESSIONAL.
YOU'RE READY FOR--
HOLY CRAP...
MAYBE THIS WASN'T SUCH A GOOD--
WAIT...
WOODY?!
#%$@&%*@#, @#$$-FACE...

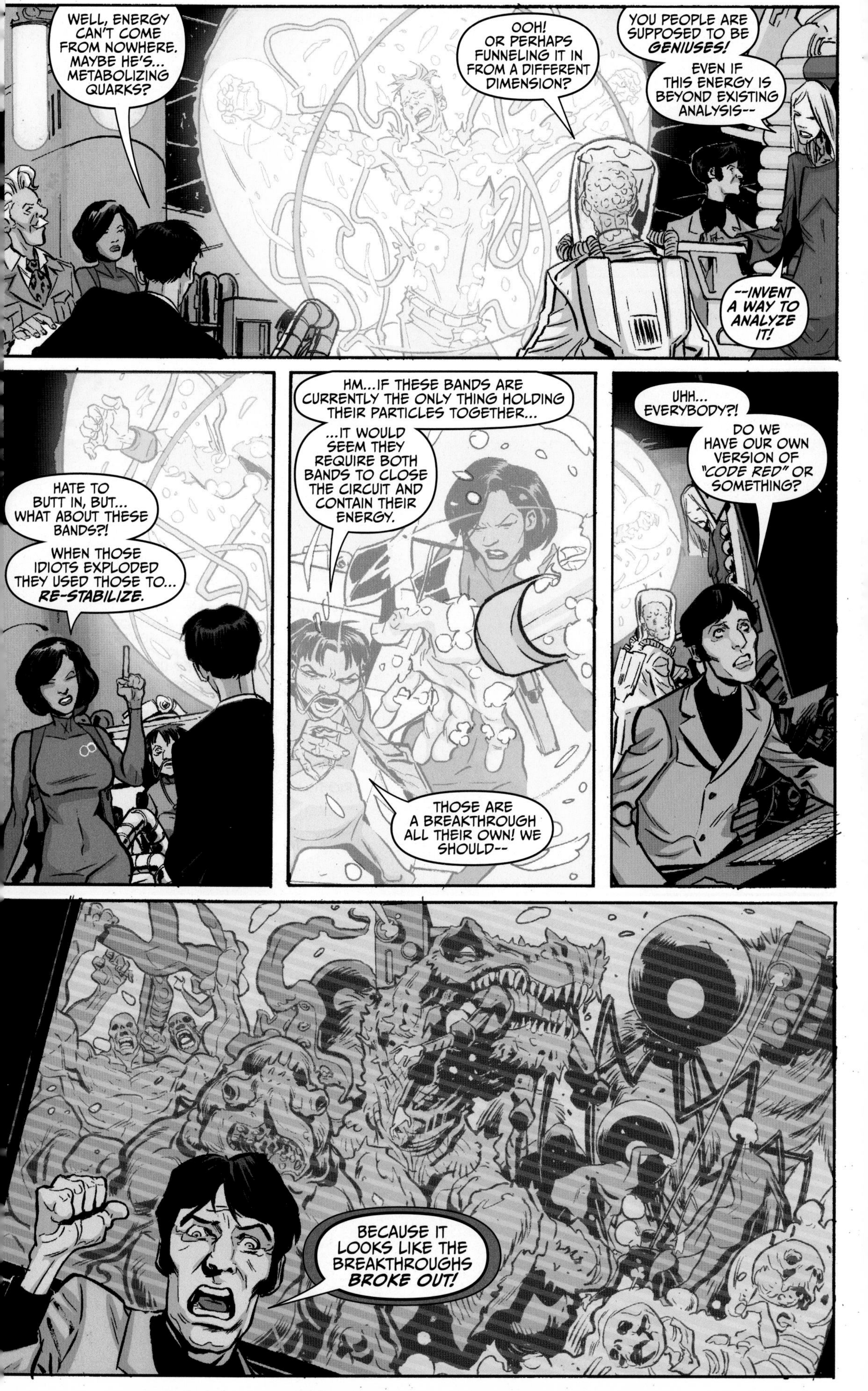
WELL, ENERGY CAN'T COME FROM NOWHERE. MAYBE HE'S... METABOLIZING QUARKS?
OOH! OR PERHAPS FUNNELING IT IN FROM A DIFFERENT DIMENSION?
YOU PEOPLE ARE SUPPOSED TO BE GENIUSES!
EVEN IF THIS ENERGY IS BEYOND EXISTING ANALYSIS--
--INVENT A WAY TO ANALYZE IT!
HATE TO BUTT IN, BUT... WHAT ABOUT THESE BANDS?!
WHEN THOSE IDIOTS EXPLODED THEY USED THOSE TO... RE-STABILIZE.
HM...IF THESE BANDS ARE CURRENTLY THE ONLY THING HOLDING THEIR PARTICLES TOGETHER...
...IT WOULD SEEM THEY REQUIRE BOTH BANDS TO CLOSE THE CIRCUIT AND CONTAIN THEIR ENERGY.
THOSE ARE A BREAKTHROUGH ALL THEIR OWN! WE SHOULD--
UHH... EVERYBODY?!
DO WE HAVE OUR OWN VERSION OF "CODE RED" OR SOMETHING?
BECAUSE IT LOOKS LIKE THE BREAKTHROUGHS BROKE OUT!

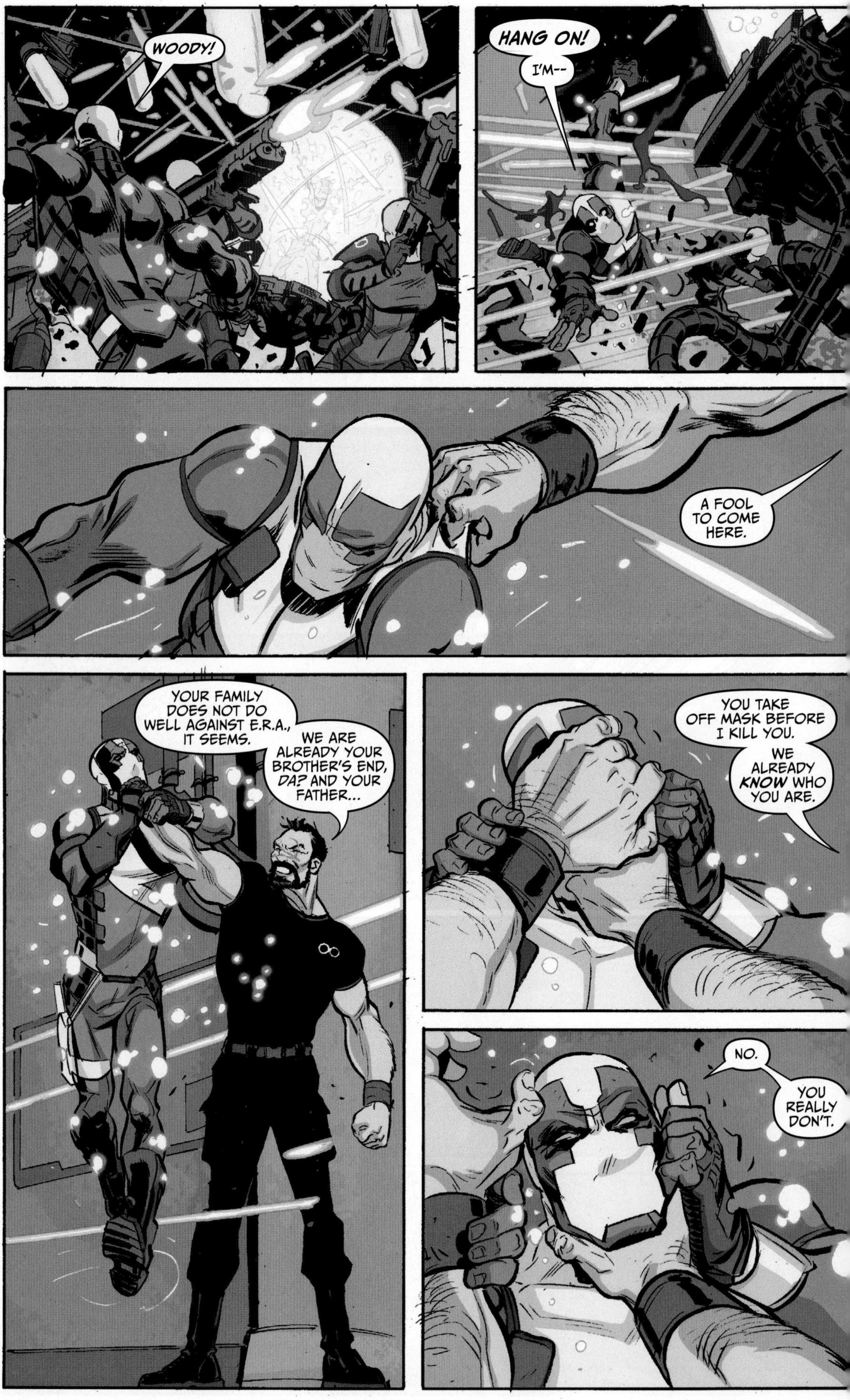
WOODY!
HANG ON!
I'M--
A FOOL TO COME HERE.
YOUR FAMILY DOES NOT DO WELL AGAINST E.R.A., IT SEEMS.
WE ARE ALREADY YOUR BROTHER'S END, DA? AND YOUR FATHER...
YOU TAKE OFF MASK BEFORE I KILL YOU.
WE ALREADY KNOW WHO YOU ARE.
NO.
YOU REALLY DON'T.

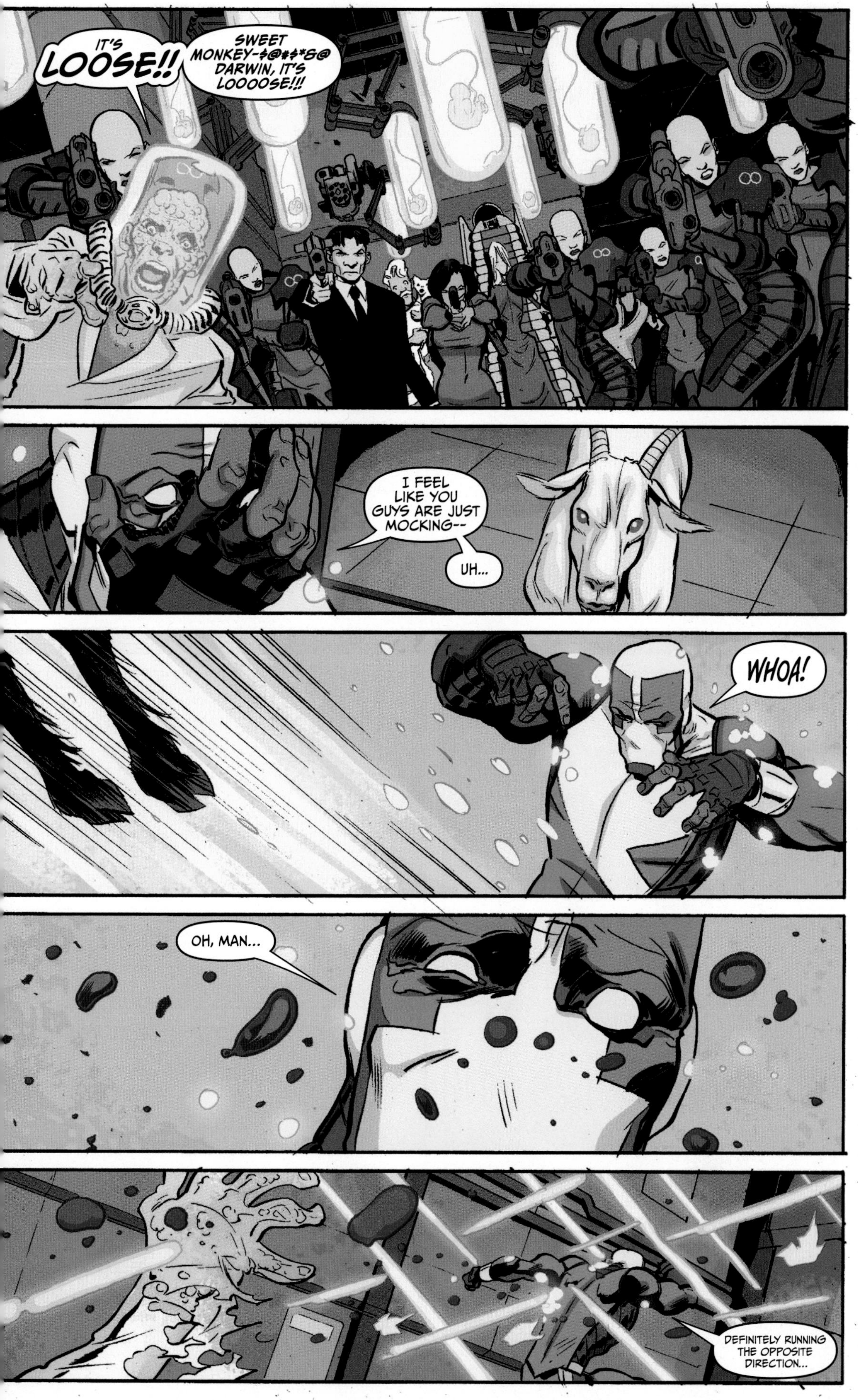
IT'S LOOSE!!
SWEET MONKEY-$@#$*&@ DARWIN, IT'S LOOOOSE!!!
I FEEL LIKE YOU GUYS ARE JUST MOCKING--
UH...
WHOA!
OH, MAN...
DEFINITELY RUNNING THE OPPOSITE DIRECTION...

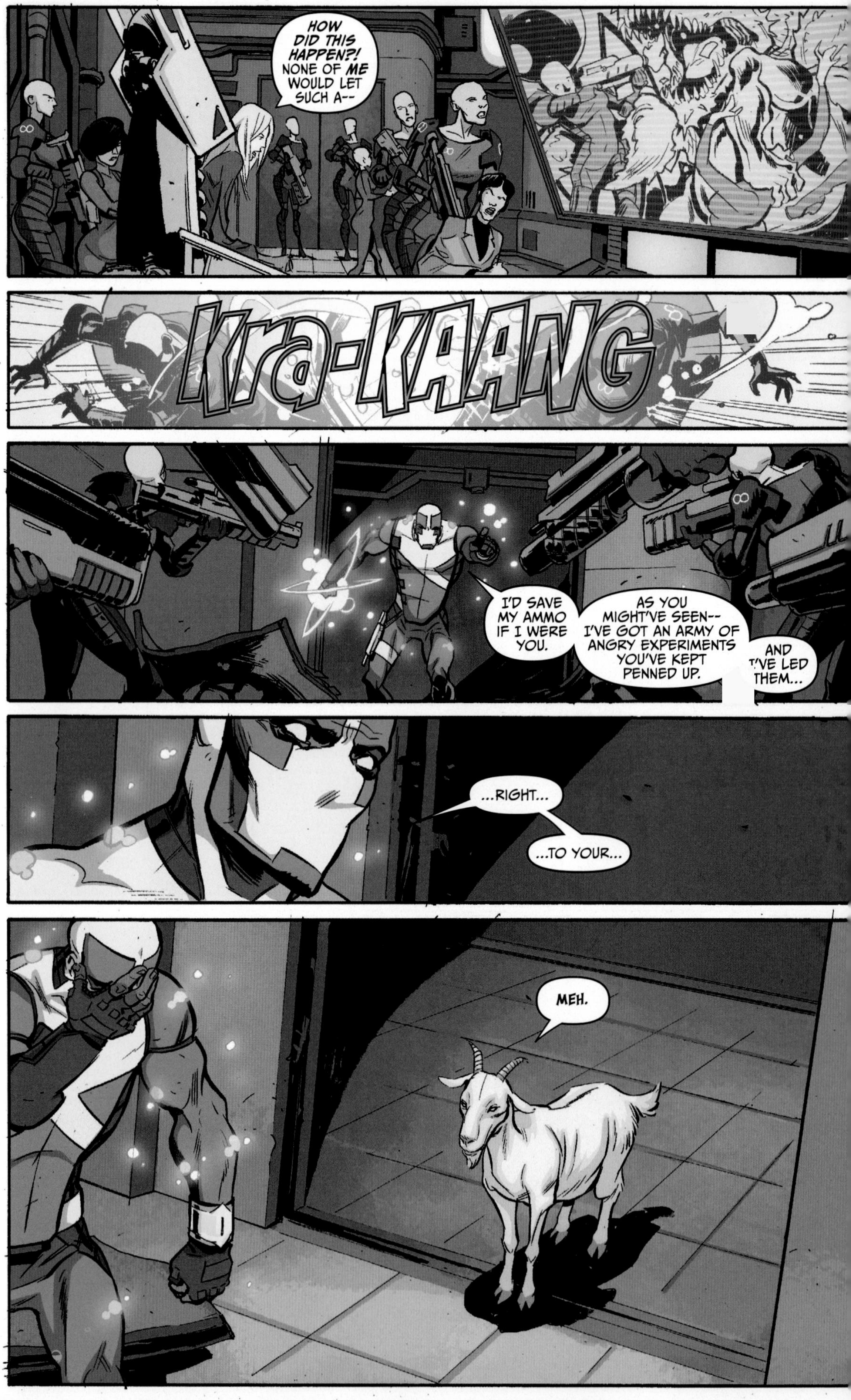
HOW DID THIS HAPPEN?! NONE OF ME WOULD LET SUCH A--
KRA-KAANG
I'D SAVE MY AMMO IF I WERE YOU.
AS YOU MIGHT'VE SEEN-- I'VE GOT AN ARMY OF ANGRY EXPERIMENTS YOU'VE KEPT PENNED UP.
AND I'VE LED THEM...
...RIGHT...
...TO YOUR...
MEH.

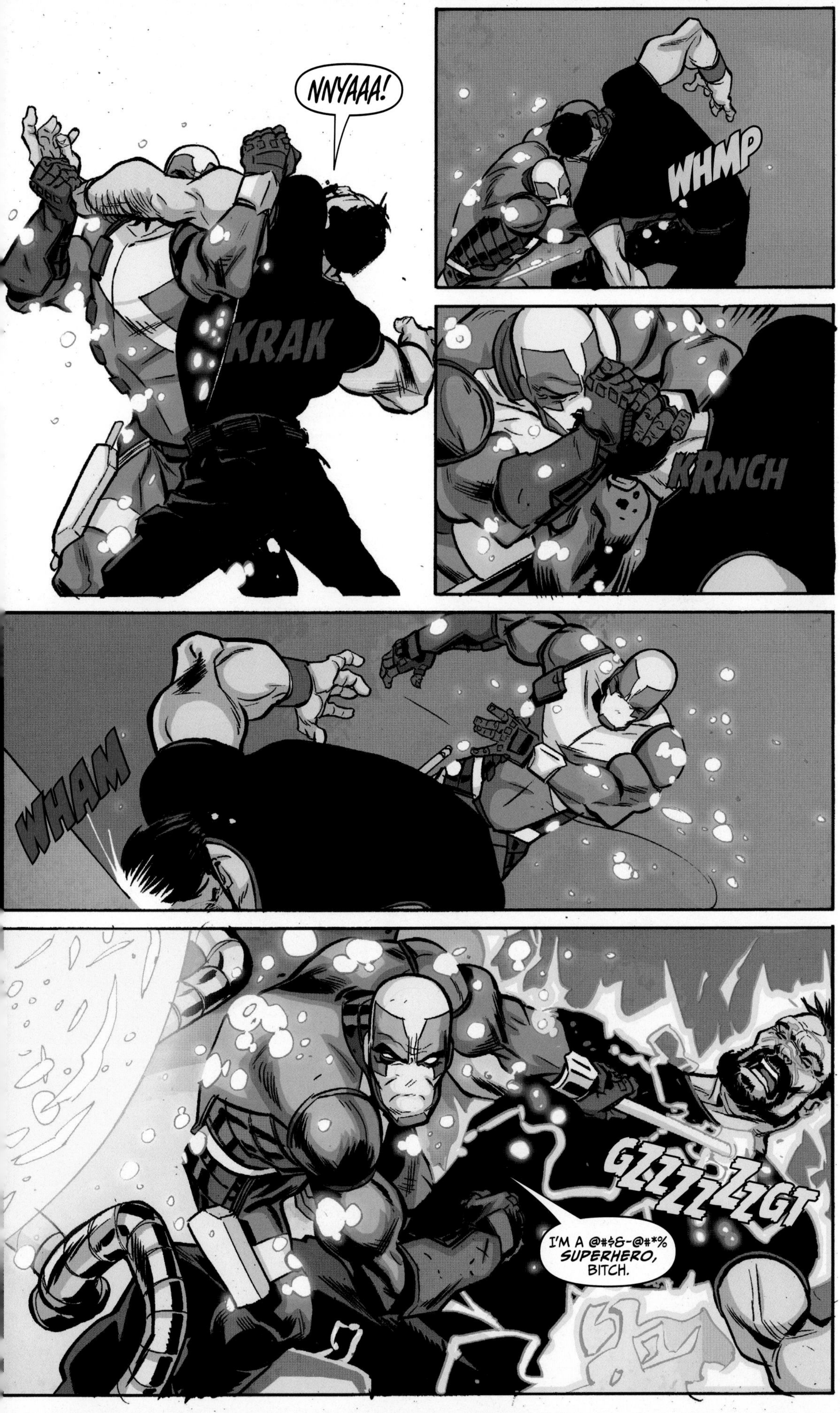
NNYAAA!
KRAK
WHMP
KRNCH
WHAM
GZZZZZZZGT
I'M A @#$&-@#*% SUPERHERO, BITCH.

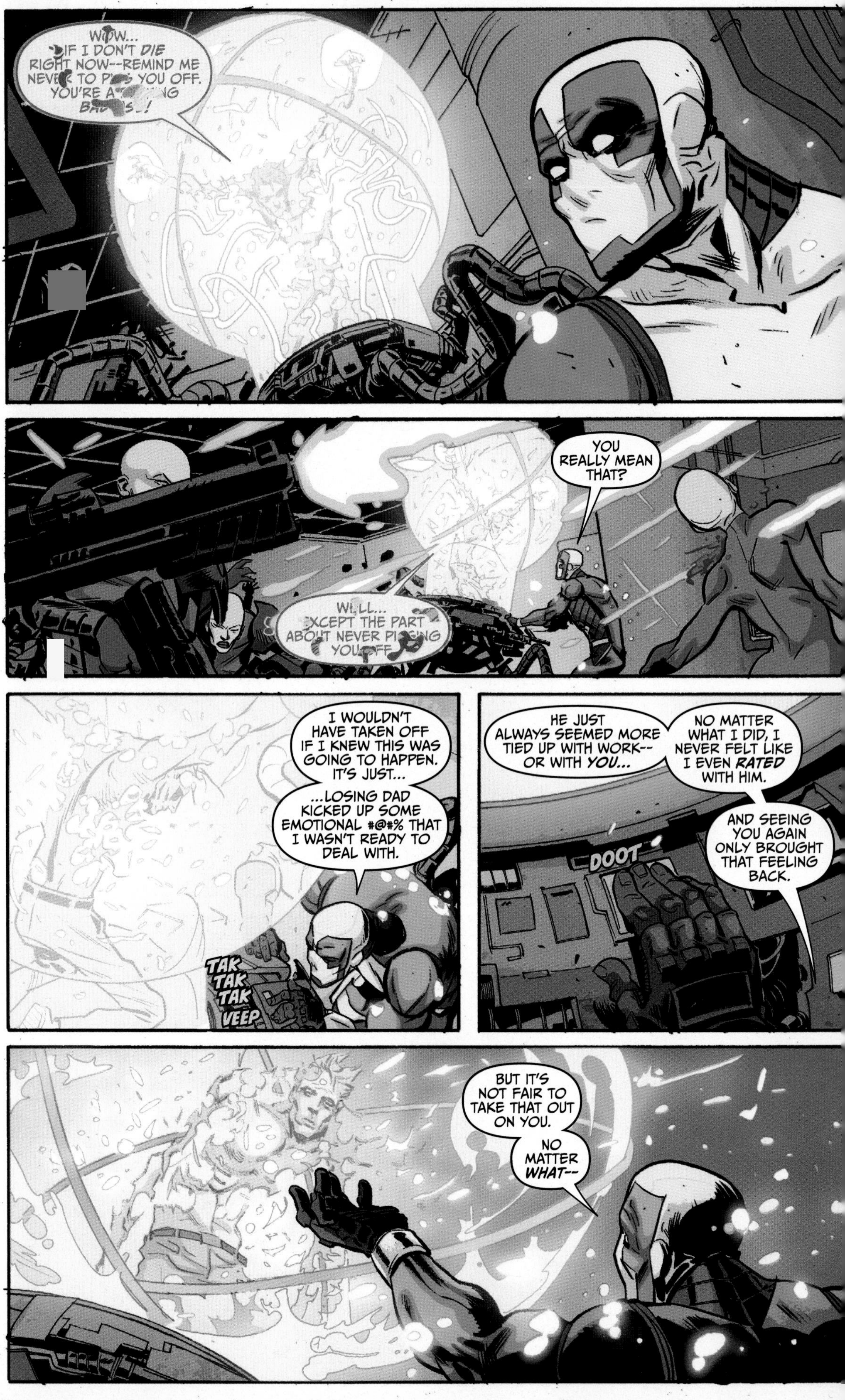
WOW...
IF I DON'T DIE RIGHT NOW--REMIND ME NEVER TO P[redacted] YOU OFF. YOU'RE A [redacted] BAD[redacted]!
YOU REALLY MEAN THAT?
WELL... EXCEPT THE PART ABOUT NEVER PI[redacted]ING YOU OFF.
I WOULDN'T HAVE TAKEN OFF IF I KNEW THIS WAS GOING TO HAPPEN. IT'S JUST...
...LOSING DAD KICKED UP SOME EMOTIONAL #@#% THAT I WASN'T READY TO DEAL WITH.
TAK TAK TAK
VEEP
HE JUST ALWAYS SEEMED MORE TIED UP WITH WORK-- OR WITH YOU...
NO MATTER WHAT I DID, I NEVER FELT LIKE I EVEN RATED WITH HIM.
DOOT
AND SEEING YOU AGAIN ONLY BROUGHT THAT FEELING BACK.
BUT IT'S NOT FAIR TO TAKE THAT OUT ON YOU.
NO MATTER WHAT--

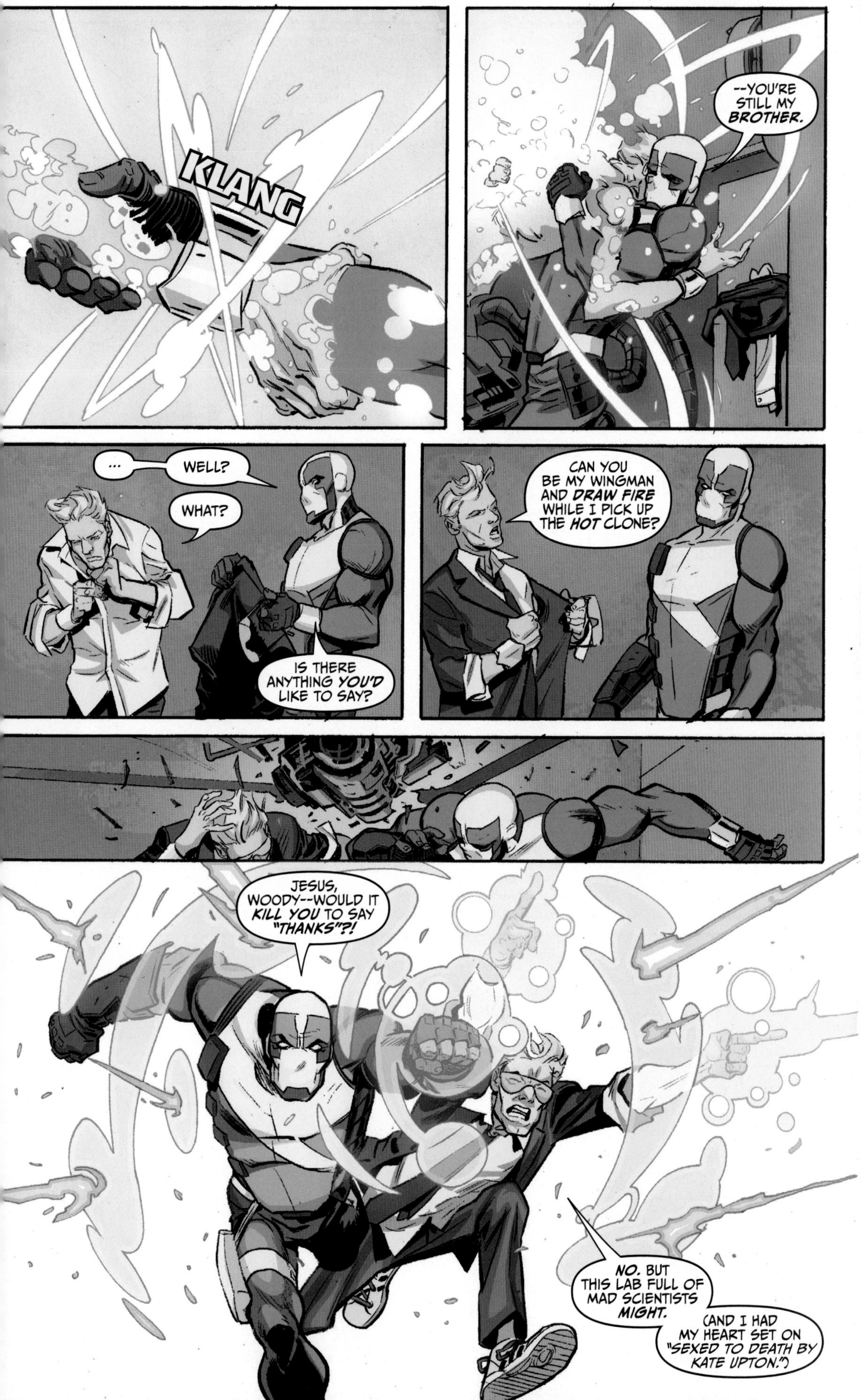
KLANG
--YOU'RE STILL MY BROTHER.
...
WELL?
WHAT?
IS THERE ANYTHING YOU'D LIKE TO SAY?
CAN YOU BE MY WINGMAN AND DRAW FIRE WHILE I PICK UP THE HOT CLONE?
JESUS, WOODY--WOULD IT KILL YOU TO SAY "THANKS"?!
NO. BUT THIS LAB FULL OF MAD SCIENTISTS MIGHT.
(AND I HAD MY HEART SET ON "SEXED TO DEATH BY KATE UPTON.")

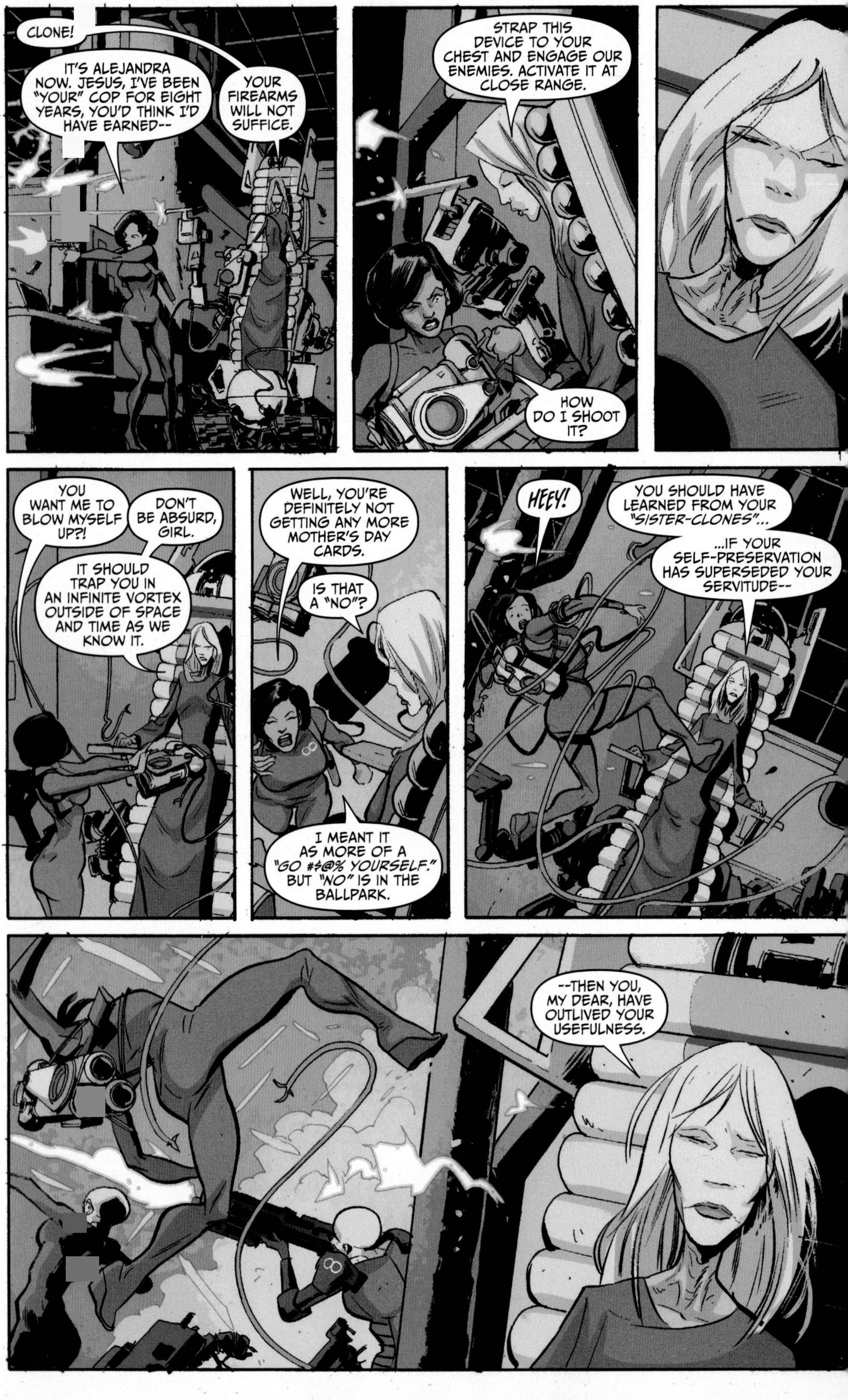
CLONE!
IT'S ALEJANDRA NOW. JESUS, I'VE BEEN "YOUR" COP FOR EIGHT YEARS, YOU'D THINK I'D HAVE EARNED--
YOUR FIREARMS WILL NOT SUFFICE.
STRAP THIS DEVICE TO YOUR CHEST AND ENGAGE OUR ENEMIES. ACTIVATE IT AT CLOSE RANGE.
HOW DO I SHOOT IT?
YOU WANT ME TO BLOW MYSELF UP?!
DON'T BE ABSURD, GIRL.
IT SHOULD TRAP YOU IN AN INFINITE VORTEX OUTSIDE OF SPACE AND TIME AS WE KNOW IT.
WELL, YOU'RE DEFINITELY NOT GETTING ANY MORE MOTHER'S DAY CARDS.
IS THAT A "NO"?
I MEANT IT AS MORE OF A *"GO #$@% YOURSELF."* BUT *"NO"* IS IN THE BALLPARK.
HEEY!
YOU SHOULD HAVE LEARNED FROM YOUR *"SISTER-CLONES"*...
...IF YOUR SELF-PRESERVATION HAS SUPERSEDED YOUR SERVITUDE--
--THEN YOU, MY DEAR, HAVE OUTLIVED YOUR USEFULNESS.

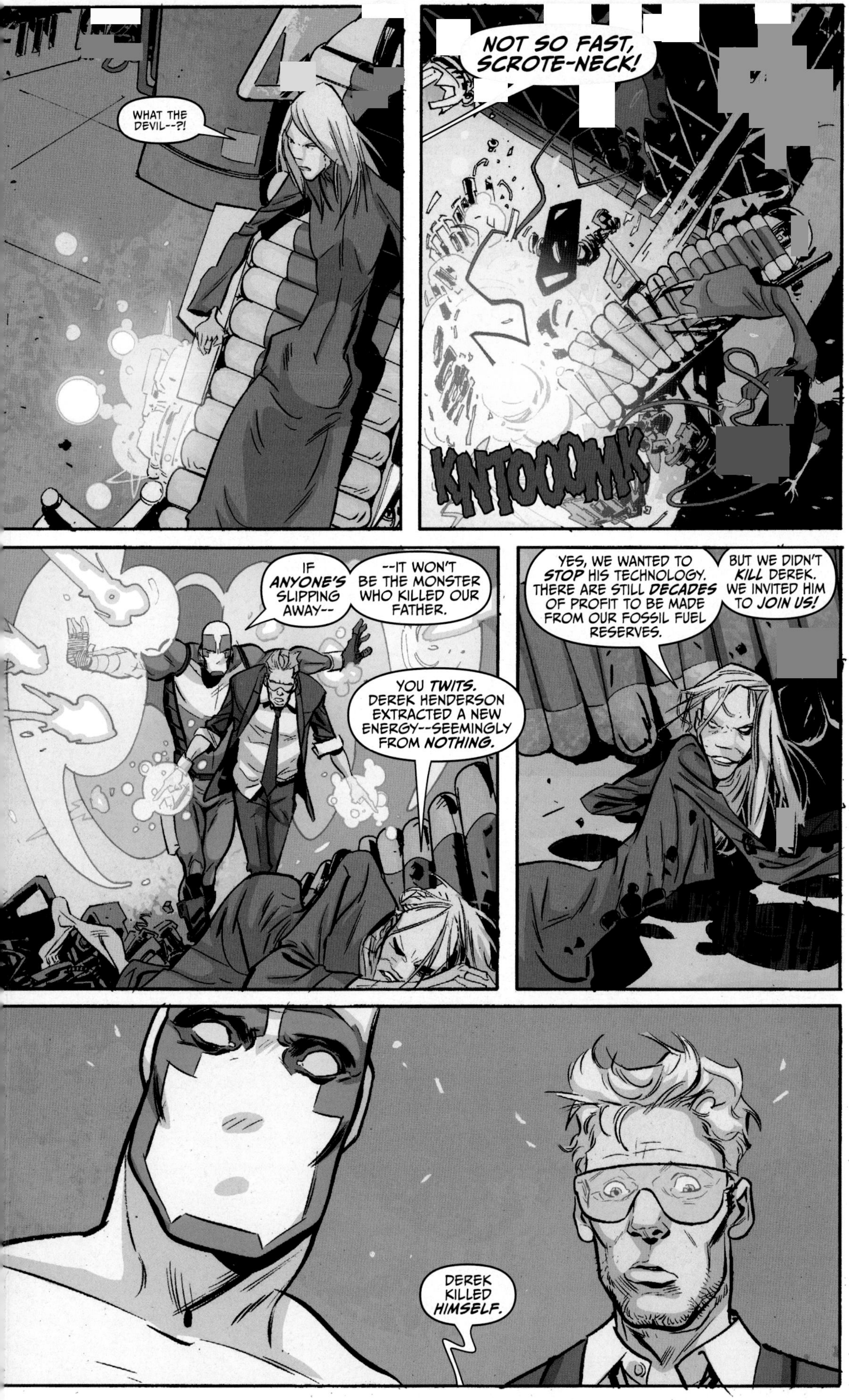
WHAT THE DEVIL--?!
NOT SO FAST, SCROTE-NECK!
KNTOOOMK
IF ANYONE'S SLIPPING AWAY--
--IT WON'T BE THE MONSTER WHO KILLED OUR FATHER.
YOU TWITS. DEREK HENDERSON EXTRACTED A NEW ENERGY--SEEMINGLY FROM NOTHING.
YES, WE WANTED TO STOP HIS TECHNOLOGY. THERE ARE STILL DECADES OF PROFIT TO BE MADE FROM OUR FOSSIL FUEL RESERVES.
BUT WE DIDN'T KILL DEREK. WE INVITED HIM TO JOIN US!
DEREK KILLED HIMSELF.

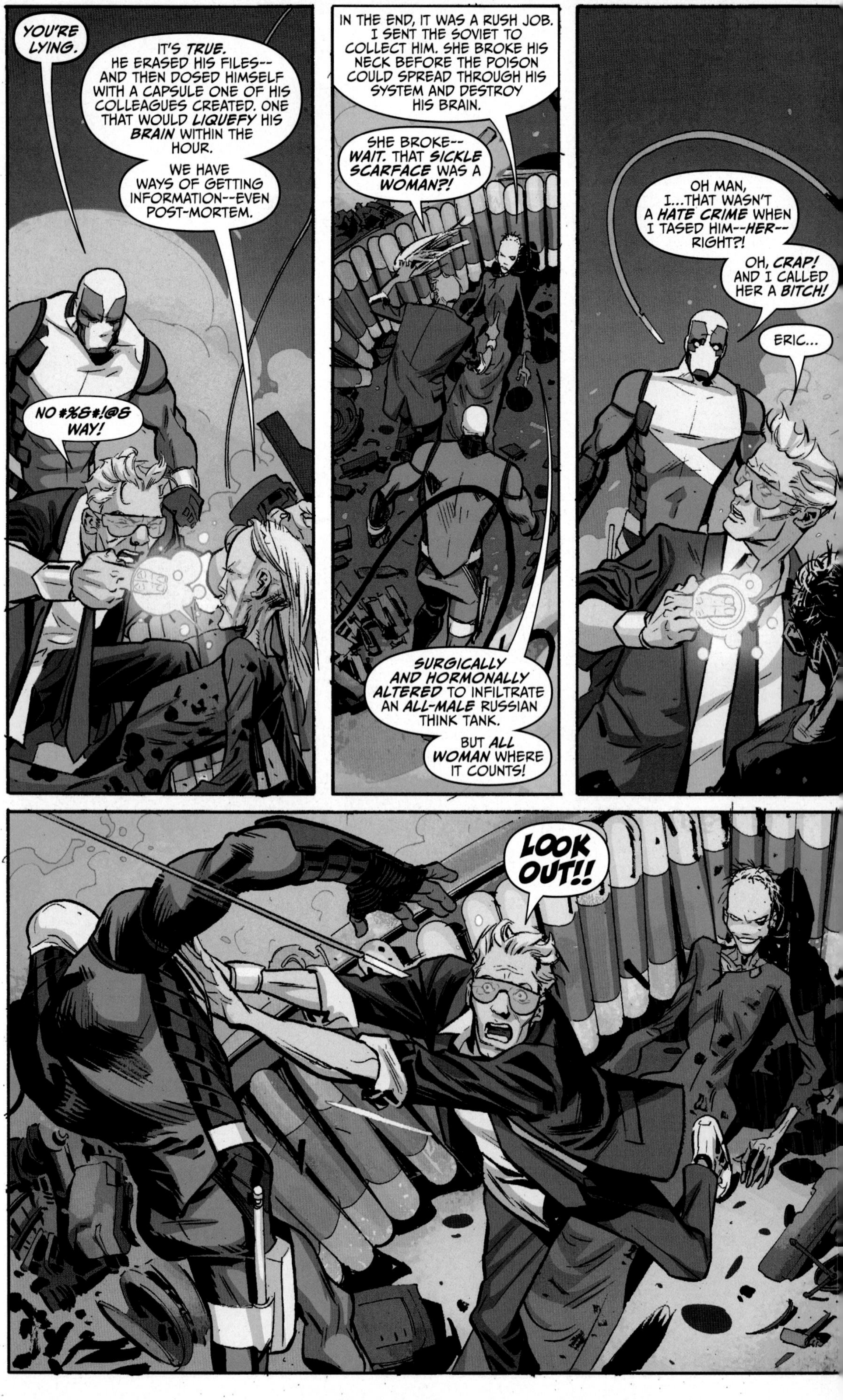
YOU'RE LYING.
IT'S TRUE. HE ERASED HIS FILES--AND THEN DOSED HIMSELF WITH A CAPSULE ONE OF HIS COLLEAGUES CREATED. ONE THAT WOULD LIQUEFY HIS BRAIN WITHIN THE HOUR.
WE HAVE WAYS OF GETTING INFORMATION--EVEN POST-MORTEM.
NO #%&#!@& WAY!
IN THE END, IT WAS A RUSH JOB. I SENT THE SOVIET TO COLLECT HIM. SHE BROKE HIS NECK BEFORE THE POISON COULD SPREAD THROUGH HIS SYSTEM AND DESTROY HIS BRAIN.
SHE BROKE--WAIT. THAT SICKLE SCARFACE WAS A WOMAN?!
SURGICALLY AND HORMONALLY ALTERED TO INFILTRATE AN ALL-MALE RUSSIAN THINK TANK.
BUT ALL WOMAN WHERE IT COUNTS!
OH MAN, I...THAT WASN'T A HATE CRIME WHEN I TASED HIM--HER--RIGHT?!
OH, CRAP! AND I CALLED HER A BITCH!
ERIC...
LOOK OUT!!

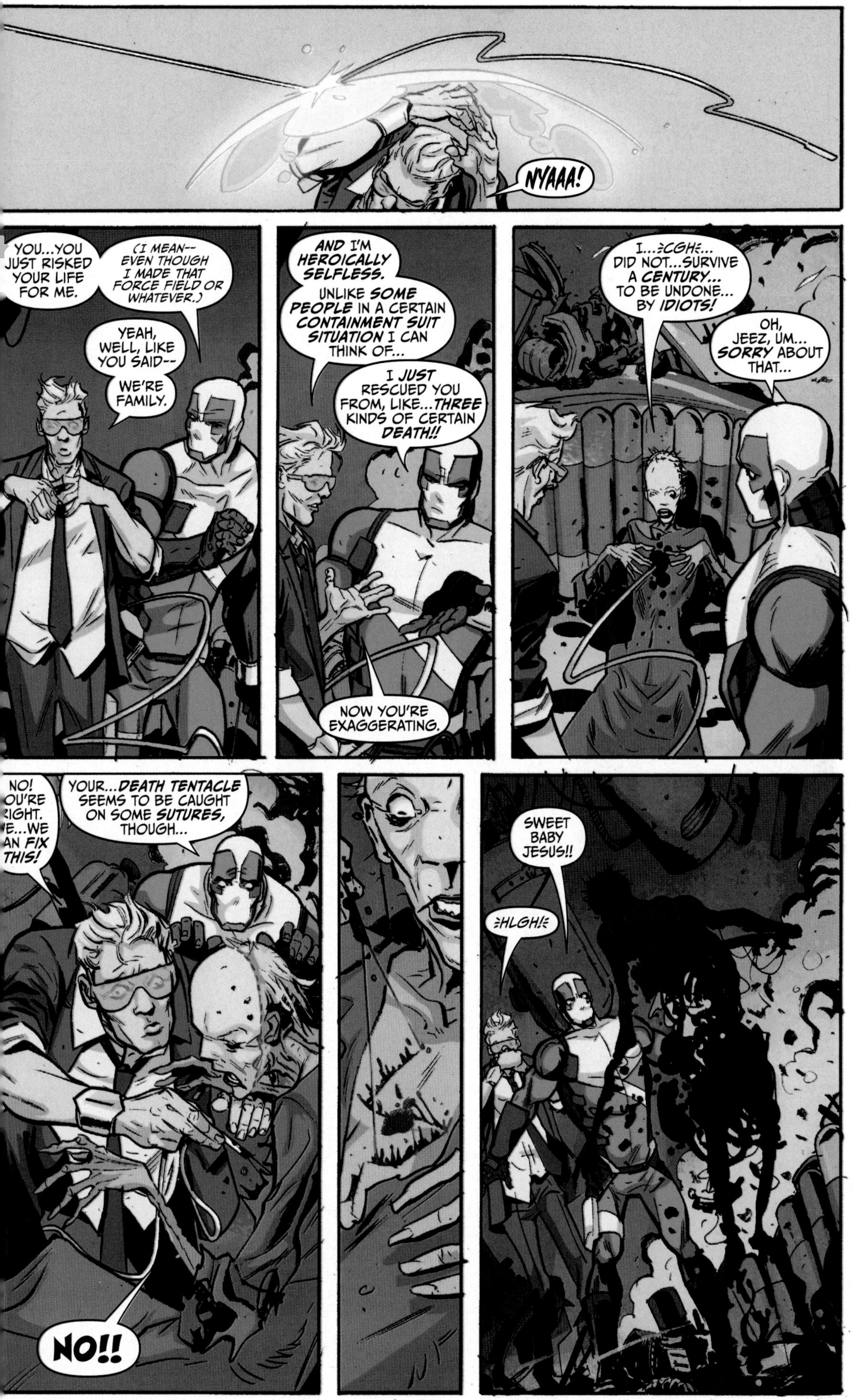
NYAAA!
YOU...YOU JUST RISKED YOUR LIFE FOR ME.
(I MEAN-- EVEN THOUGH I MADE THAT FORCE FIELD OR WHATEVER.)
YEAH, WELL, LIKE YOU SAID--
WE'RE FAMILY.
AND I'M HEROICALLY SELFLESS.
UNLIKE SOME PEOPLE IN A CERTAIN CONTAINMENT SUIT SITUATION I CAN THINK OF...
I JUST RESCUED YOU FROM, LIKE...THREE KINDS OF CERTAIN DEATH!!
NOW YOU'RE EXAGGERATING.
I...ECGHE... DID NOT...SURVIVE A CENTURY... TO BE UNDONE... BY IDIOTS!
OH, JEEZ, UM... SORRY ABOUT THAT...
NO! YOU'RE RIGHT. WE...WE CAN FIX THIS!
YOUR...DEATH TENTACLE SEEMS TO BE CAUGHT ON SOME SUTURES, THOUGH...
NO!!
SWEET BABY JESUS!!
EHLGH!E

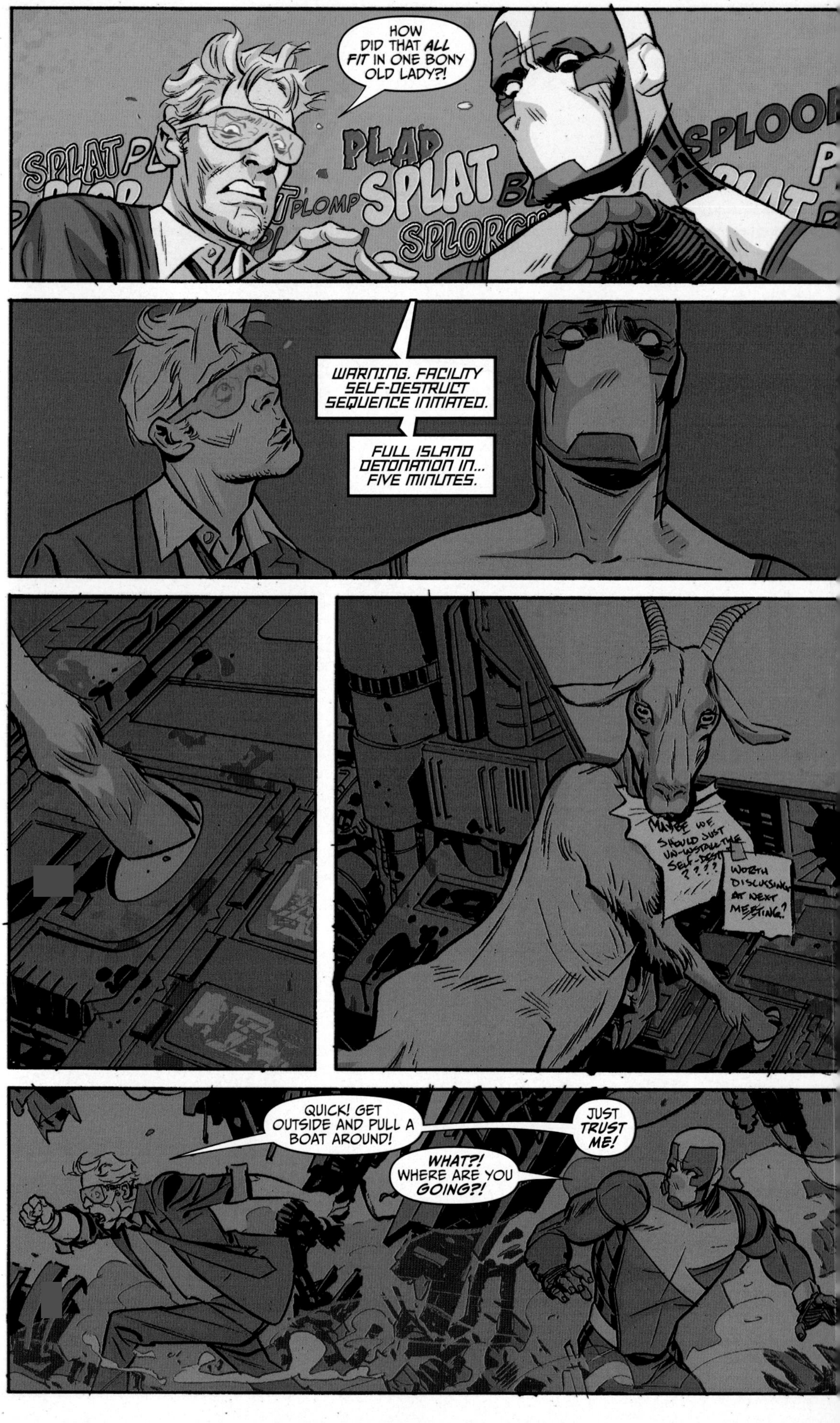

HOW DID THAT *ALL* *FIT* IN ONE BONY OLD LADY?!
SPLAT
PLAD
PLOMP
SPLAT
WARNING. FACILITY SELF-DESTRUCT SEQUENCE INITIATED.
FULL ISLAND DETONATION IN... FIVE MINUTES.
MAYBE WE SHOULD JUST UN-INSTALL THE SELF-DEST
????
WORTH DISCUSSING AT NEXT MEETING?
QUICK! GET OUTSIDE AND PULL A BOAT AROUND!
WHAT?! WHERE ARE YOU *GOING?!*
JUST *TRUST* *ME!*

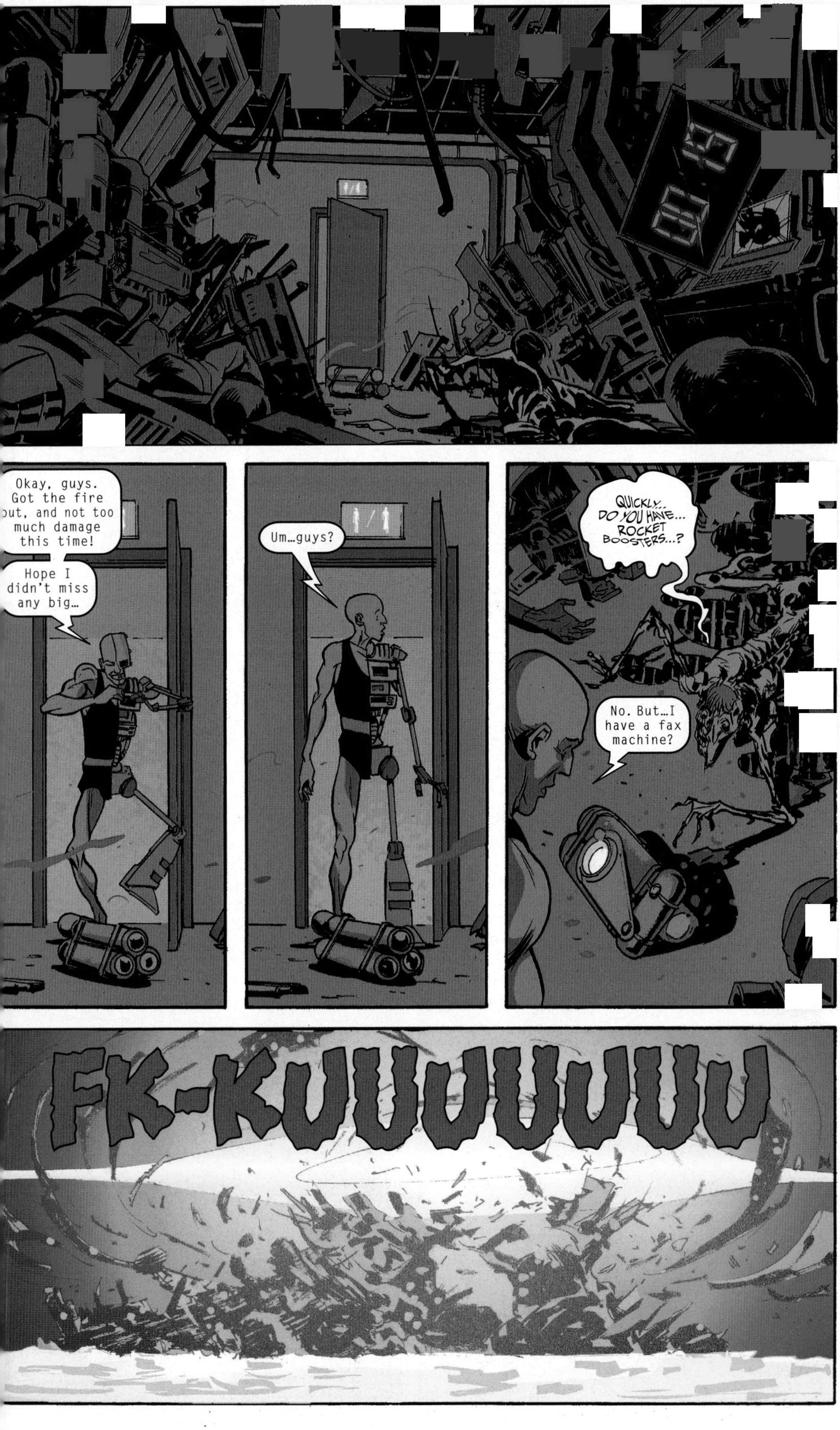

Okay, guys. Got the fire out, and not too much damage this time!
Hope I didn't miss any big…
Um…guys?
QUICKLY... DO YOU HAVE... ROCKET BOOSTERS...?
No. But…I have a fax machine?
FK-KUUUUUUU

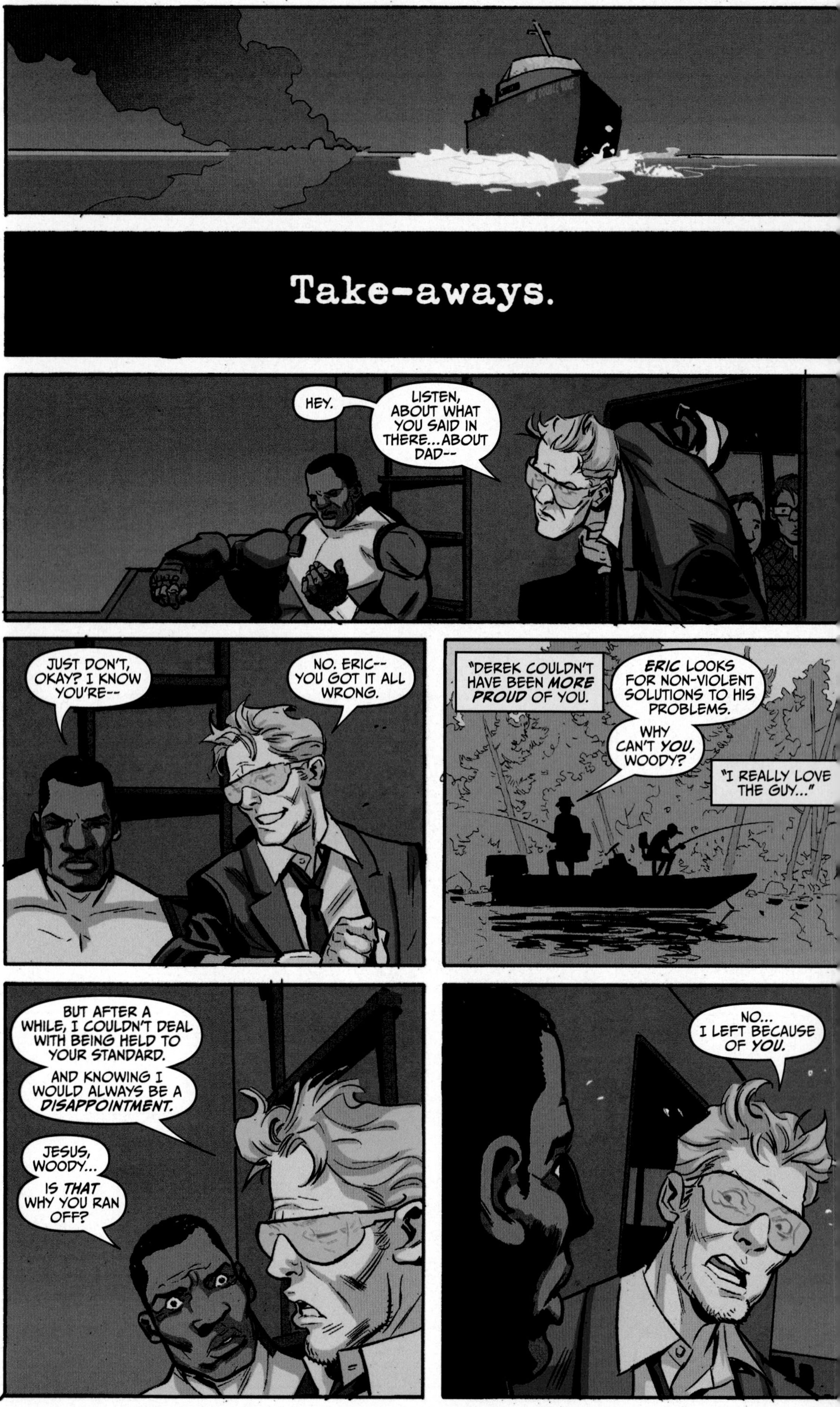
Take-aways.
HEY.
LISTEN, ABOUT WHAT YOU SAID IN THERE...ABOUT DAD--
JUST DON'T, OKAY? I KNOW YOU'RE--
NO. ERIC-- YOU GOT IT ALL WRONG.
"DEREK COULDN'T HAVE BEEN MORE PROUD OF YOU.
ERIC LOOKS FOR NON-VIOLENT SOLUTIONS TO HIS PROBLEMS.
WHY CAN'T YOU, WOODY?
"I REALLY LOVE THE GUY..."
BUT AFTER A WHILE, I COULDN'T DEAL WITH BEING HELD TO YOUR STANDARD.
AND KNOWING I WOULD ALWAYS BE A DISAPPOINTMENT.
JESUS, WOODY...
IS THAT WHY YOU RAN OFF?
NO... I LEFT BECAUSE OF YOU.

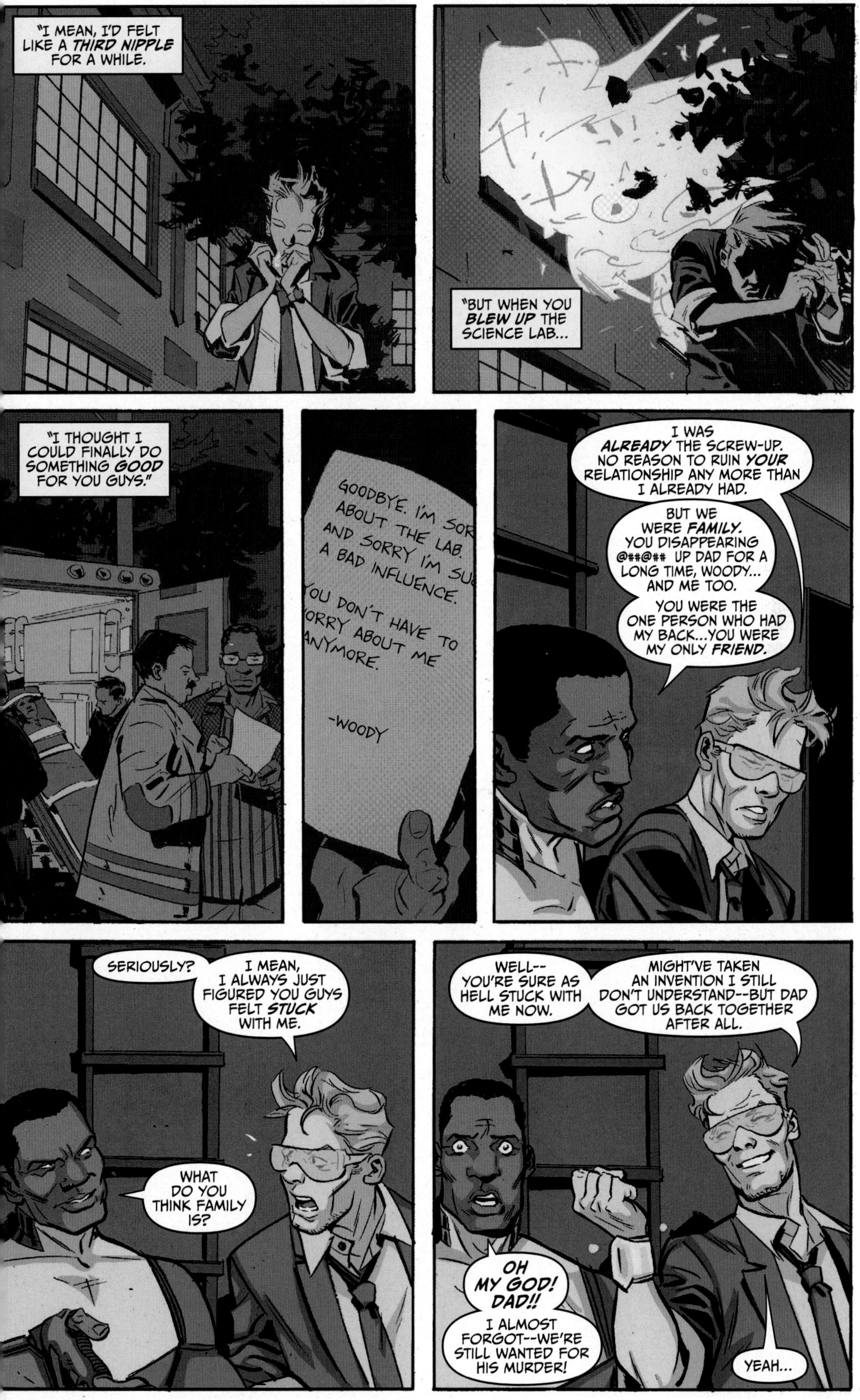
"I MEAN, I'D FELT LIKE A THIRD NIPPLE FOR A WHILE.
"BUT WHEN YOU BLEW UP THE SCIENCE LAB...
"I THOUGHT I COULD FINALLY DO SOMETHING GOOD FOR YOU GUYS."
GOODBYE. I'M SOR ABOUT THE LAB. AND SORRY I'M SU A BAD INFLUENCE.
OU DON'T HAVE TO ORRY ABOUT ME NYMORE.
-WOODY
I WAS ALREADY THE SCREW-UP. NO REASON TO RUIN YOUR RELATIONSHIP ANY MORE THAN I ALREADY HAD.
BUT WE WERE FAMILY. YOU DISAPPEARING @##@## UP DAD FOR A LONG TIME, WOODY... AND ME TOO.
YOU WERE THE ONE PERSON WHO HAD MY BACK...YOU WERE MY ONLY FRIEND.
SERIOUSLY?
I MEAN, I ALWAYS JUST FIGURED YOU GUYS FELT STUCK WITH ME.
WHAT DO YOU THINK FAMILY IS?
WELL-- YOU'RE SURE AS HELL STUCK WITH ME NOW.
MIGHT'VE TAKEN AN INVENTION I STILL DON'T UNDERSTAND--BUT DAD GOT US BACK TOGETHER AFTER ALL.
OH MY GOD! DAD!!
I ALMOST FORGOT--WE'RE STILL WANTED FOR HIS MURDER!
YEAH...

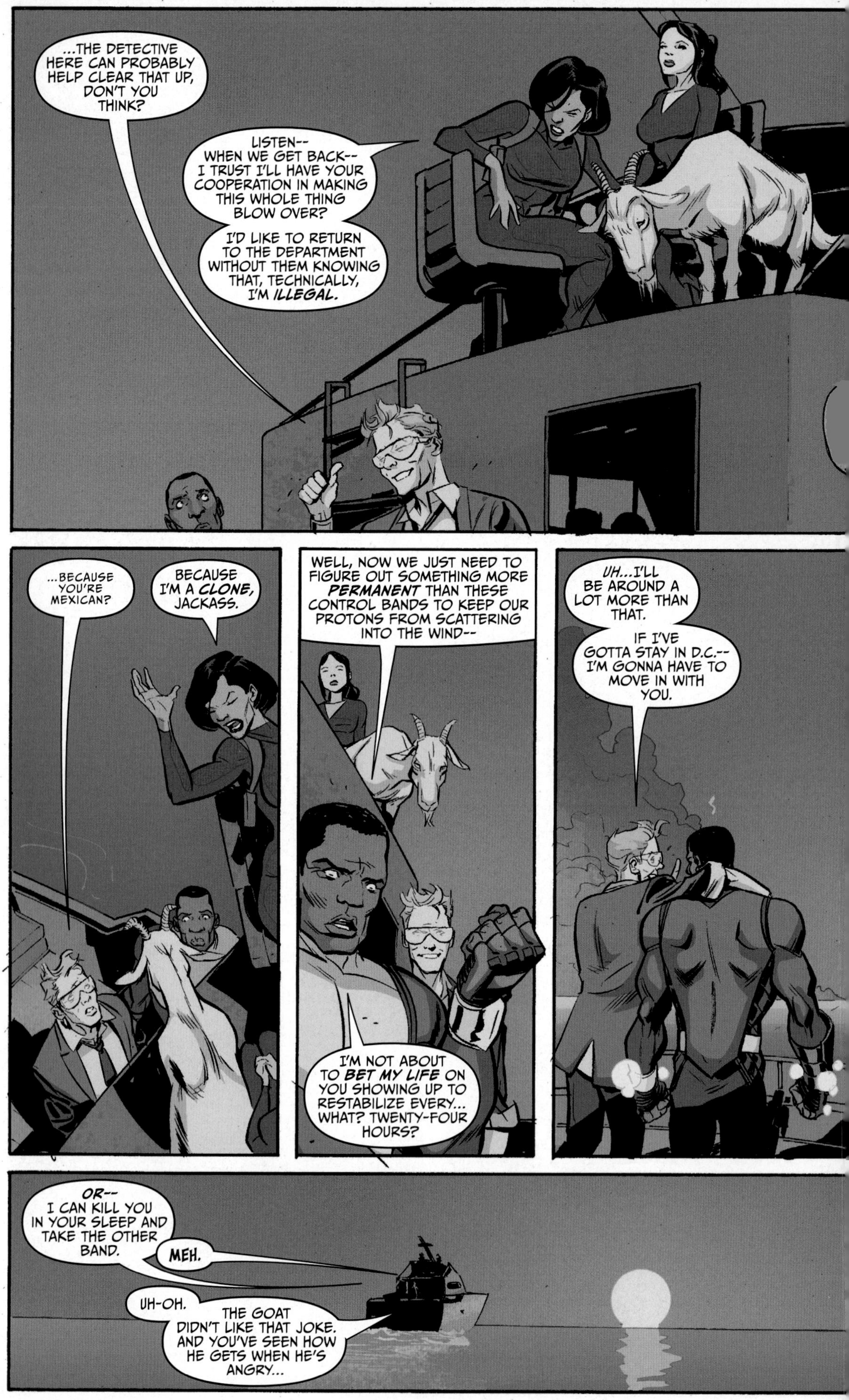
...THE DETECTIVE HERE CAN PROBABLY HELP CLEAR THAT UP, DON'T YOU THINK?
LISTEN-- WHEN WE GET BACK-- I TRUST I'LL HAVE YOUR COOPERATION IN MAKING THIS WHOLE THING BLOW OVER?
I'D LIKE TO RETURN TO THE DEPARTMENT WITHOUT THEM KNOWING THAT, TECHNICALLY, I'M *ILLEGAL.*
...BECAUSE YOU'RE MEXICAN?
BECAUSE I'M A *CLONE,* JACKASS.
WELL, NOW WE JUST NEED TO FIGURE OUT SOMETHING MORE *PERMANENT* THAN THESE CONTROL BANDS TO KEEP OUR PROTONS FROM SCATTERING INTO THE WIND--
I'M NOT ABOUT TO *BET MY LIFE* ON YOU SHOWING UP TO RESTABILIZE EVERY... WHAT? TWENTY-FOUR HOURS?
*UH...*I'LL BE AROUND A LOT MORE THAN THAT.
IF I'VE GOTTA STAY IN D.C.-- I'M GONNA HAVE TO MOVE IN WITH YOU.
OR-- I CAN KILL YOU IN YOUR SLEEP AND TAKE THE OTHER BAND.
MEH.
UH-OH.
THE GOAT DIDN'T LIKE THAT JOKE. AND YOU'VE SEEN HOW HE GETS WHEN HE'S ANGRY...

Actually, land's the other way.

Quantum and Woody

will return in:

"In Security"

GALLERY

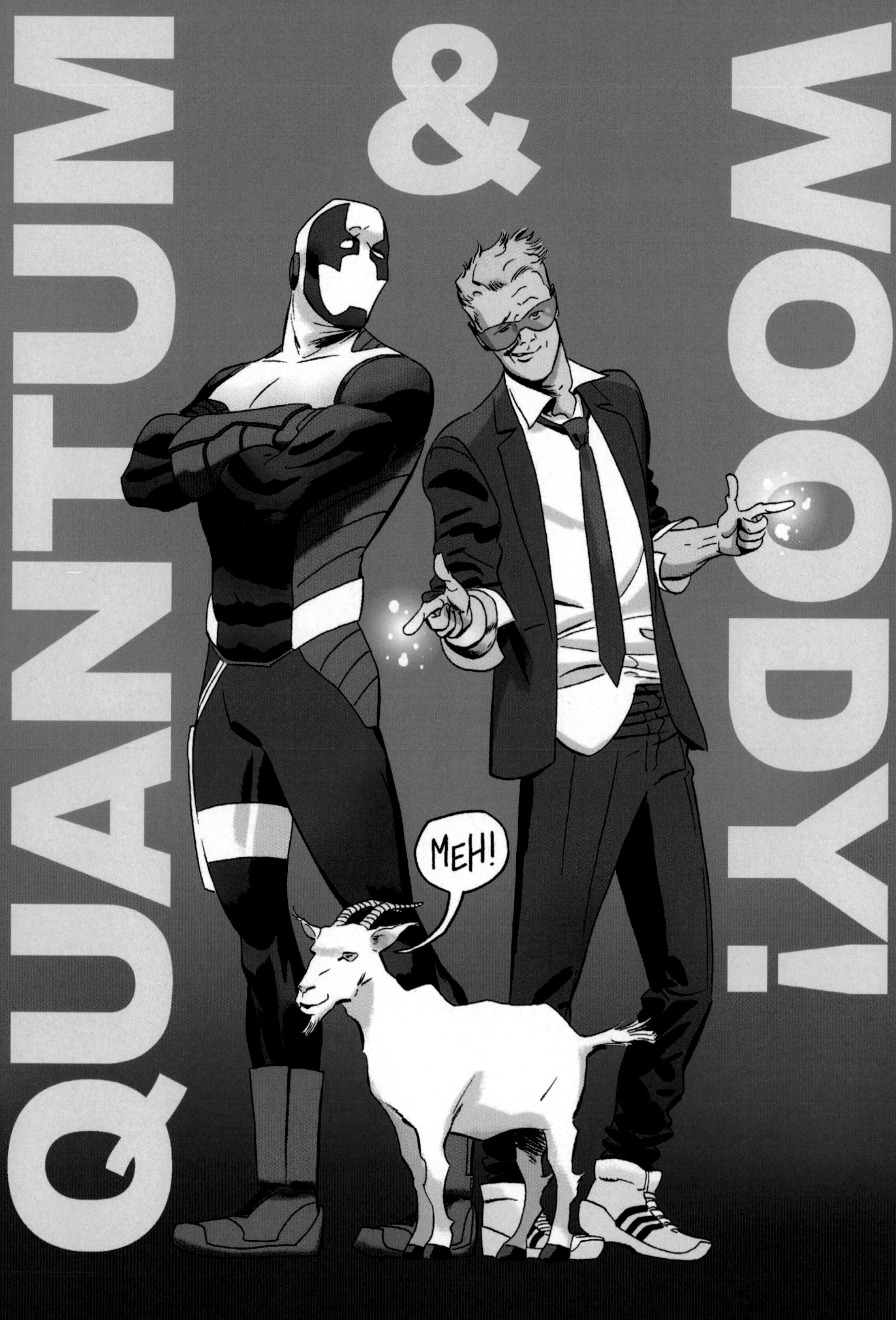

QUANTUM
&
WOODY!
MEH!

QUANTUM AND WOODY #1 PULLBOX VARIANT
Cover by MARCOS MARTIN

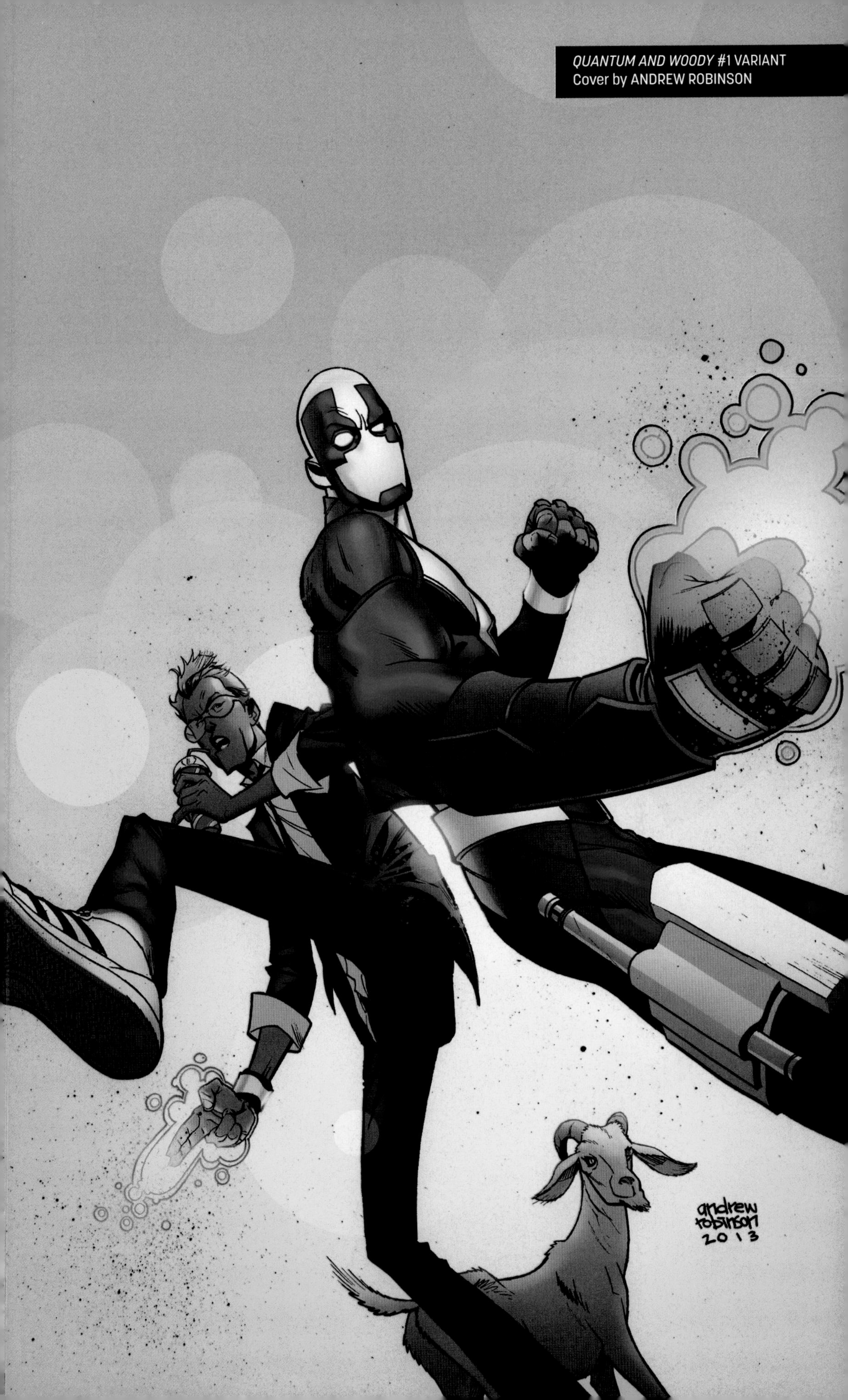
andrew robinson 2013

QUANTUM AND WOODY #1 VARIANT
Cover by ANDREW ROBINSON

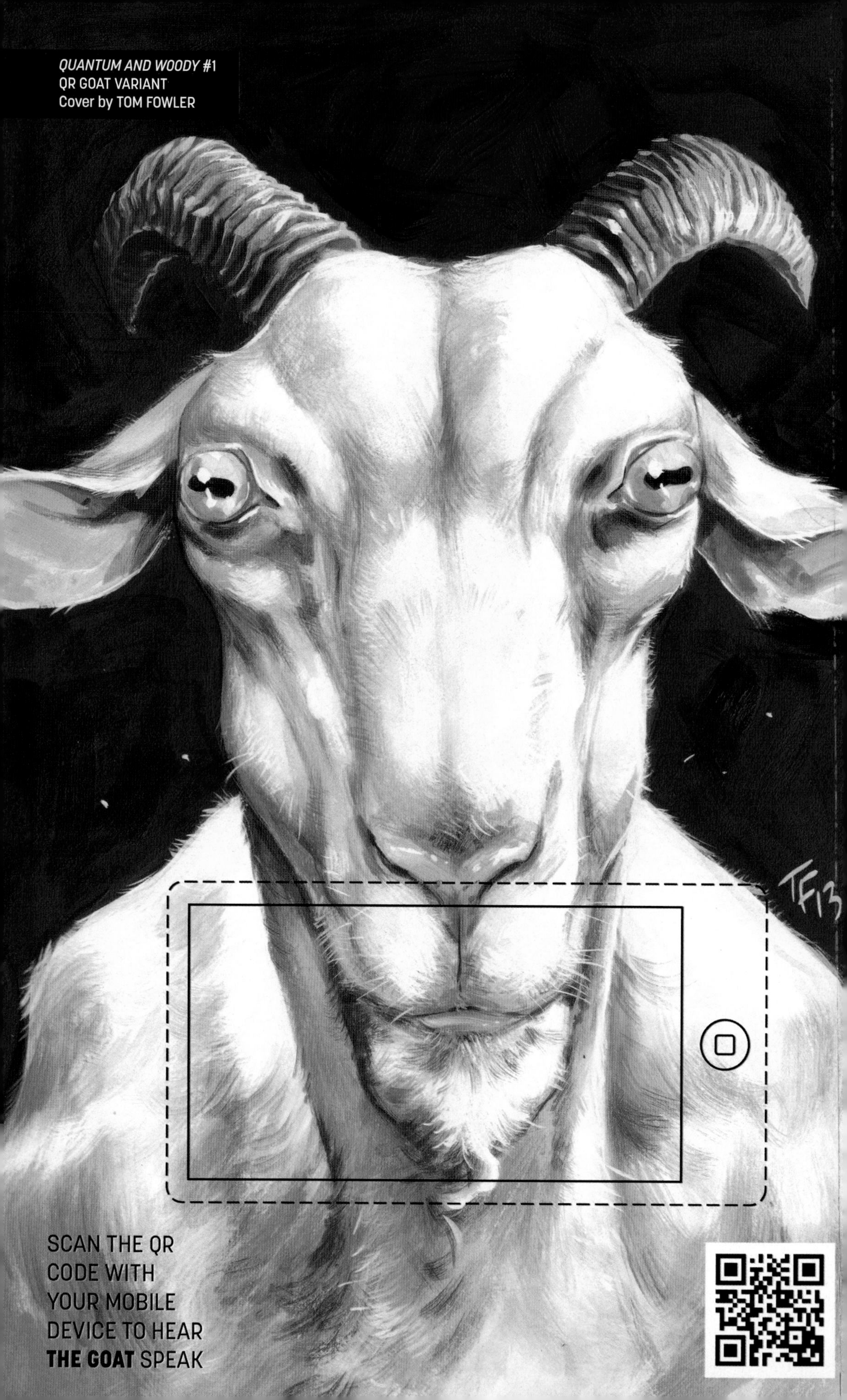
SCAN THE QR
CODE WITH
YOUR MOBILE
DEVICE TO HEAR
THE GOAT SPEAK

QUANTUM AND WOODY #1
QR GOAT VARIANT
Cover by TOM FOWLER

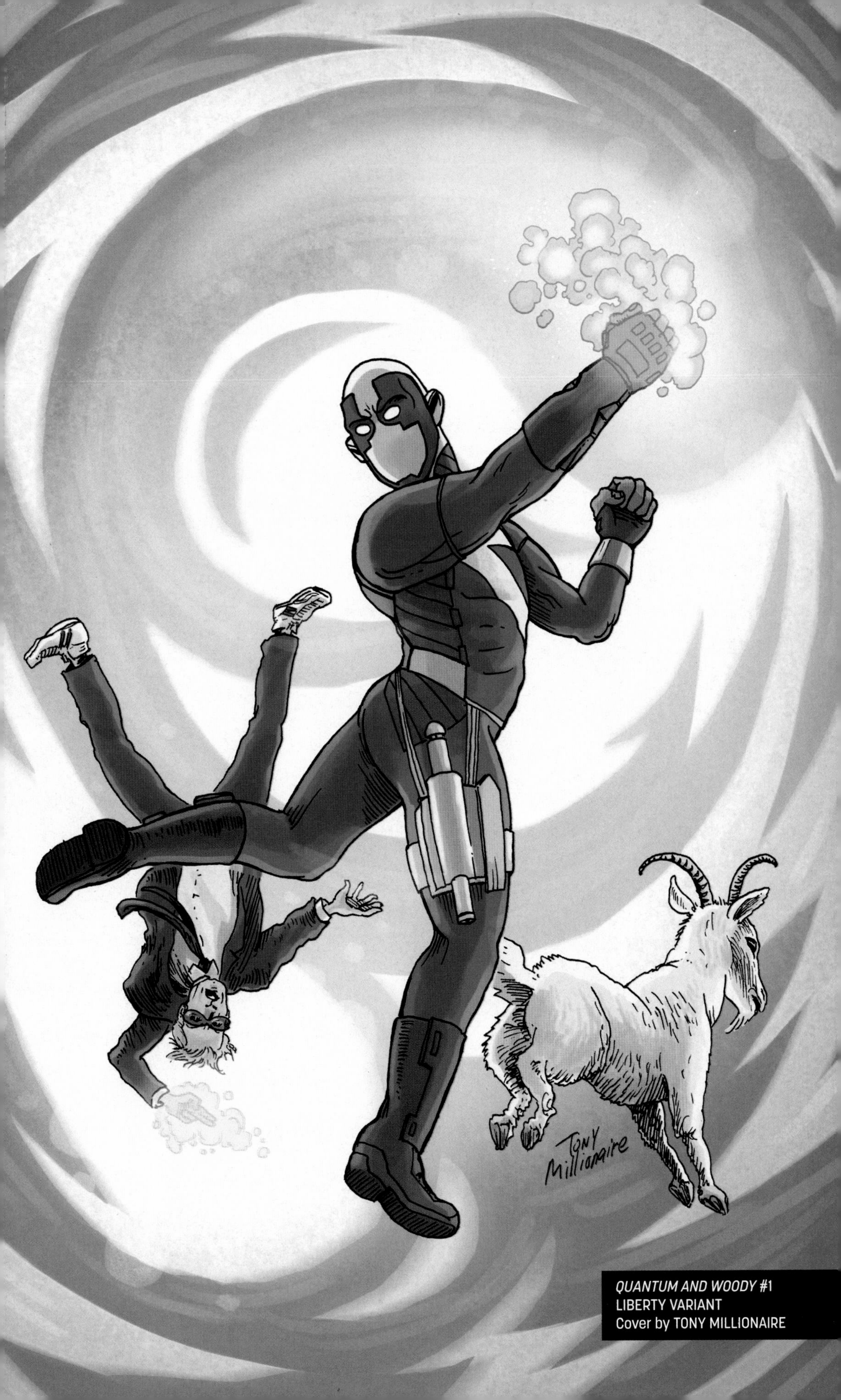
TONY
Millionaire

QUANTUM AND WOODY #1
LIBERTY VARIANT
Cover by TONY MILLIONAIRE

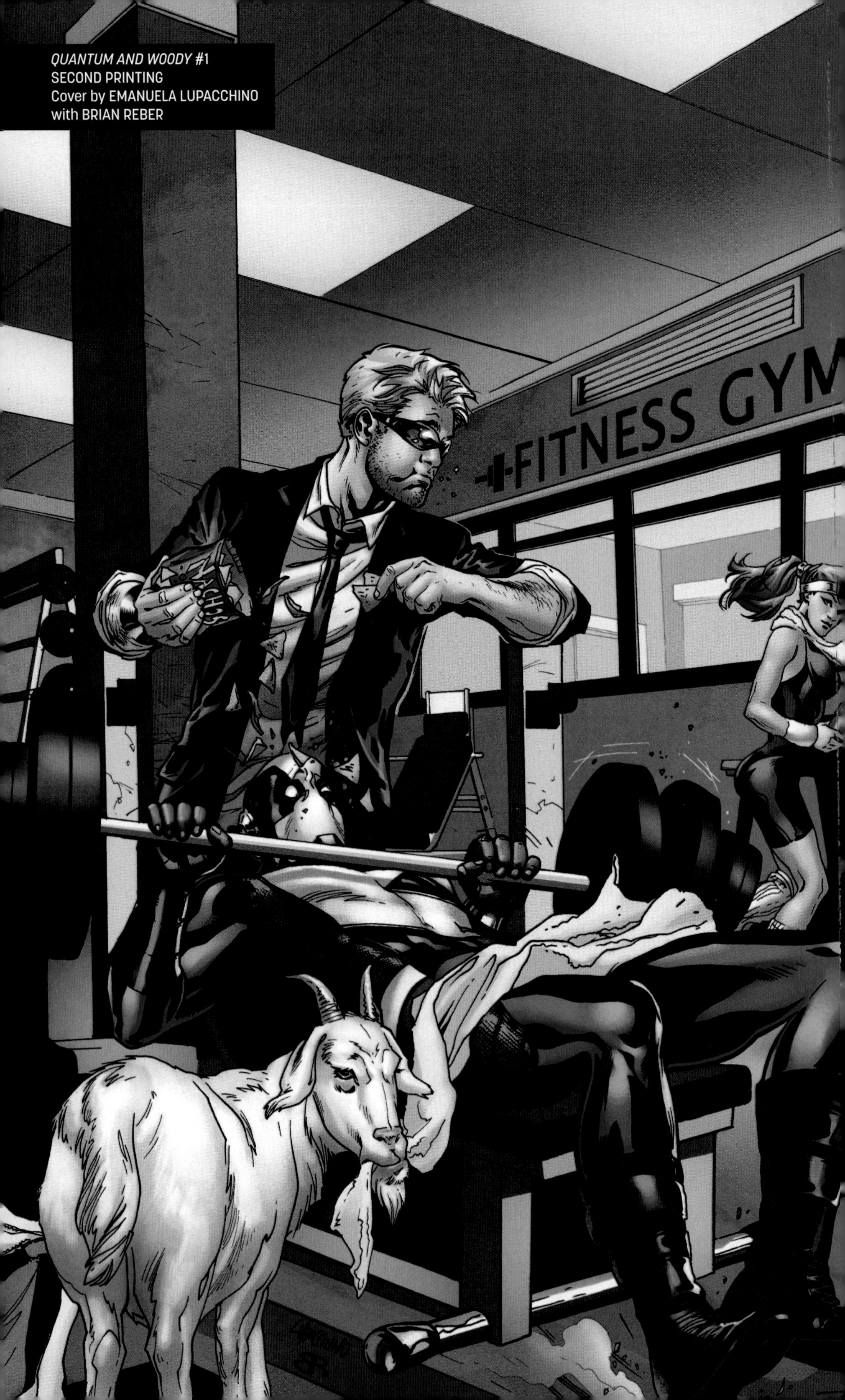
FITNESS GYM

QUANTUM AND WOODY #1
SECOND PRINTING
Cover by EMANUELA LUPACCHINO
with BRIAN REBER

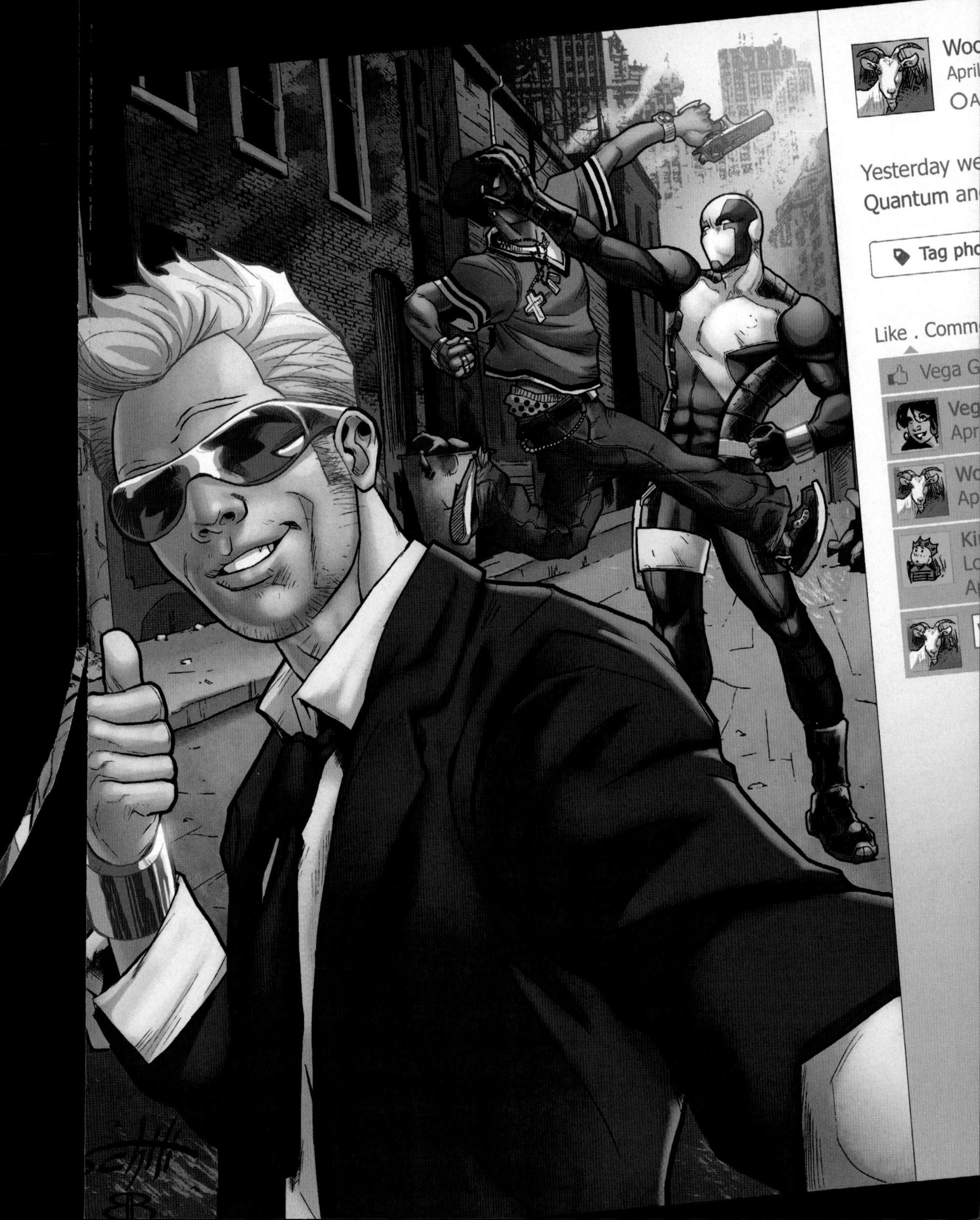

Woo
April
Yesterday we
Quantum an
Tag pho
Like . Comm
Vega G
Veg
Apr
Wo
Ap
Ki

QUANTUM AND WOODY #2 VARIANT
Cover by TOM FOWLER

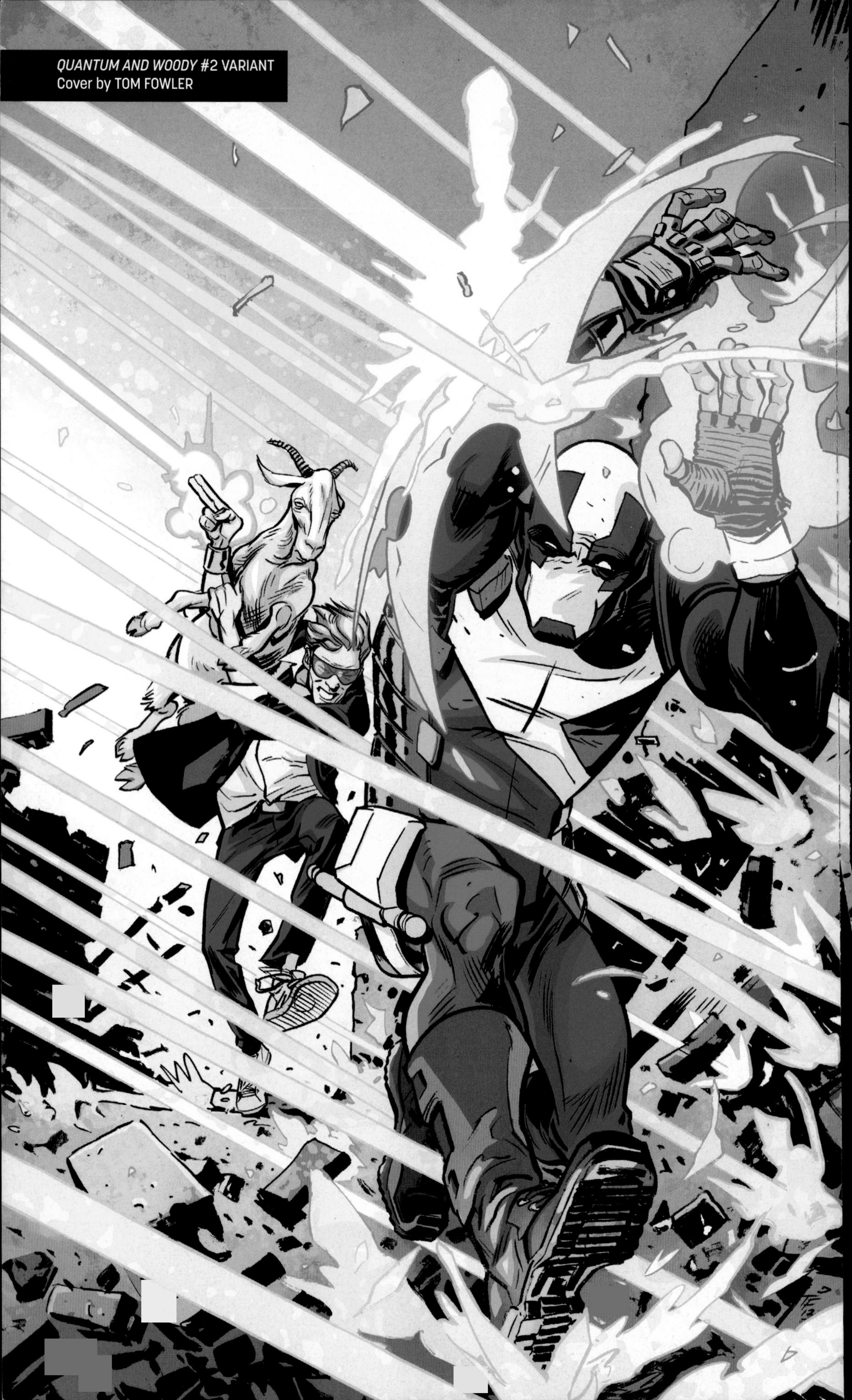

QUANTUM AND WOODY #2 VARIANT
Cover by RIAN HUGHES

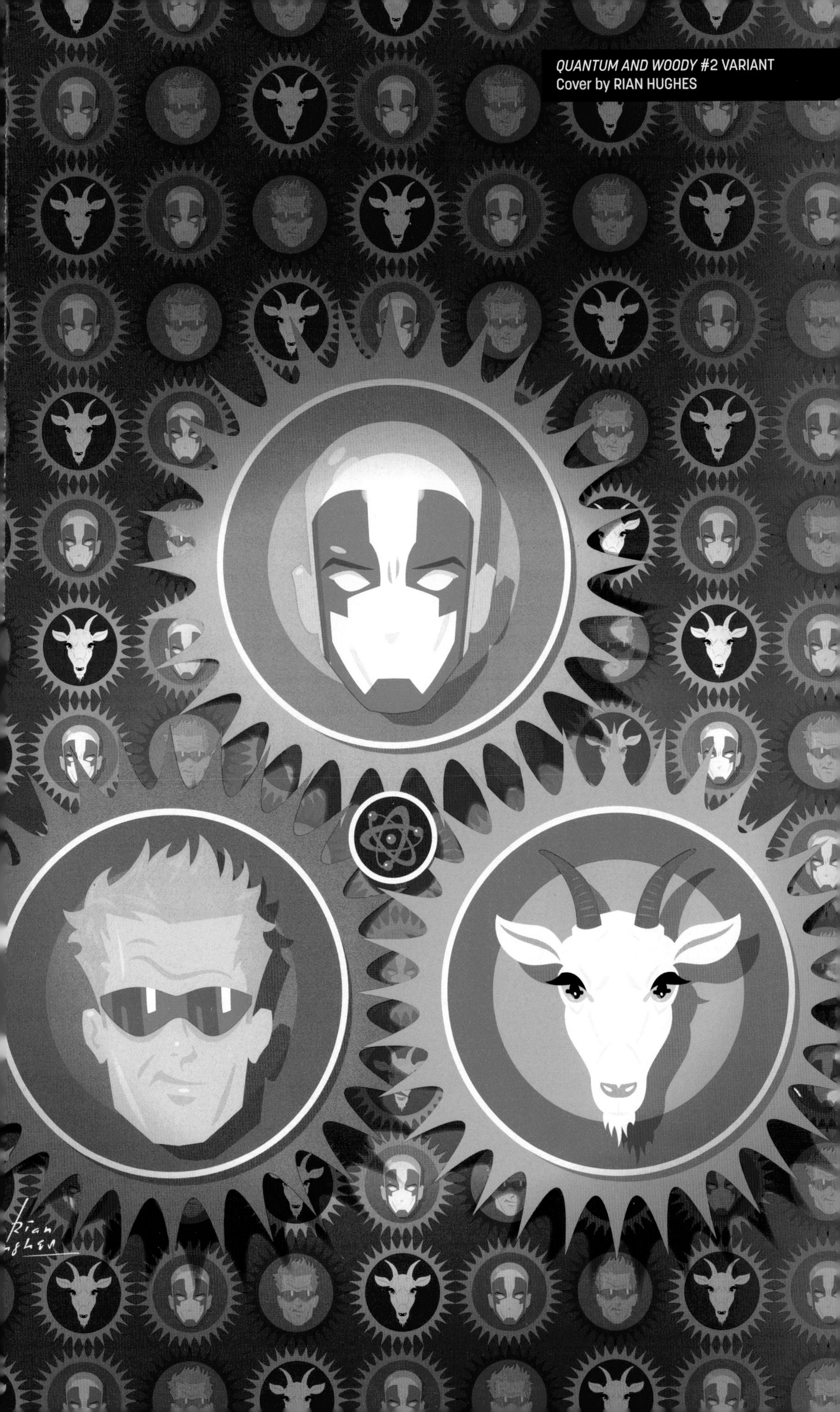

QUANTUM AND WOODY #3 VARIANT
Cover by JUAN DOE

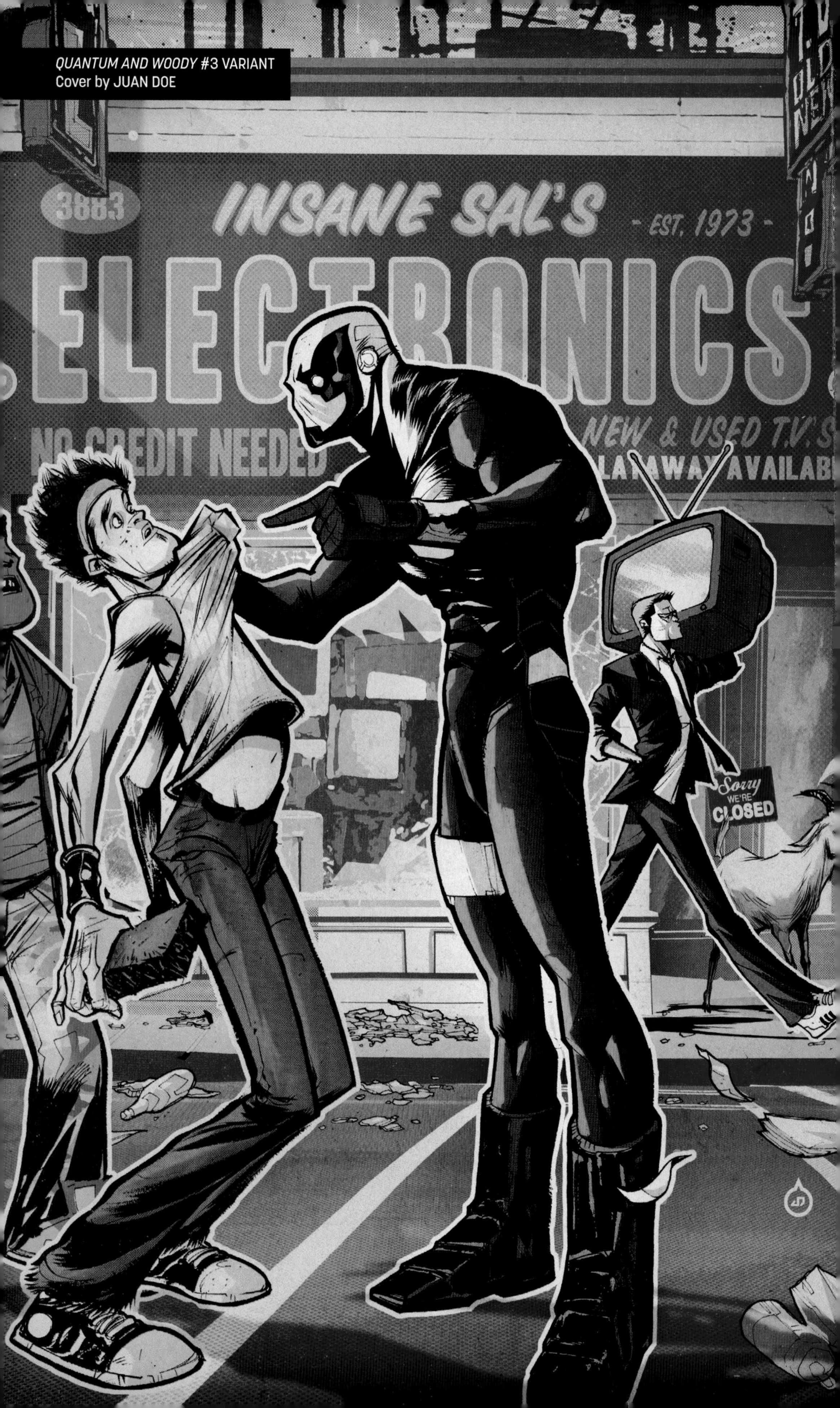
3883
INSANE SAL'S
- EST. 1973 -
ELECTRONICS
NO CREDIT NEEDED
NEW & USED T.V.'S
LAYAWAY AVAILABLE
Sorry
WE'RE
CLOSED

THE LEGENDARY QUANTUM AND WOODY!

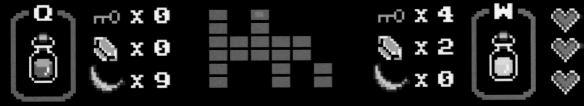

IT'S DANGEROUS TO GO
ALONE! TAKE THIS!

QUANTUM AND WOODY #4
VALIANT LEVEL TWO 8-BIT VARIANT
Cover by DONOVAN SANTIAGO

C[redacted]IM AND WOODY #4 GOAT VARIANT
Cover by ROB GUILLORY

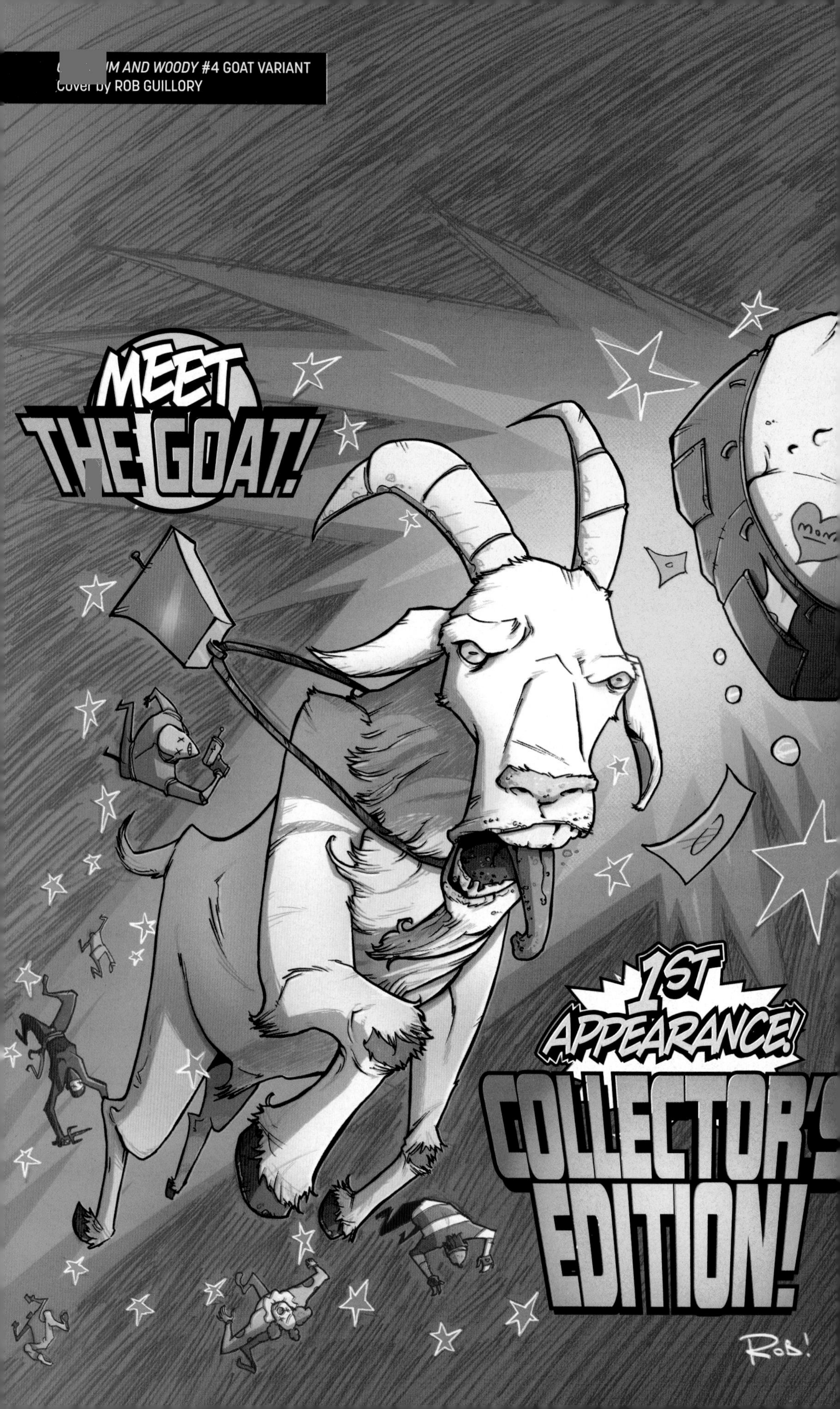

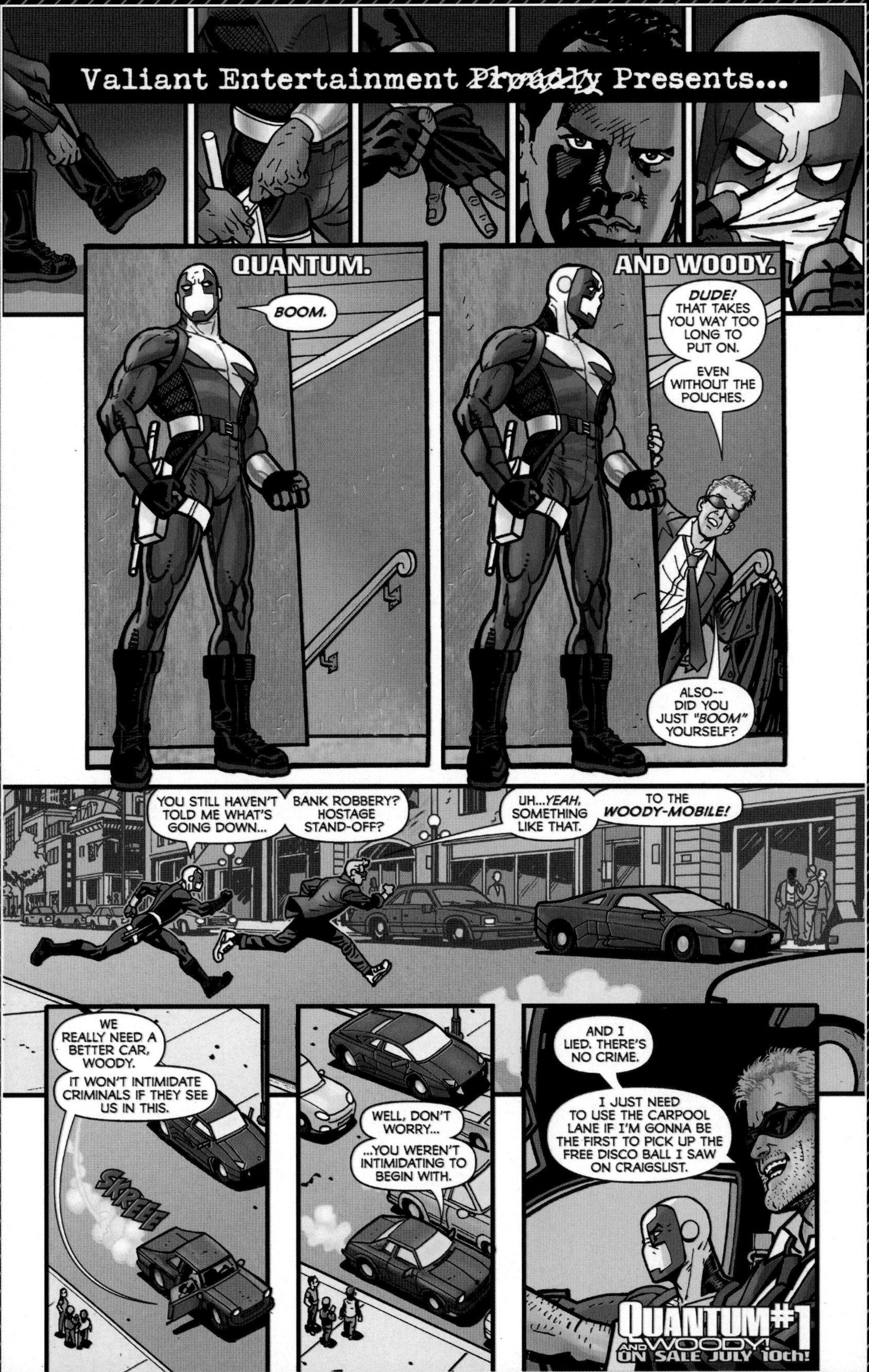
Valiant Entertainment Proudly Presents...
QUANTUM.
BOOM.
AND WOODY.
DUDE! THAT TAKES YOU WAY TOO LONG TO PUT ON.
EVEN WITHOUT THE POUCHES.
ALSO-- DID YOU JUST "BOOM" YOURSELF?
YOU STILL HAVEN'T TOLD ME WHAT'S GOING DOWN...
BANK ROBBERY? HOSTAGE STAND-OFF?
UH...YEAH, SOMETHING LIKE THAT.
TO THE WOODY-MOBILE!
WE REALLY NEED A BETTER CAR, WOODY.
IT WON'T INTIMIDATE CRIMINALS IF THEY SEE US IN THIS.
SKREEE
WELL, DON'T WORRY...
...YOU WEREN'T INTIMIDATING TO BEGIN WITH.
AND I LIED. THERE'S NO CRIME.
I JUST NEED TO USE THE CARPOOL LANE IF I'M GONNA BE THE FIRST TO PICK UP THE FREE DISCO BALL I SAW ON CRAIGSLIST.
QUANTUM AND WOODY! #1
ON SALE JULY 10th!

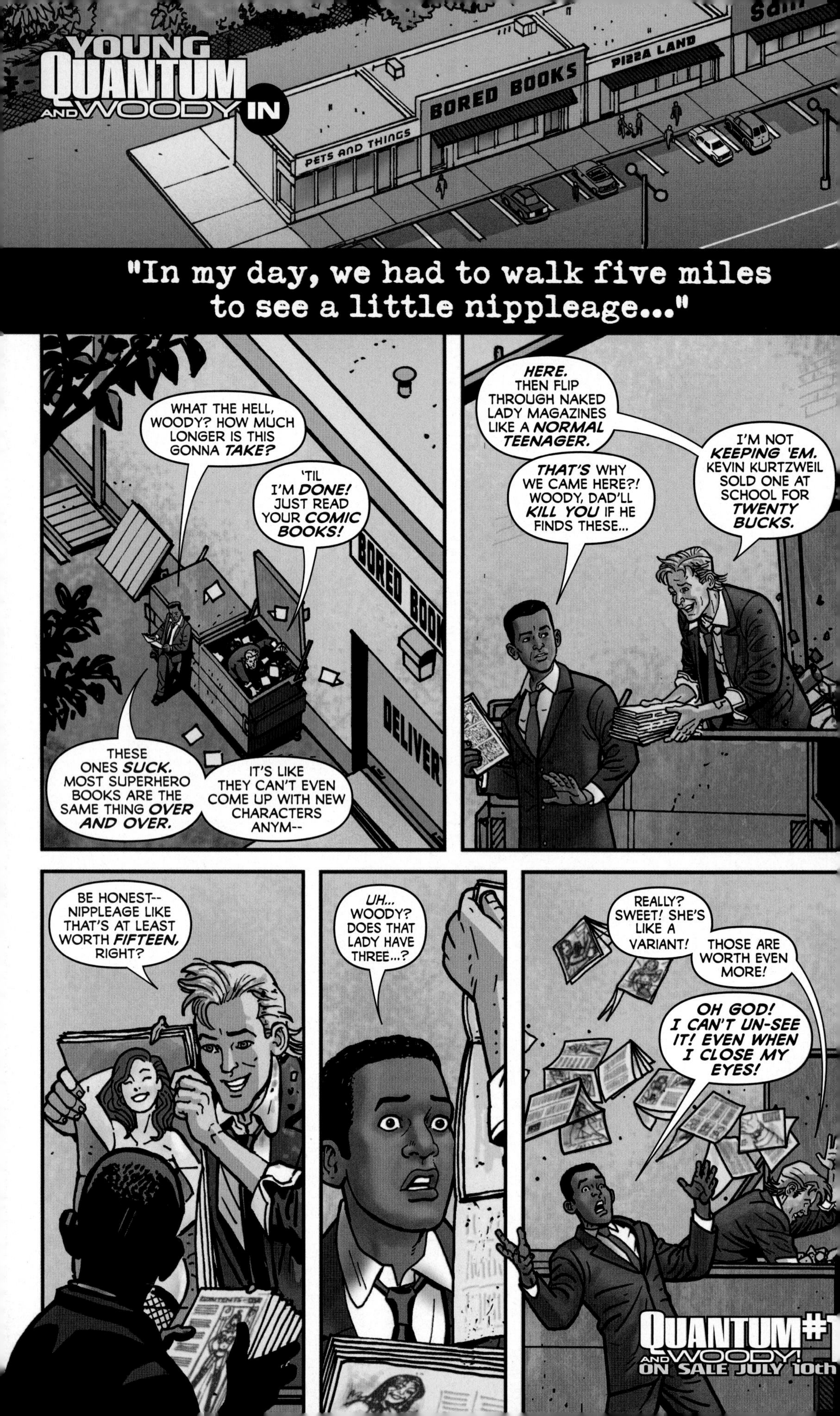

YOUNG QUANTUM AND WOODY IN
PETS AND THINGS
BORED BOOKS
PIZZA LAND
"In my day, we had to walk five miles to see a little nippleage..."
WHAT THE HELL, WOODY? HOW MUCH LONGER IS THIS GONNA TAKE?
'TIL I'M DONE! JUST READ YOUR COMIC BOOKS!
BORED BOOK
DELIVERY
THESE ONES SUCK. MOST SUPERHERO BOOKS ARE THE SAME THING OVER AND OVER.
IT'S LIKE THEY CAN'T EVEN COME UP WITH NEW CHARACTERS ANYM--
HERE. THEN FLIP THROUGH NAKED LADY MAGAZINES LIKE A NORMAL TEENAGER.
THAT'S WHY WE CAME HERE?! WOODY, DAD'LL KILL YOU IF HE FINDS THESE...
I'M NOT KEEPING 'EM. KEVIN KURTZWEIL SOLD ONE AT SCHOOL FOR TWENTY BUCKS.
BE HONEST-- NIPPLEAGE LIKE THAT'S AT LEAST WORTH FIFTEEN, RIGHT?
UH... WOODY? DOES THAT LADY HAVE THREE...?
REALLY? SWEET! SHE'S LIKE A VARIANT!
THOSE ARE WORTH EVEN MORE!
OH GOD! I CAN'T UN-SEE IT! EVEN WHEN I CLOSE MY EYES!
QUANTUM AND WOODY! #1
ON SALE JULY 10th

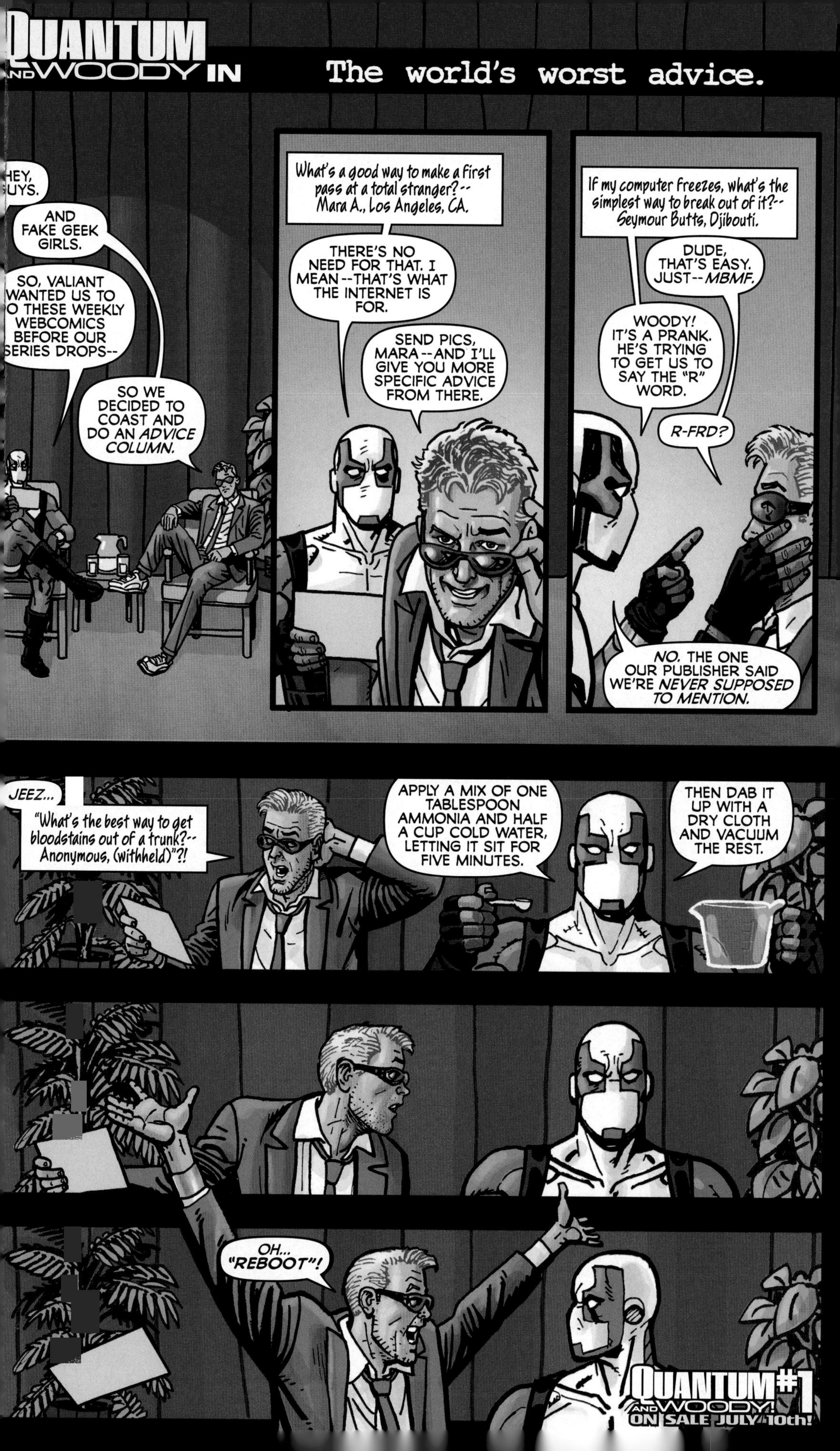
QUANTUM AND WOODY IN
The world's worst advice.
HEY, UYS.
AND FAKE GEEK GIRLS.
SO, VALIANT WANTED US TO O THESE WEEKLY WEBCOMICS BEFORE OUR SERIES DROPS--
SO WE DECIDED TO COAST AND DO AN ADVICE COLUMN.
What's a good way to make a first pass at a total stranger?-- Mara A., Los Angeles, CA.
THERE'S NO NEED FOR THAT. I MEAN--THAT'S WHAT THE INTERNET IS FOR.
SEND PICS, MARA--AND I'LL GIVE YOU MORE SPECIFIC ADVICE FROM THERE.
If my computer freezes, what's the simplest way to break out of it?-- Seymour Butts, Djibouti.
DUDE, THAT'S EASY. JUST--MBMF.
WOODY! IT'S A PRANK. HE'S TRYING TO GET US TO SAY THE "R" WORD.
R-FRD?
NO. THE ONE OUR PUBLISHER SAID WE'RE NEVER SUPPOSED TO MENTION.
JEEZ...
"What's the best way to get bloodstains out of a trunk?-- Anonymous, (withheld)"?!
APPLY A MIX OF ONE TABLESPOON AMMONIA AND HALF A CUP COLD WATER, LETTING IT SIT FOR FIVE MINUTES.
THEN DAB IT UP WITH A DRY CLOTH AND VACUUM THE REST.
OH... "REBOOT"!
QUANTUM AND WOODY! #1
ON SALE JULY 10th!

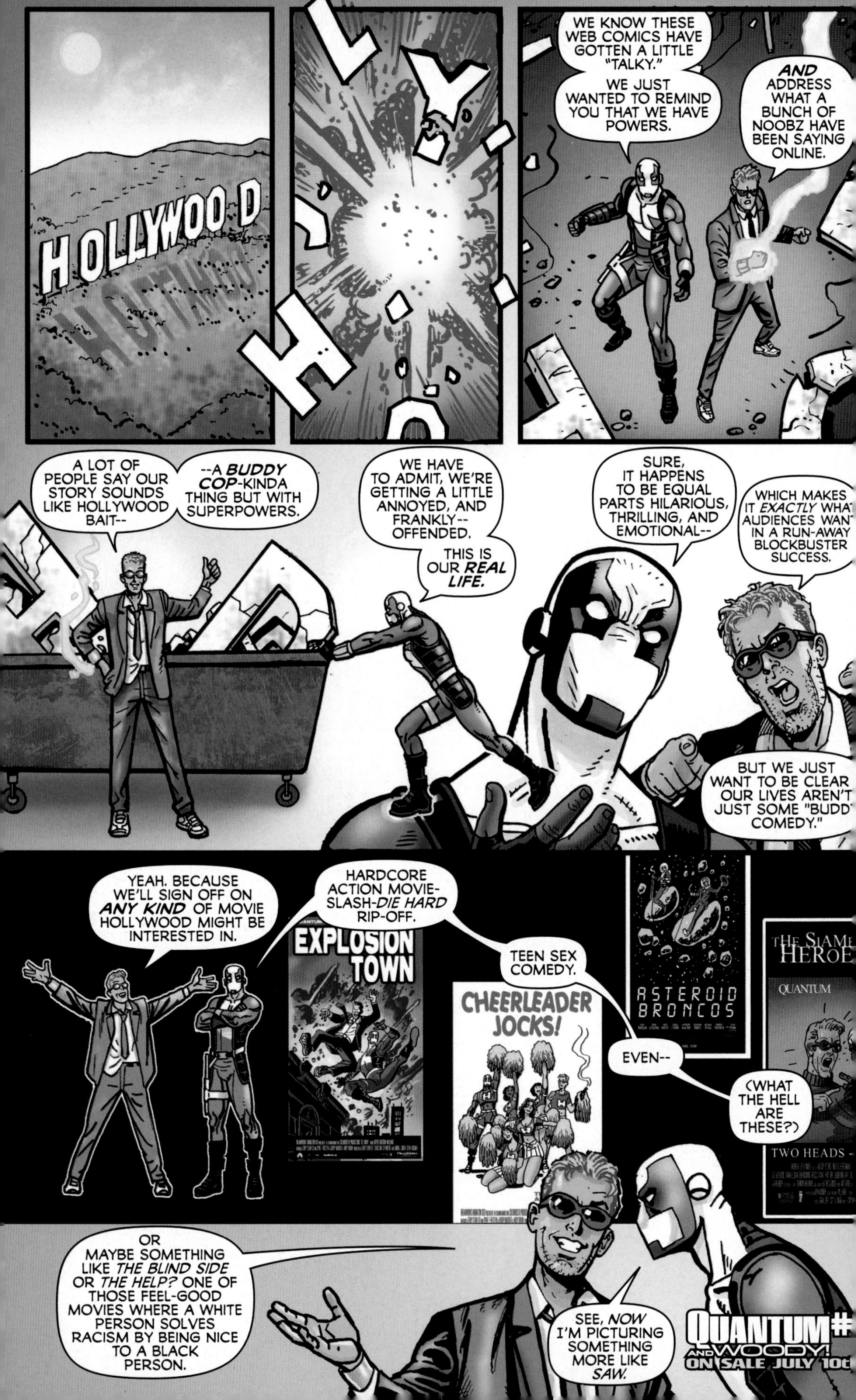
HOLLYWOOD
WE KNOW THESE WEB COMICS HAVE GOTTEN A LITTLE "TALKY."
WE JUST WANTED TO REMIND YOU THAT WE HAVE POWERS.
AND ADDRESS WHAT A BUNCH OF NOOBZ HAVE BEEN SAYING ONLINE.
A LOT OF PEOPLE SAY OUR STORY SOUNDS LIKE HOLLYWOOD BAIT--
--A BUDDY COP-KINDA THING BUT WITH SUPERPOWERS.
WE HAVE TO ADMIT, WE'RE GETTING A LITTLE ANNOYED, AND FRANKLY-- OFFENDED.
THIS IS OUR REAL LIFE.
SURE, IT HAPPENS TO BE EQUAL PARTS HILARIOUS, THRILLING, AND EMOTIONAL--
WHICH MAKES IT EXACTLY WHAT AUDIENCES WANT IN A RUN-AWAY BLOCKBUSTER SUCCESS.
BUT WE JUST WANT TO BE CLEAR OUR LIVES AREN'T JUST SOME "BUDD COMEDY."
YEAH. BECAUSE WE'LL SIGN OFF ON ANY KIND OF MOVIE HOLLYWOOD MIGHT BE INTERESTED IN.
HARDCORE ACTION MOVIE-SLASH-DIE HARD RIP-OFF.
EXPLOSION TOWN
TEEN SEX COMEDY.
CHEERLEADER JOCKS!
ASTEROID BRONCOS
EVEN--
THE SIAME HEROE
QUANTUM
(WHAT THE HELL ARE THESE?)
TWO HEADS
OR MAYBE SOMETHING LIKE THE BLIND SIDE OR THE HELP? ONE OF THOSE FEEL-GOOD MOVIES WHERE A WHITE PERSON SOLVES RACISM BY BEING NICE TO A BLACK PERSON.
SEE, NOW I'M PICTURING SOMETHING MORE LIKE SAW.
QUANTUM AND WOODY! #
ON SALE JULY 10

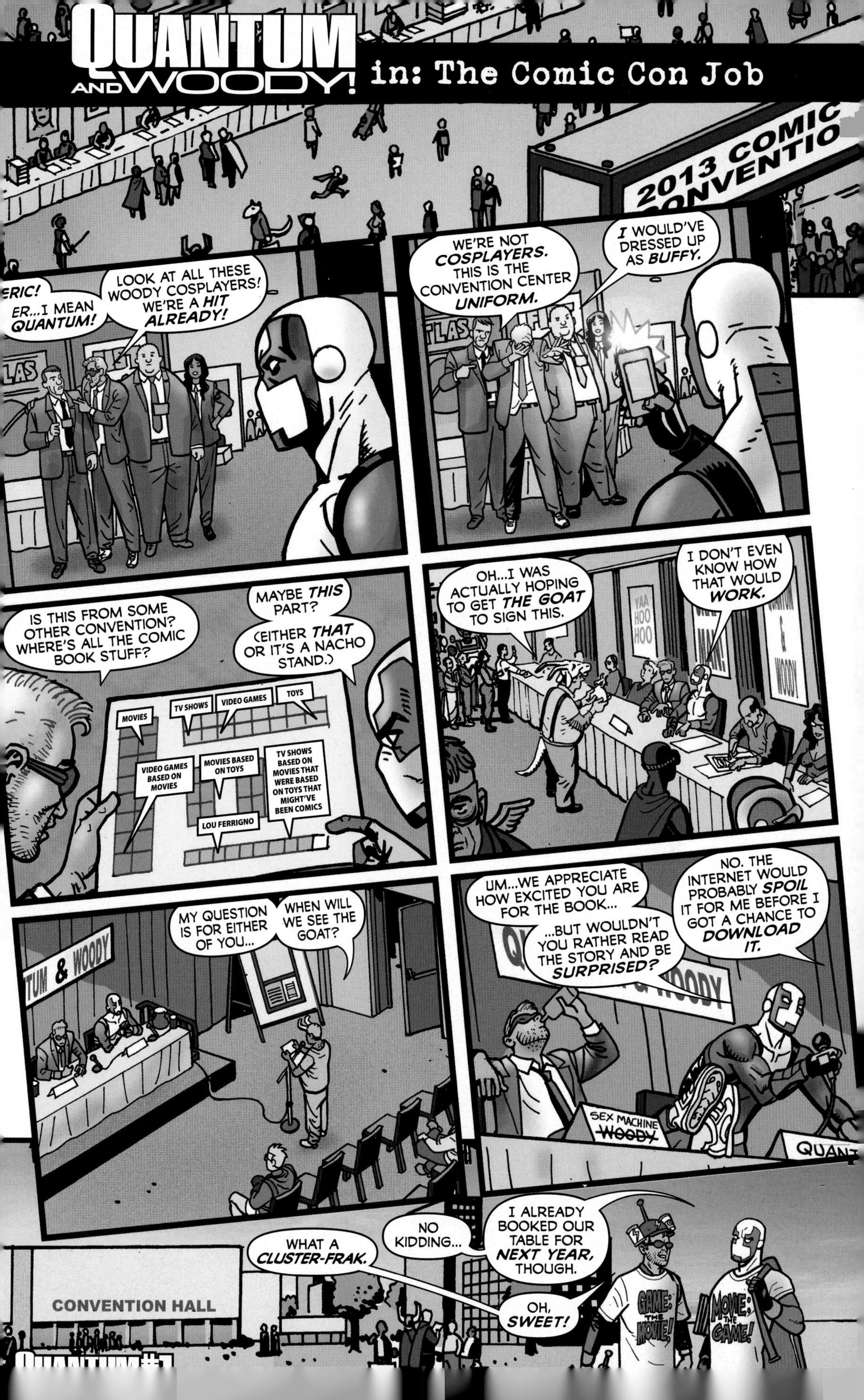
QUANTUM AND WOODY! in: The Comic Con Job
2013 COMIC CONVENTION
ERIC!
ER...I MEAN QUANTUM!
LOOK AT ALL THESE WOODY COSPLAYERS! WE'RE A HIT ALREADY!
WE'RE NOT COSPLAYERS. THIS IS THE CONVENTION CENTER UNIFORM.
I WOULD'VE DRESSED UP AS BUFFY.
IS THIS FROM SOME OTHER CONVENTION? WHERE'S ALL THE COMIC BOOK STUFF?
MAYBE THIS PART?
(EITHER THAT OR IT'S A NACHO STAND.)
MOVIES
TV SHOWS
VIDEO GAMES
TOYS
VIDEO GAMES BASED ON MOVIES
MOVIES BASED ON TOYS
TV SHOWS BASED ON MOVIES THAT WERE BASED ON TOYS THAT MIGHT'VE BEEN COMICS
LOU FERRIGNO
OH...I WAS ACTUALLY HOPING TO GET THE GOAT TO SIGN THIS.
I DON'T EVEN KNOW HOW THAT WOULD WORK.
YAA HOO HOO
QUANTUM & WOODY
MY QUESTION IS FOR EITHER OF YOU...
WHEN WILL WE SEE THE GOAT?
TUM & WOODY
UM...WE APPRECIATE HOW EXCITED YOU ARE FOR THE BOOK...
...BUT WOULDN'T YOU RATHER READ THE STORY AND BE SURPRISED?
NO. THE INTERNET WOULD PROBABLY SPOIL IT FOR ME BEFORE I GOT A CHANCE TO DOWNLOAD IT.
SEX MACHINE WOODY
QUANT
CONVENTION HALL
WHAT A CLUSTER-FRAK.
NO KIDDING...
I ALREADY BOOKED OUR TABLE FOR NEXT YEAR, THOUGH.
OH, SWEET!
GAME: THE MOVIE!
MOVIE: THE GAME!

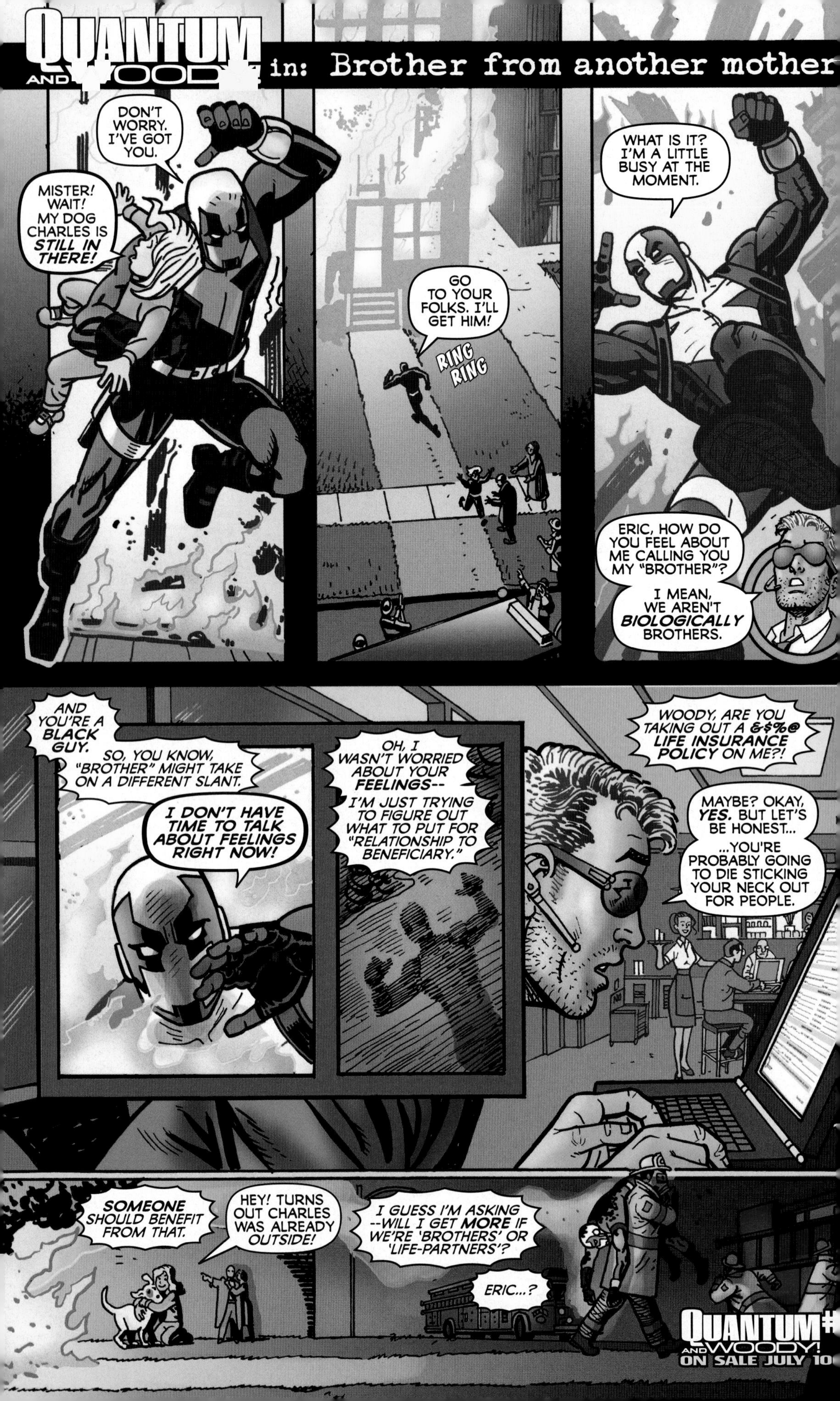

QUANTUM AND WOOD
in: Brother from another mother
DON'T WORRY. I'VE GOT YOU.
MISTER! WAIT! MY DOG CHARLES IS STILL IN THERE!
GO TO YOUR FOLKS. I'LL GET HIM!
RING RING
WHAT IS IT? I'M A LITTLE BUSY AT THE MOMENT.
ERIC, HOW DO YOU FEEL ABOUT ME CALLING YOU MY "BROTHER"?
I MEAN, WE AREN'T BIOLOGICALLY BROTHERS.
AND YOU'RE A BLACK GUY.
SO, YOU KNOW, "BROTHER" MIGHT TAKE ON A DIFFERENT SLANT.
I DON'T HAVE TIME TO TALK ABOUT FEELINGS RIGHT NOW!
OH, I WASN'T WORRIED ABOUT YOUR FEELINGS--
I'M JUST TRYING TO FIGURE OUT WHAT TO PUT FOR "RELATIONSHIP TO BENEFICIARY."
WOODY, ARE YOU TAKING OUT A &$%@ LIFE INSURANCE POLICY ON ME?!
MAYBE? OKAY, YES. BUT LET'S BE HONEST...
...YOU'RE PROBABLY GOING TO DIE STICKING YOUR NECK OUT FOR PEOPLE.
SOMEONE SHOULD BENEFIT FROM THAT.
HEY! TURNS OUT CHARLES WAS ALREADY OUTSIDE!
I GUESS I'M ASKING --WILL I GET MORE IF WE'RE 'BROTHERS' OR 'LIFE-PARTNERS'?
ERIC...?
QUANTUM AND WOODY! #
ON SALE JULY 10

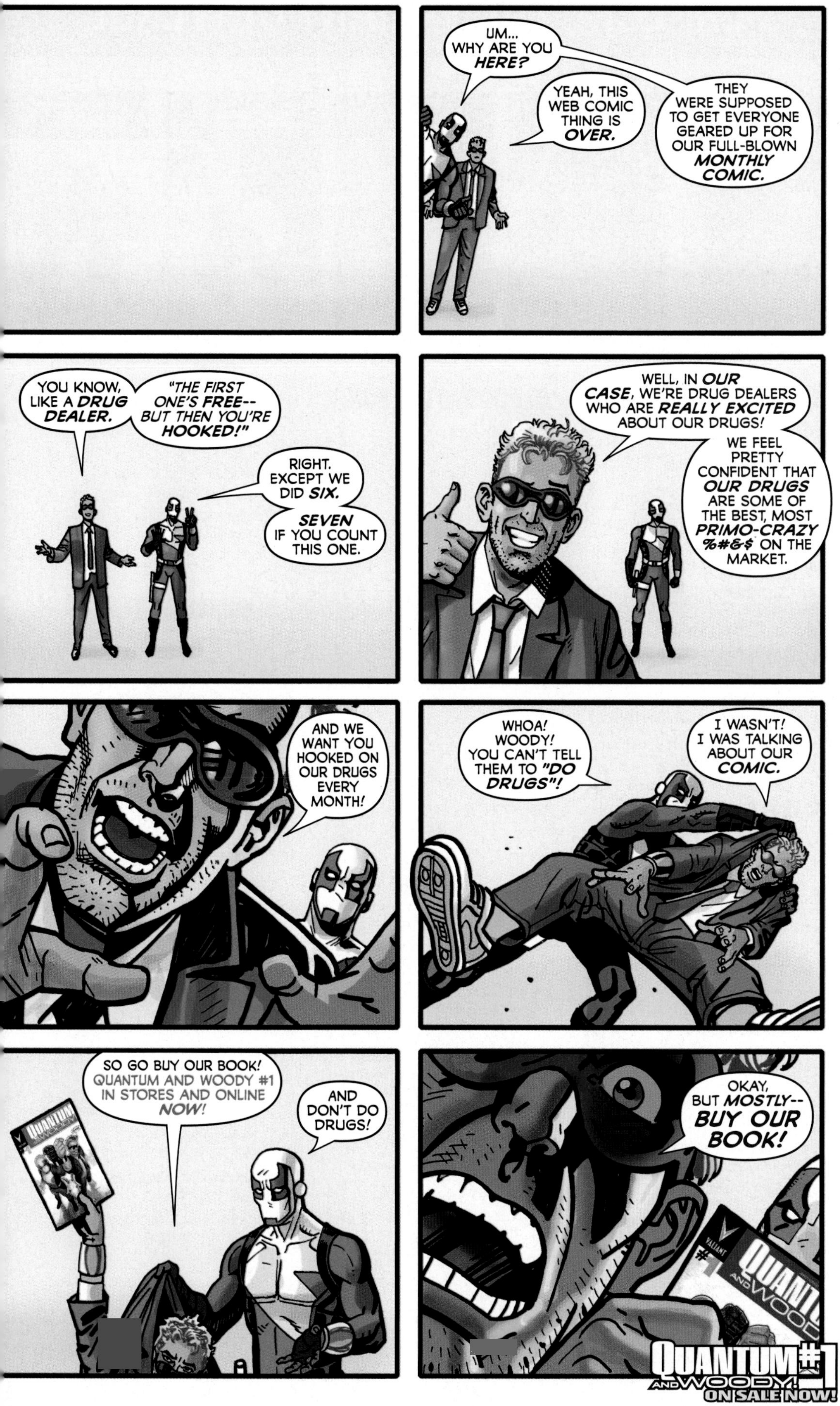
UM... WHY ARE YOU HERE?
YEAH, THIS WEB COMIC THING IS OVER.
THEY WERE SUPPOSED TO GET EVERYONE GEARED UP FOR OUR FULL-BLOWN MONTHLY COMIC.
YOU KNOW, LIKE A DRUG DEALER.
"THE FIRST ONE'S FREE-- BUT THEN YOU'RE HOOKED!"
RIGHT. EXCEPT WE DID SIX.
SEVEN IF YOU COUNT THIS ONE.
WELL, IN OUR CASE, WE'RE DRUG DEALERS WHO ARE REALLY EXCITED ABOUT OUR DRUGS!
WE FEEL PRETTY CONFIDENT THAT OUR DRUGS ARE SOME OF THE BEST, MOST PRIMO-CRAZY %#&$ ON THE MARKET.
AND WE WANT YOU HOOKED ON OUR DRUGS EVERY MONTH!
WHOA! WOODY! YOU CAN'T TELL THEM TO "DO DRUGS"!
I WASN'T! I WAS TALKING ABOUT OUR COMIC.
SO GO BUY OUR BOOK! QUANTUM AND WOODY #1 IN STORES AND ONLINE NOW!
AND DON'T DO DRUGS!
OKAY, BUT MOSTLY-- BUY OUR BOOK!
QUANTUM AND WOODY! #1
ON SALE NOW!

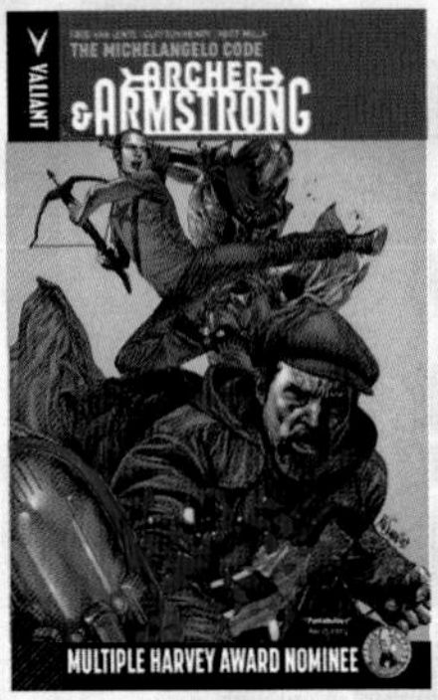
VALIANT
THE MICHELANGELO CODE
ARCHER & ARMSTRONG
MULTIPLE HARVEY AWARD NOMINEE
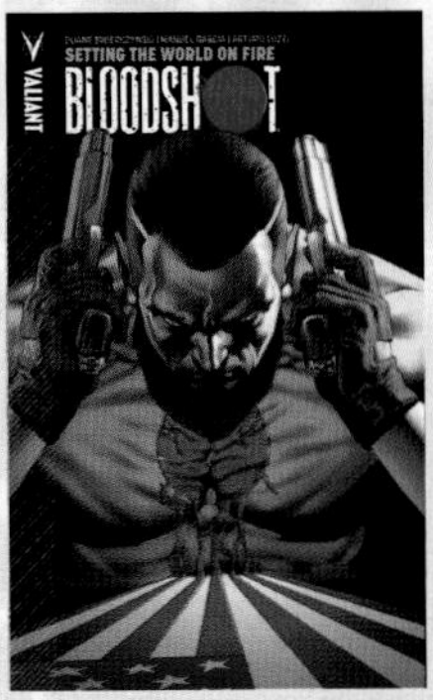
VALIANT
SETTING THE WORLD ON FIRE
BLOODSHOT
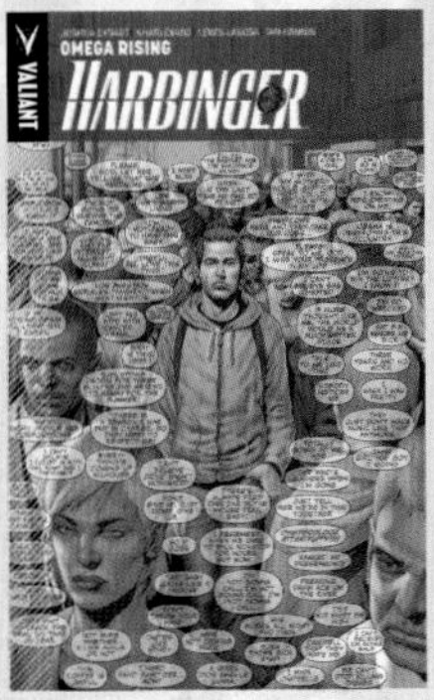
VALIANT
OMEGA RISING
HARBINGER
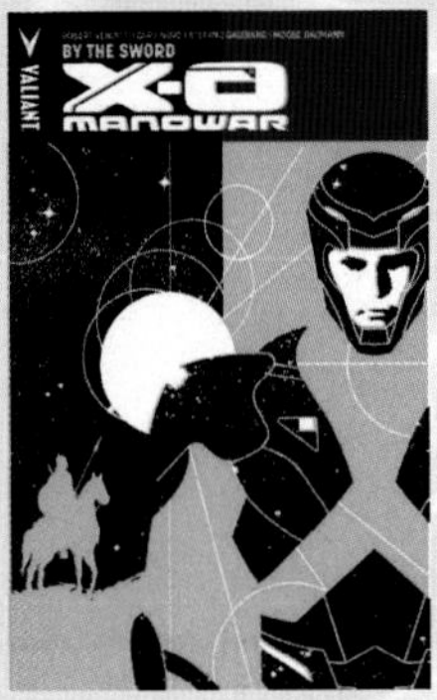
VALIANT
BY THE SWORD
X-O MANOWAR
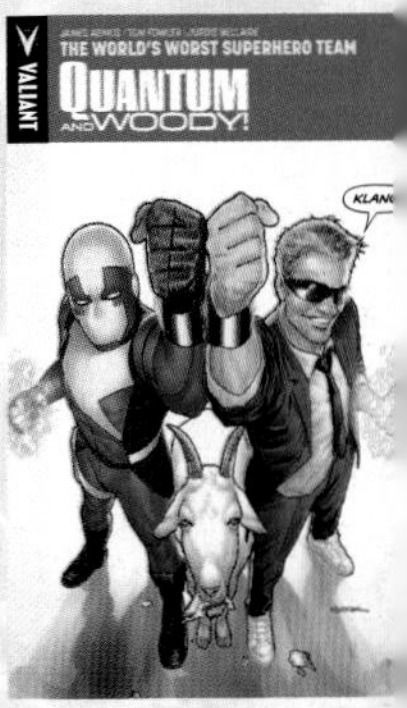
VALIANT
THE WORLD'S WORST SUPERHERO TEAM
QUANTUM AND WOODY!

ARCHER & ARMSTRONG

Volume 1: The Michelangelo Code
ISBN: 9780979640988

Volume 2: Wrath of the Eternal Warrior
ISBN: 9781939346049

Volume 3: Far Faraway
ISBN: 9781939346148

Volume 4: Sect Civil War
ISBN: 9781939346254

Volume 5: Mission: Improbable
ISBN: 9781939346353

Volume 6: American Wasteland
ISBN: 9781939346421

Volume 7: The One Percent and Other Tales
ISBN: 9781939346537

ARMOR HUNTERS

Armor Hunters
ISBN: 9781939346452

Armor Hunters: Bloodshot
ISBN: 9781939346469

Armor Hunters: Harbinger
ISBN: 9781939346506

Unity Vol. 3: Armor Hunters
ISBN: 9781939346445

X-O Manowar Vol. 7: Armor Hunters
ISBN: 9781939346476

BLOODSHOT

Volume 1: Setting the World on Fire
ISBN: 9780979640964

Volume 2: The Rise and the Fall
ISBN: 9781939346032

Volume 3: Harbinger Wars
ISBN: 9781939346124

Volume 4: H.A.R.D. Corps
ISBN: 9781939346193

Volume 5: Get Some!
ISBN: 9781939346315

Volume 6: The Glitch and Other Tales
ISBN: 9781939346711

BLOODSHOT REBORN

Volume 1: Colorado
ISBN: 9781939346674

Volume 2: The Hunt
ISBN: 9781939346827

Volume 3: The Analog Man
ISBN: 9781682151334

BOOK OF DEATH

Book of Death
ISBN: 9781939346971

Book of Death: The Fall of the Valiant Universe
ISBN: 9781939346988

DEAD DROP

ISBN: 9781939346858

THE DEATH-DEFYING DOCTOR MIRAGE

Volume 1
ISBN: 9781939346490

Volume 2: Second Lives
ISBN: 9781682151297

THE DELINQUENTS

ISBN: 9781939346513

DIVINITY

ISBN: 9781939346766

ETERNAL WARRIOR

Volume 1: Sword of the Wild
ISBN: 9781939346209

Volume 2: Eternal Emperor
ISBN: 9781939346292

Volume 3: Days of Steel
ISBN: 9781939346742

WRATH OF THE ETERNAL WARRIOR

Volume 1: Risen
ISBN: 9781682151235

HARBINGER

Volume 1: Omega Rising
ISBN: 9780979640957

Volume 2: Renegades
ISBN: 9781939346025

Volume 3: Harbinger Wars
ISBN: 9781939346117

Volume 4: Perfect Day
ISBN: 9781939346155

Volume 5: Death of a Renegade
ISBN: 9781939346339

Volume 6: Omegas
ISBN: 9781939346384

HARBINGER WARS

Harbinger Wars
ISBN: 9781939346094

Bloodshot Vol. 3: Harbinger Wars
ISBN: 9781939346124

Harbinger Vol. 3: Harbinger Wars
ISBN: 9781939346117

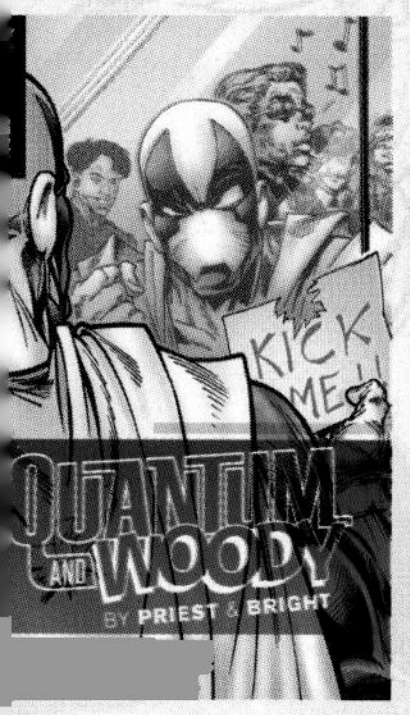
KICK ME
QUANTUM AND WOODY
BY PRIEST & BRIGHT
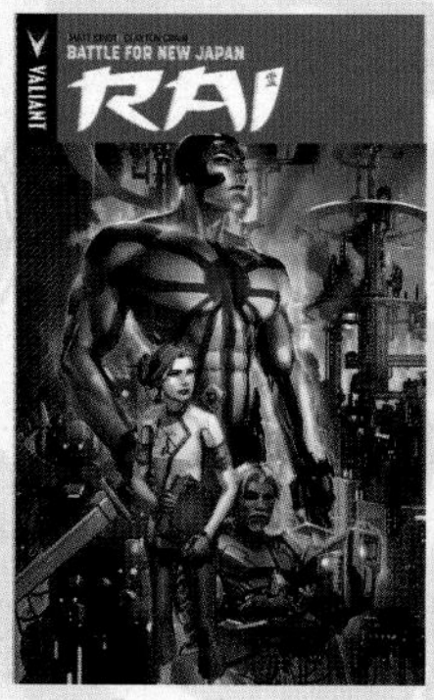
VALIANT
BATTLE FOR NEW JAPAN
RAI
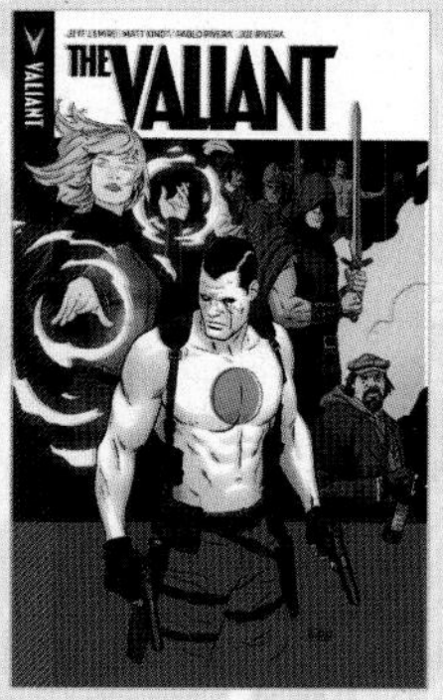
VALIANT
THE VALIANT
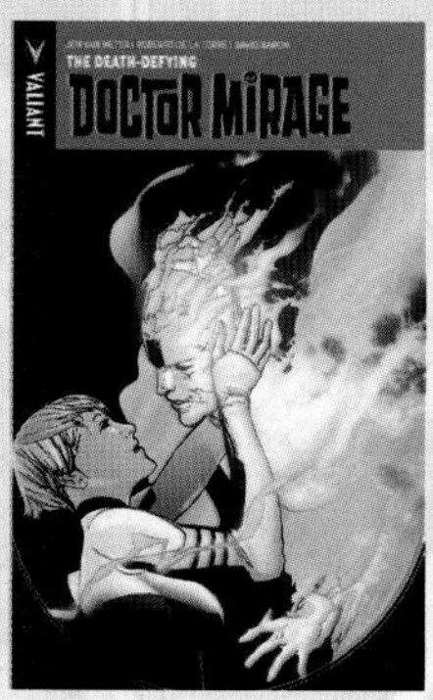
VALIANT
THE DEATH-DEFYING
DOCTOR MIRAGE
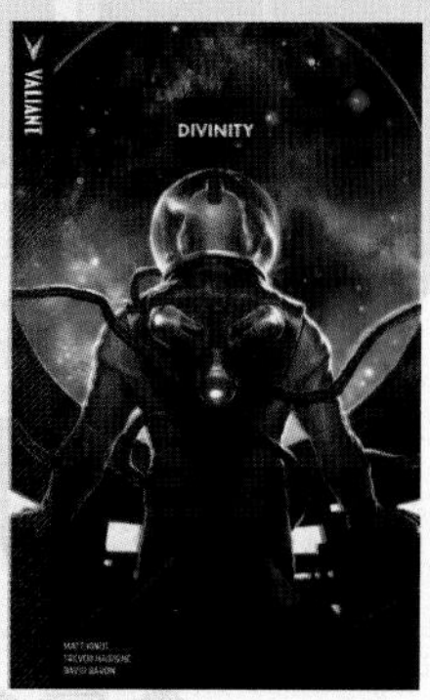
VALIANT
DIVINITY

MPERIUM

lume 1: Collecting Monsters
BN: 9781939346759

lume 2: Broken Angels
BN: 9781939346896

lume 3: The Vine Imperative
BN: 9781682151112

INJAK

lume 1: Weaponeer
BN: 9781939346667

lume 2: The Shadow Wars
BN: 9781939346940

lume 3: Operation: Deadside
BN: 9781682151259

UANTUM ND WOODY

lume 1: The World's Worst Superhero Team
BN: 9781939346186

lume 2: In Security
BN: 9781939346230

lume 3: Crooked Pasts, Present Tense
BN: 9781939346391

lume 4: Quantum and Woody Must Die!
N: 9781939346629

UANTUM AND WOODY Y PRIEST & BRIGHT

lume 1: Klang
N: 9781939346780

lume 2: Switch
N: 9781939346803

lume 3: And So...
N: 9781939346865

lume 4: Q2 - The Return
N: 9781682151099

RAI

Volume 1: Welcome to New Japan
ISBN: 9781939346414

Volume 2: Battle for New Japan
ISBN: 9781939346612

Volume 3: The Orphan
ISBN: 9781939346841

SHADOWMAN

Volume 1: Birth Rites
ISBN: 9781939346001

Volume 2: Darque Reckoning
ISBN: 9781939346056

Volume 3: Deadside Blues
ISBN: 9781939346162

Volume 4: Fear, Blood, And Shadows
ISBN: 9781939346278

Volume 5: End Times
ISBN: 9781939346377

IVAR, TIMEWALKER

Volume 1: Making History
ISBN: 9781939346636

Volume 2: Breaking History
ISBN: 9781939346834

Volume 3: Ending History
ISBN: 9781939346995

UNITY

Volume 1: To Kill a King
ISBN: 9781939346261

Volume 2: Trapped by Webnet
ISBN: 9781939346346

Volume 3: Armor Hunters
ISBN: 9781939346445

Volume 4: The United
ISBN: 9781939346544

Volume 5: Homefront
ISBN: 9781939346797

Volume 6: The War-Monger
ISBN: 9781939346902

Volume 7: Revenge of the Armor Hunters
ISBN: 9781682151136

THE VALIANT

ISBN: 9781939346605

VALIANT ZEROES AND ORIGINS

ISBN: 9781939346582

X-O MANOWAR

Volume 1: By the Sword
ISBN: 9780979640940

Volume 2: Enter Ninjak
ISBN: 9780979640995

Volume 3: Planet Death
ISBN: 9781939346087

Volume 4: Homecoming
ISBN: 9781939346179

Volume 5: At War With Unity
ISBN: 9781939346247

Volume 6: Prelude to Armor Hunters
ISBN: 9781939346407

Volume 7: Armor Hunters
ISBN: 9781939346476

Volume 8: Enter: Armorines
ISBN: 9781939346551

Volume 9: Dead Hand
ISBN: 9781939346650

Volume 10: Exodus
ISBN: 9781939346933

Volume 11: The Kill List
ISBN: 9781682151273

EXPLORE THE VALIANT UNIVERSE

VALIANT
JOSHUA DYSART BARRY KITSON CLAYTON HENRY KHARI EVANS RAFA SANDOVAL
HARBINGER
DELUXE EDITION 2

VALIANT
ROBERT VENDITTI MATT KINDT JOSHUA DYSART JOE HARRIS ROBERT GILL DOUG BRAITHWAITE DIEGO BERNARD TREVOR HAIRSINE STEPHEN SEGOVIA
ARMOR HUNTERS
DELUXE EDITION

VALIANT
JIM SHOOTER | DAVID LAPHAM
CHILDREN OF THE EIGHTH DAY
HARBINGER

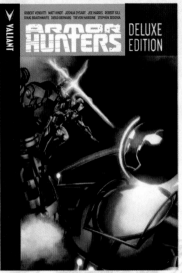

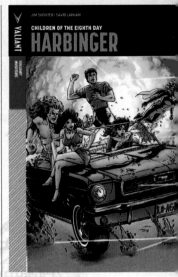

Omnibuses

Archer & Armstrong: The Complete Classic Omnibus
ISBN: 9781939346872
Collecting ARCHER & ARMSTRONG (1992) #0-26, ETERNAL WARRIOR (1992) #25 along with ARCHER & ARMSTRONG: THE FORMATION OF THE SECT.

Quantum and Woody: The Complete Classic Omnibus
ISBN: 9781939346360
Collecting QUANTUM AND WOODY (1997) #0, 1-21 and #32, THE GOAT: H.A.E.D.U.S. #1, and X-O MANOWAR (1996) #16

X-O Manowar Classic Omnibus Vol. 1
ISBN: 9781939346308
Collecting X-O MANOWAR (1992) #0-30, ARMORINES #0, X-O DATABASE #1, as well as material from SECRETS OF THE VALIANT UNIVERSE #1

Deluxe Editions

Archer & Armstrong Deluxe Edition Book 1
ISBN: 9781939346223
Collecting ARCHER & ARMSTRONG #0-13

Archer & Armstrong Deluxe Edition Book 2
ISBN: 9781939346957
Collecting ARCHER & ARMSTRONG #14-25, ARCHER & ARMSTRONG: ARCHER #0 and BLOODSHOT AND H.A.R.D. CORPS #20-21.

Armor Hunters Deluxe Edition
ISBN: 9781939346728
Collecting Armor Hunters #1-4, Armor Hunters: Aftermath #1, Armor Hunters: Bloodshot #1-3, Armor Hunters: Harbinger #1-3, Unity #8-11, and X-O MANOWAR #23-29

Bloodshot Deluxe Edition Book 1
ISBN: 9781939346216
Collecting BLOODSHOT #1-13

Bloodshot Deluxe Edition Book 2
ISBN: 9781939346810
Collecting BLOODSHOT AND H.A.R.D. CORPS #14-23, BLOODSHOT #24-25, BLOODSHOT #0, BLOODSHOT AND H.A.R.D. CORPS: H.A.R.D. CORPS #0, along with ARCHER & ARMSTRONG #18-19

Book of Death Deluxe Edition
ISBN: 9781682151150
Collecting BOOK OF DEATH #1-4, BOOK OF DEATH: THE FALL OF BLOODSHOT #1, BOOK OF DEATH: THE FALL OF NINJAK #1, BOOK OF DEATH: THE FALL OF HARBINGER #1, and BOOK OF DEATH: THE FALL OF X-O MANOWAR #1.

Divinity Deluxe Edition
ISBN: 97819393460993
Collecting DIVNITY #1-4

Harbinger Deluxe Edition Book 1
ISBN: 9781939346131
Collecting HARBINGER #0-14

Harbinger Deluxe Edition Book 2
ISBN: 9781939346773
Collecting HARBINGER #15-25, HARBINGER: OMEGAS #1-3, and HARBINGER: BLEEDING MONK #0

Harbinger Wars Deluxe Edition
ISBN: 9781939346322
Collecting HARBINGER WARS #1-4, HARBINGER #11-14, and BLOODSHOT #10-13

Ivar, Timewalker Deluxe Edition Book 1
ISBN: 9781682151198
Collecting IVAR, TIMEWALKER #1-12

Quantum and Woody Deluxe Edition Book 1
ISBN: 9781939346681
Collecting QUANTUM AND WOODY #1-12 and QUANTUM AND WOODY: THE GOAT #0

Q2: The Return of Quantum and Woody Deluxe Edition
ISBN: 9781939346568
Collecting Q2: THE RETURN OF QUANTUM AND WOODY #1-5

Rai Deluxe Edition Book 1
ISBN: 9781682151174
Collecting RAI #1-12, along with material from RAI #1 PLUS EDITION and RAI #5 PLUS EDITION

Shadowman Deluxe Edition Book 1
ISBN: 9781939346438
Collecting SHADOWMAN #0-10

Shadowman Deluxe Edition Book 2
ISBN: 9781682151075
Collecting SHADOWMAN #11-16, SHADOWMAN #13X, SHADOWMAN: END TIMES #1-3 and PUNK MAMBO #0

Unity Deluxe Edition Book 1
ISBN: 9781939346575
Collecting UNITY #0-14

The Valiant Deluxe Edition
ISBN: 97819393460986
Collecting THE VALIANT #1-4

X-O Manowar Deluxe Edition Book 1
ISBN: 9781939346100
Collecting X-O MANOWAR #1-14

X-O Manowar Deluxe Edition Book 2
ISBN: 9781939346520
Collecting X-O MANOWAR #15-22, and UNITY #1-

X-O Manowar Deluxe Edition Book 3
ISBN: 9781682151310
Collecting X-O MANOWAR #23-29 and ARMOR HUNTERS #1-4.

Valiant Masters

Bloodshot Vol. 1 - Blood of the Machine
ISBN: 9780979640933

H.A.R.D. Corps Vol. 1 - Search and Destroy
ISBN: 9781939346285

Harbinger Vol. 1 - Children of the Eighth Day
ISBN: 9781939346483

Ninjak Vol. 1 - Black Water
ISBN: 9780979640971

Rai Vol. 1 - From Honor to Strength
ISBN: 9781939346070

Shadowman Vol. 1 - Spirits Within
ISBN: 9781939346018

QUANTUM AND WOODY BY PRIEST & BRIGHT | READING ORDER

VALIANT
KICK ME!!
QUANTUM AND WOODY
BY PRIEST & BRIGHT
VOL 1: KLANG

Quantum and Woody by Priest & Bright
Vol. 1: Klang

VALIANT
QUANTUM AND WOODY
BY PRIEST & BRIGHT
VOL 2: SWITCH

Quantum and Woody
by Priest & Bright
Vol. 2: Switch

VALIANT
QUANTUM AND WOODY
BY PRIEST & BRIGHT
VOL 3: AND SO...

Quantum and Woody
by Priest & Bright
Vol. 3: And So...

One of the funniest superhero omics ever..." - Kotaku

A fun ride.... Unmissable."
Wired

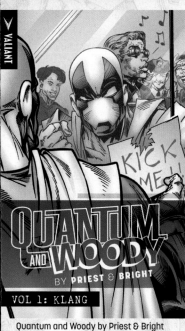

VALIANT
QUANTUM AND WOODY
BY PRIEST & BRIGHT
VOL 4: Q2 - THE RETURN

Quantum and Woody
by Priest & Bright
Vol. 4: Q2–The Return

The complete collected adventures of the original world's worst superhero team - now in trade paperback!

From legendary creators

CHRISTOPHER PRIEST (*Black Panther, Deadpool*) and **MD BRIGHT** (*Green Lantern, Iron Man*)

VALIANT®

QUANTUM AND WOODY!

VOLUME TWO: **IN SECURITY**

SO... TWO SUPERHEROES, A CLONE, AND A GOAT MOVE INTO A JUNIOR TWO-BEDROOM...

Eric and Woody have had their lives turned upside down. What do you do when the most annoying person in your life is also the only thing keeping you alive? You move in with him! And his goat. And his barely legal clone girlfriend. Besides, every team of heroes needs a secret headquarters... and this one has a slightly used hot tub. Plus: Quantum gets a job - as an on-staff superhero for Magnum Security!

Collecting QUANTUM AND WOODY #5-8 by acclaimed writer James Asmus (*Thief of Thieves*) and rising star Ming Doyle (*Mara*), get ready to kiss that security deposit goodbye when the world's worst superhero team shacks up for their next down-and-out adventure!

TRADE PAPERBACK
ISBN: 978-1-939346-23-0

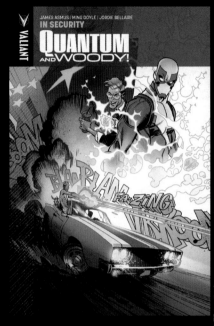

VALIANT
JAMES ASMUS | MING DOYLE | JORDIE BELLAIRE
IN SECURITY
QUANTUM AND WOODY!
FA-ZING

QUANTUM AND WOODY!

VOLUME THREE: **CROOKED PASTS, PRESENT TENSE**

THERE'S A NEW SCOURGE SWEEPING THE STREETS OF THE BIG CITY - ROBO-CRIME!

Eric needs to know he can trust Woody – and that means Woody needs to get a job, open a bank account, sign up for a library card, and do all the things a responsible adult does. But when a new gang of rogue mad-scientist super-criminals launch a wave of robot-enabled mega-crimes, will Woody stop them...or join them?

Plus: the return of Edison's Radical Acquisitions and the thrilling secret origin of... the one and only Goat!

Collecting QUANTUM AND WOODY #9-12 and QUANTUM AND WOODY: THE GOAT #0, the world's worst superhero team unleashes a volatile new batch of high-stakes hijinks right here with an all-new collection of adventures from award-winning writer James Asmus (*Thief of Thieves*) and acclaimed artists Tom Fowler (*Hulk: Season One*), Kano (*Gotham Central*), and Wilfredo Torres (*The Shadow: Year One*)!

TRADE PAPERBACK
ISBN: 978-1-939346-39-1

VALIANT
JAMES ASMUS | TOM FOWLER | KANO | WILFREDO TORRES
CROOKED PASTS, PRESENT TENSE
QUANTUM AND WOODY!
NOMINATED FOR SIX 2014 HARVEY AWARDS

THE MOST HARVEY AWARD NOMINATIONS OF 2014!

"The ultimate buddy comedy... QUANTUM AND WOODY is bar none." - Ain't It Cool News

"★★★★★... Everyone needs more QUANTUM AND WOODY in their lives." - Comic Vine

"10/10... Everything you could ask for in a comic." - Inside Pulse

"It's great stuff." - MTV Geek

VALIANT
#1
JAMES ASMUS | TOM FOWLER | JORDIE BELLAIRE
QUANTUM AND WOODY!
VALIANT
#2
JAMES ASMUS | TOM FOWLER | JORDIE BELLAIRE
QUANTUM AND WOODY!
VALIANT
#3
JAMES ASMUS | TOM FOWLER | JORDIE BELLAIRE
QUANTUM AND WOODY!
VALIANT
#4
JAMES ASMUS | TOM FOWLER | JORDIE BELLAIRE
QUANTUM AND WOODY!

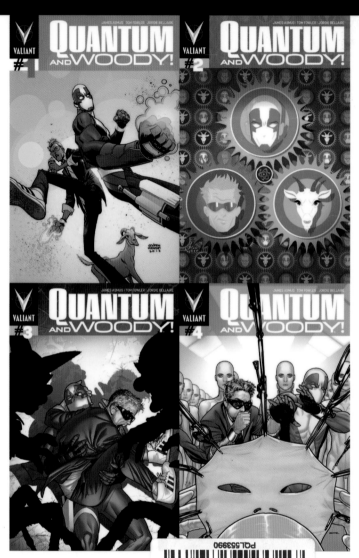

THOSE GUYS ARE

Once upon a time, Eric and Woody Henderson were inseparable. Adopted brothers. Best friends. Brilliant minds. Years later, they are estranged siblings, petty rivals, and washed-up failures. But when their father's murder leads them into the throes of a life-altering scientific accident, Eric and Woody will find themselves with a whole new purpose - and a perfectly legitimate reason to wear costumes and fight crime. Go big or go home, folks! Quantum and Woody are coming! (And, yes, there is a goat, too.)

Collecting QUANTUM AND WOODY #1-4 by creators James Asmus (*Thief of Thieves*) and Tom Fowler (*Hulk: Season One*), start reading here to jump into the action-packed, zeitgeist-shredding exploitation stunt comic that Comic Book Resources calls "yet another critically acclaimed hit for Valiant Comics."

VALIANT®
RATED T+ | www.valiantuniverse.com
9 781939 346186
50999
US $9.99